THE BOOK OF

WHERE?

A GAZETTEER OF
PLACES REAL AND IMAGINARY

Compiled and edited by
Rodney Dale

INDEX

To my wife, family and friends

This edition first published in 2004 by CRW Publishing Limited,
69 Gloucester Crescent, London NW1 7EG
This edition published for Index Books Ltd 2005

ISBN 1 904919 21 9

Text copyright © Rodney Dale 2004

Rodney Dale has asserted his right under the Copyright Designs and Patents Act
1988 to be identified as the author of this work.

Typeset and designed in Bliss by Bookcraft Limited, Stroud, Gloucestershire
Printed and bound in China by Imago

Contents

Acknowledgements

Many people have helped to bring this book into being, and I am particularly indebted to Charlotte Edwards in my office for her crucial part in marshalling the computer files and keeping everything in order as the project developed. I would also like to thank my sister Steve Puttick who produced an early organisational framework for the book, and Meredith MacArdle and Nick and Sue Webb, some of whose research is to be found in Part 2.

Others have provided and confirmed information, made comments, and generally facilitated the work: Stephen Adamson, Mags Barrett-Jolley, Anne Challis, Peter Drake, Christopher Dunn, Lindsay Goddard, Mark Hatcher, Gina Keene, Michael and Valerie Grosvenor Myer, and Georgia Parkes.

A book such as this stands or falls by its design, and I would like to thank John Button of Bookcraft Ltd, and typesetter Matt Gavan, for an especially creative relationship. Proofreader Graham Frankland's contribution to the reader's wellbeing has been more than helpful – having said which my shoulders accept the usual author's burden as the place where the buck stops.

And for their faith, patience, and ever-cheerful encouragement, Marcus Clapham, Clive Reynard and Ken Webb – in other words, CRW.

Introduction

> I keep six honest serving men
> (They taught me all I knew);
> Their names are What and Why and When
> And How and Where and Who.
>
> Rudyard Kipling

The Book of Where? is the second in the present series, following as it does *When?*, and preceding *Who?* and *What?* All gradually came into being when I was in that delightful garden at Probus in Cornwall, contemplating the raised Cornwall-shaped bed on whose surface is laid geological specimens from various parts of the Duchy. I envisaged an account of the materials from which matter, and hence the universe, is made; then the universe itself, then the earth, then its peoples, and so on and so on, until *The Book of Where?* emerged as part of the Grand Scheme.

The book is in two Parts. **Part 1** is the A to Z, listing a variety of places, real and imaginary, in alphabetical order. **Part 2** presents the tables where information is arranged in categories. The scope of such a work is enormous, but one purpose to inform the arrangement has been to help those solving crosswords and other types of puzzle.

No doubt the book will be used in many different ways for many different purposes, and I will welcome comments and feedback – preferably by e-mail.

Rodney Dale
Haddenham, Cambridgeshire 2004
info@fernhouse.com

Abbreviations

=	generally indicates a translation
AC	administrative county
ACT	Australian Capital Territory (Australia)
aet	aged
Afr	(The continent of) Africa
aka	also known as
Am	(The continent of) America
AS	Australian slang
Asa	(The continent of) Asia
b	born
BCE	before the common era (aka BC)
C	century, county
c	about
CB	citizens' band, county borough
CE	common era (aka AD)
cf	compare
d	died
DoL	A country that drives on the left (very often a member or former member of the British Commonwealth)
et al	and others
Eur	(The continent of) Europe
IC	Suffix to a country's internet address
ICR	International Car Registration mark
ID	Independence Day
inter alia	among others
ND	National Day
NSW	New South Wales (Australia)
NT	Northern Territory (Australia)
NZ	New Zealand
Oce	(The continent of) Oceania
OE	Old English
PC	political(ly) correct(ness)
PNG	Papua New Guinea
pron	pronounced
pt	part
Qld	Queensland (Australia)
qv	which see
RN	Royal Navy

RS	rhyming slang
SA	South Australia (Australia)
Tas	Tasmania (Australia)
TLA	three-letter abbreviation
UA	unitary authority
UK	United Kingdom of Great Britain and Northern Ireland
US(A)	United States (of America)
vi	see below
Vic	Victoria (Australia)
vs	see above
WA	Western Australia (Australia)
WW1	World War 1
WW2	World War 2

Part 1   A–Z

A note on alphabetical order

In the following pages and for the purposes of keeping important material together, some of the highlighted panels may be slightly out of alphabetical order with the main text entries.

Aachen
City and spa in North Rhine-Westphalia, Germany; the northern capital of Charlemagne's empire.

Aalborg
City and port in Denmark in North Jutland.

Aalu
See Elysian Fields.

Aarau
Capital of Aargau canton in North Switzerland; capital of the Helvetic Republic 1798–1803.

Aarau
Capital of the Swiss Canton (*qv*) of Aargau.

Abadan
A port in South West Iran, on an island in the Shatt-al-Arab delta.

Abbots Bromley

A village in Staffordshire, England, where one of the rare European animal dances – the Horn Dance – dating back to at least August 1226 is performed annually. Originally danced at the Barthelmy Fair, it now takes place on Wakes Monday: the first Monday after 4 September (unless 4 September is a Sunday, in which case the Dance is on 12 September). The side comprises 12 men: the six Deermen, who carry the reindeer antlers (on iron frames, and weighing between 16 and 25 pounds); the other six are the stock figures: the Hobbyhorse, the Fool, Maid Marian, and the Bowman, and the two musicians who respectively play the melodeon and the triangle. The horns are normally kept in the church, and drawn at 8am on the day of the Dance, which covers some 10 miles and a dozen locations. For nigh on 200 years, the Lead Deerman has been a member of the Fowell family, and he is responsible for choosing the rest of the side.

Abdera
Whence came Democritus, the scoffing or laughing philosopher, hence Abderian laughter.

Aberdeen
'The Granite City' in North East Scotland, administrative centre of Grampian region on the North Sea; centre for processing North Sea oil and gas; university established 1494.

Aberfan
Welsh mining village near Merthyr Tydfil where, on 21 October 1966, by the gross negligence of the National Coal Board, a coal tip slumped on to the village school killing 144 people, mostly children.

Aberystwyth
A Welsh resort on Cardigan Bay, where you will find University College, Aberystwyth and the National Library of Wales, one of the six UK copyright libraries.

Abilene
A city in central Texas; major trading centre for cotton, grain, livestock, with timber mills and food processing plants.

Abingdon
A market town in Southern England, in Oxfordshire. It was once the county town of Berkshire, but lost that honour to Reading when it rebuffed the railway (cf Stamford).

Aboukir Bay
A bay on the North coast of Egypt, where the Nile enters the Mediterranean: site of the battle of the Nile, where Nelson defeated the French fleet in 1798, and Napoleon defeated the Turks the following year.

Above board
In the open, honest; card players who keep their hands above the table are less likely to be cheating.

Above the line
1   In adagencyspeak, activities normally associated with promotion, such as advertising.
2   In accountancyspeak, money used for current expenditure, or a payment made by its due date (cf Below the line).

Abroholos
Brazil – a frequent coastal squall May through August between Cabo de Sao Tome and Cabo Frio; see Winds.

Abruzzi

A region of South central Italy between the Apennines and the Adriatic: separated from the former administrative region Abruzzi e Molise in 1965.

Abu Dhabi

An oil-rich sheikhdom of South East Arabia, on the south coast of the Persian Gulf. Capital of the United Arab Emirates, consisting principally of the port of Abu Dhabi and a desert hinterland.

Abu Simbel

A former village in Southern Egypt: site of two temples of Rameses II, which were moved to higher ground (1966–67) before the area behind the Aswan High Dam was flooded.

Abydos

An ancient town in central Egypt: site of many temples and tombs; an ancient Greek colony on the Asiatic side of the Dardanelles (Hellespont): scene of the legend of Hero and Leander.

Abyssinia

Former name for Ethiopia.

Academy

Named after Academos, originally a garden near Athens where taught Plato (?427–?347BCE), pupil of Socrates (?470–399BCE) and teacher of Aristotle (384–322BCE), the triumvirate regarded as the founders of western philosophy.

Acadia; Acadie

Once a French settlement in Canada, now part of Nova Scotia and New Brunswick.

Accadin

A Sicilian fountain supposed to have divinatory powers, in that genuine writings thrown into it floated, whereas bogus writings sank.

Aceldama

In the New Testament, the place near Jerusalem which was said to have been bought with the 30 pieces of silver paid to Judas for betraying Jesus (Matt 27:8, Acts 1:19).

Achaean League

A confederation of Achaean cities formed in the early third century BCE, which became a political and military force in Greece, directed particularly against Macedonian domination of the Peloponnesus.

Achernar
The only bright star in the constellation Eridanus, visible only in the southern hemisphere, named for a river in ancient mythology; see Astral Constellations.

Acheron
Greek myth – one of the rivers in Hades over which the souls of the dead were ferried by Charon.

Aconcagua
A mountain in West Argentina, the highest peak in the Andes and in the western hemisphere.

Acre
1 A territory of west Brazil, mostly unexplored tropical forests, acquired from Bolivia in 1903, capital Rio Branco.
2 A city and port in North Israel, strategically situated in the Bay of Acre in the east Mediterranean, taken and retaken during the Crusades between 1104 and 1291, again by the Turks (1517), by Egypt (1832), and by the Turks again (1839).

Acropolis
(Greek = city on high) in Ancient Greece, an isolated ground on which stood the religious and administrative centre of a town or city, serving also as a citadel in times of war. The most famous is the Acropolis of Athens on which stand the Propylæa, Parthenon and Erectheum and the restored temple of Athena Nike.

Acrux
Alpha star in Crux; see Astral Constellations.

Actium
Ancient Greek town which overlooked the naval battle at which Octavian's fleet under the control of Agrippa defeated that of Mark Antony and Cleopatra (31BCE).

Acubens
Alpha star in Cancer; see Astral Constellations.

Adams
A mountain in the Cascade Range, SW Washington; height: 12,307 ft (3,751 m)

Addis Ababa
Founded in 1887; capital of Ethiopia from 1896; 8,000 ft (2,400 m) above sea level.

Adelaide
Capital of South Australia; Port Adelaide, 11 km (7 miles) away on St Vincent Gulf, handles the bulk of the country's exports.

Adélie Coast; Adélie Land
A part of Antarctica between Wilkes Land and George V Land; under French sovereignty.

Adhara
A significant star in Canis Major; see Astral Constellations.

Adige
A river in Northern Italy, flowing south-east to the Adriatic; length 220 miles (354 km).

Adirondack Mountains
Mountain range in NE New York State. Highest peak: Mount Marcy, 5,344 ft (1,629 m).

Admiralty House
In Sydney, Australia, the official residence of the Governor-General.

Admiralty Islands
Part of Papua New Guinea, a group of about forty volcanic and coral islands in the Bismarck Archipelago, SW Pacific Ocean.

Adriatic Sea
An arm of the Mediterranean between Italy and the former Yugoslavia.

Aduwa; Adowa
A town in North Ethiopia where Emperor Menelik II defeated the Italians in 1896.

Aegean Islands
The islands of the Aegean Sea, including the Cyclades, Dodecanese, Euboea and Sporades, the majority of which are under Greek administration.

Aegean Sea
An arm of the Mediterranean Sea between Greece and Turkey.

Ægina
A rocky island in the Saronic Gulf, near where the Athenians won the naval battle of Salamis against the fleet of Xerxes 480BCE.

Aegospotami
River of ancient Thrace which flowed into the Hellespont. At its mouth the Spartan fleet under Lysander defeated the Athenians in 405BCE, ending the Peloponnesian War.

Aejej
Morocco – a whirlwind in the Morocco desert; see Winds.

Aeolis
The ancient name for the coastal region of NW Asia Minor including island of Lesbos settled by the Aeolian Greeks.

Ain (Ein)
An Arabic spring or natural fountain; where it forms an oasis, the specific name of the place is taken from a person or associated flora or fauna, and preceded by 'Ain'.

Ain
A significant star in Taurus; see Astral Constellations.

Akrab
A significant star in Scorpius; see Astral Constellations.

Al Bali
A significant star in Aquarius; see Astral Constellations.

Al Na'ir
Alpha star in Grus; see Astral Constellations.

Al Niyat
A significant star in Scorpius; see Astral Constellations.

Alabama
An American State; see United States of America.

Alaska
An American State; see United States of America.

Albany
State capital of New York; see United States of America.

Albert Square
The fictional setting for the BBC1 soap *EastEnders*, centring on the Queen Vic(toria) public house.

Albireo
A significant star in Cygnus; see Astral Constellations.

Alchiba
Alpha star in Corvus; see Astral Constellations.

Alcor
A significant star in Ursa Major; see Astral Constellations.

Alcyone
A significant star in Taurus; see Astral Constellations.

Aldebaran
Alpha star in Taurus; see Astral Constellations.

Alderamin
Alpha star in Cepheus; see Astral Constellations.

Aldhafera
A significant star in Leo; see Astral Constellations.

Alfirk
A significant star in Cepheus; see Astral Constellations.

Algedi
Alpha star in Capricornus; see Astral Constellations.

Algieba
A significant star in Leo; see Astral Constellations.

Algol
A significant star in Perseus; see Astral Constellations.

Alhena, Mebsouta
A significant star in Gemini; see Astral Constellations.

Alice Springs
'A town like Alice', NT Australia, capital of the former Central Territory in the Macdonnell Ranges, named after Lody Alice Todd, wife of Sir Charles Todd who supervised the construction of the Overland Telegraph Line in the 1870s.

Alioth
A significant star in Ursa Major; see Astral Constellations.

Alkaid
A significant star in Ursa Major; see Astral Constellations.

Alkes
Alpha star in Crater; see Astral Constellations.

All Round Will's Mother's
A circuitous route to attain a comparatively simple result, sometimes literally; sometimes figuratively – though who Will was and where his mother lived I have not yet been able to ascertain; see Wrekin, and *cf* G K Chesterton: 'The Rolling English Road' (1914).

Allegheny Mountains (Alleghenies)
In the US, part of the Appalachian chain, running NNE to SSW, parallel to and W of the Blue Ridge Mountains in Pennsylvania, western Maryland and western Virginia.

Almaak
A significant star in Andromeda; see Astral Constellations.

Alnilam
A significant star in Orion; see Astral Constellations.

Aloha State
Nickname of the State of Hawaii; see United States of America.

Alph
The sacred river of Xanadu, the summer residence of Kublai Khan some 180 miles north of Beijing; it was immortalised through Coleridge's poem Kubla Khan (1816).

Alphard
Alpha star in Hydra; see Astral Constellations.

Alphecca
Alpha star in Corona Borealis; see Astral Constellations.

Alpheratz
Alpha star in Andromeda; see Astral Constellations.

Alrischa
Alpha star in Pisces; see Astral Constellations.

Altair
1   Alpha star in Aquila; see Astral Constellations.
2   A significant star in Capricornus; see Astral Constellations.

Altdorf
Capital of the Swiss Canton (qv) of Uri.

Amazon

River in S America (Portuguese name Rio Amazônas), the world's largest river system, and its longest river after the Nile. It rises in the Peruvian Andes as the Rio Masrañón and flows to the east into the Atlantic Ocean in NE Brazil; its tributaries drain areas of Bolivia, Brazil, Colombia, Ecuador, Peru and Venezuela. Its length in round figures is 4,000 miles (6,440 km) and it drains an area for some 2,250,000 square miles (5.8×10^6 km^2).

Ambridge
1   A town in Pennsylvania.
2   The home of the Archer family of Brookfield Farm (formerly Wimberton Farm), a BBC sound soap (The Archers) running since 1950 in the Midlands, and country-wide from the following year. The programme is recognised for incorporating advice for farmers, and now for a wider public, in a low-key way. The signature tune is Barwick Green, a maypole dance from My Native Heath by Arthur Wood.

American River

Rises in the Sierra Nevada Mountains in NE California, and flows south west to join the Sacramento River at Sacramento. Its historical importance is the discovery therein of gold by John A Sutter in 1849, which led to the Great Gold Rush.

Amindivi Islands

See Lakshadweep.

Amirante Islands

An archipelago of coral islands in the West Indian Ocean; they belong to the Seychelles, and are generally leased to coconut growers.

Amritsar

City in the Punjab in North-west India founded in 1577 by Ram Das, 4th Sikh guru, its Golden Shrine and is the centre of the Sikh faith.

Amsterdam

Since 1808 capital of the Netherlands, in North Holland province, on the Rivers Amstel and IJ. Note, however, that the seat of government is The Hague ('s Gravenhage or Den Haag). It is a seaport of great importance, linked since 1876 to the North Sea by a canal.

Amu Darya River

Rises in the Pamirs I central Asia, it flows through the Hindu Kush, Turkmenistan and Uzbekistan to a great delta flowing into the Aral Sea.

Amundsen Sea

Part of the South Pacific Ocean, whose coast is on Ellsworth Land in Antarctica.

Amur River

In North-East Asia (called in Chinese Hei-Lung Chiang), it rises in North Mongolia and flows through Mongolia, Russia and China to the Seas of Okhotsk; it is a natural border of Manchuria.

Andromeda

The Chained Lady; see Astral Constellations.

Angel Falls

Waterfall on the Caroni River, South-East Venezuela, probably the highest in the world at 3,211ft (979m), about three times as high as the Eiffel Tower. Named after the pilot Jimmy Angel who discovered them in 1935.

Ankaa

Alpha star in Phoenix; see Astral Constellations.

Annapolis
State capital of Maryland; see United States of America.

Antares
Alpha star in Scorpius (Scorpio); see Astral Constellations.

Antlia
The Air Pump; see Astral Constellations.

Antonine Wall

A defensive wall about 36 miles long, built in 140–142CE, between Carriden (on the Forth) to Old Kilpatrick (on the Clyde), by Lollius Urbicus, Roman governor of Britain under the Emperor Antoninus Pius. It was built of turf, with a ditch on the Scottish side and periodic forts. It was abandoned after half a century or so.

Antrim
A county of Northern Ireland.

Apache State
Nickname of the State of Arizona; see United States of America.

Apennines
(Italian Appennino); a range of mountains in Italy from the Maritime Alps to the Straits of Messina, a distance of some 650 miles (1,050 km). The highest peak is Monte Corno (9,560 ft (2,914 m)).

Appenzell
Capital of the Swiss half-Canton (*qv*) of Appenzell Inner-Rhoden.

Appian Way
Begun *c*312BCE by the censor Appius Claudius Cæcus; it connects Rome to Brundusium (Brindisi). Some 350 miles (550m) long, it is known as 'the queen of long distance roads'.

Appleby
A municipal borough and county town of Westmorland (now Cumbria) near the River Eden and at the foot of Dufton Fells, formerly a border stronghold, and today noted for its annual horse fair.

Appleton Layer
A layer in the ionosphere (*qv*) (also called the F-layer) discovered by the British physicist Sir Edward Appleton (1892–1963). It is 150–1000m above the surface of the earth, contains a high proportion of free electrons, and aids long-range radio transmission. See also Heaviside layer.

Appomattox
A village in central Virginia where, on 9 April 1865, the American Civil War came to an end when the Confederates under Robert E Lee surrendered to the Unionists under Ulysses S Grant.

Apus
The Bird of Paradise; see Astral Constellations.

Aquarius
The Water Bearer; see Astral Constellations.

Aquila
The Eagle; see Astral Constellations.

Aquilo
Ancient Rome – a northwesterly wind; see Winds.

Aquilon
North Wind – a Shakespearean epithet; see Winds.

Ara
The Altar; see Astral Constellations.

Arcturus
Alpha star in Boötes; see Astral Constellations.

Aries
The Ram; see Astral Constellations.

Arizona
An American State; see United States of America.

Arkansas
An American State; see United States of America.

Armagh
A county of Northern Ireland.

Arneb
Alpha star in Lepus; see Astral Constellations.

Arthur's Seat
The summit (823ft (250m) asl) of a large hill roughly 1,650 yards (1.5km) in diameter to the east of Edinburgh (*qv*) in the Holyrood District. Once used for archery practice, the ground was called in Gaelic *Ard-na-said* (the height of arrows), from which its modern name derives.

Asellus australis
A significant star in Cancer; see Astral Constellations.

Asellus borealis
A significant star in Cancer; see Astral Constellations.

Ashram
1   A Hindu holy man's retreat.
2   A house for destitutes.

Asphaltic Lake
Another name for the Dead Sea (*qv*), where asphalt is found in abundance both on the water and on the banks.

Asteroids
Minor planets; chunks of rock in orbit around the Sun, mainly between the orbits of Mars and Jupiter, but there are enough between the Earth and Mars to cause astronomers, or the tabloids, concern from time to time. The largest is Ceres (diameter 670 miles; 1,025 km) which would have a devastating effect were it to strike Earth; some believe that a catastrophic impact brought the age of the dinosaurs to an abrupt end.

Aswan Dam
Built on the River Nile in Egypt in 1902 and twice raised; the Swan High Dam was built 4 miles (6 km) upstream from the original dam in 1971, and the reservoir Lake Nasser now extends 300 miles (480 km) from the First to the Third Cataract.

Atlanta
State capital of Georgia; see United States of America.

Atlantic City
A resort in South-East New Jersey on an Island in the Atlantic Coast, Absecon Beach.

Atlantic Intercoastal Waterway
A system of inland waterways some 1,550 miles (2,500 km) in length on the East coast of America between Cape Cod and Florida Bay.

Atlantic Ocean
The world's second largest ocean, extending as it does from the Arctic to the Antarctic Oceans. Its area is 31,500,000 square miles (81,600,000 km^2), and its greatest depth 30,250 feet (5.73 miles, 9,220 m).

Atlantis
Historically, a large mythical island or continent in the Atlantic Ocean which sank below the waves, giving endless excitement to those with pet theories as to where it was and is, especially makers of television documentaries. After the discovery of America, that continent was briefly identified as Atlantis; latterly, it has been identified it as the volcanic island Stronghyle in the Eastern Mediterranean, submerged about 1,500BCE.

Atria
Alpha star in Triangulum Australe; see Astral Constellations.

Augusta
State capital of Maine; see United States of America.

Auld Reekie
(Scottish = Old Smoky) the City of Edinburgh, in the days when its perpetual blanket of smoke echoed that over London (The Smoke).

Aulis
An ancient harbour in Boeotia, whence the Greeks are supposed to have sailed to wage the Trojan war.

Auriga
The Charioteer; see Astral Constellations.

Auster
See Ostria.

Austin
State capital of Texas; see United States of America.

Austronesia
The islands of the Central and South Pacific, including Indonesia, Melanesia, Micronesia and Polynesia.

Austru
Romania – an east or southeast wind, cold in winter; it may be a local name for a foehn wind; see Winds.

Avalon
1 In Celtic legend, an island paradise in the western seas.
2 In the Arthurian Legend, the place whither Morgan Le Fay bore the mortally wounded King Arthur, and where he is buried. Its identification as Glastonbury (qv) is due to shaky etymology.

Babel, or Tower of Babel

In the Old Testament [Gen 11:1–10], a tower that the then monolingual people of the Earth decided to build – perhaps in Babylon (hence the name) – to reach from Earth to Heaven, whereupon Yahweh, for some reason, decided to 'confound their language, that they might not understand one another's speech'. This move has hindered international co-operation ever since, and added untold millions to the European Community budget, for every document has to be presented in every member language.

Ayers Rock
See Uluru.

Backs, The
Popular name for Queen's Road, Cambridge (England), so-called because the backs of certain colleges (Trinity Hall, Clare, King's, Queens') can be seen therefrom. It is famous for its display of crocuses, daffodils and other spring flowers.

Badger State
Nickname of the State of Wisconsin; see United States of America.

Bad-I-Sad-O-Bist-Roz
Afghanistan – a hot and dry northwesterly wind June through September; see Winds.

Baffin Bay; Baffin Island
Baffin Island is the largest island in the Canadian Arctic, between Hudson Bay and Greenland, from which it is separated by Baffin Bay. William Baffin (c1584–1622) was an English navigator, pilot on board *Discovery* (Capt Robert Bylot) seeking the Northwest Passage) in 1615–16.

Bag End
In *The Lord of the Rings,* the name of the home of the two Hobbits, Bilbo Baggins and Frodo, located in Northfarthing, a part of The Shire. It stands in the side of The Hill, where at the bottom runs the river The Water, through the Hobbit village Hobbiton.

Baguio
A hurricane; see Winds.

Baja California
(Spanish = drop or fall; *pron* baa-haa) – In the US, also known as Lower California, is part of Mexico, from whose main mass it is separated by the Gulf of California.

Bali wind
East Java – a strong east wind; see Winds.

Balolo moon
The annelid balolo (or palolo or paolo) worm (*Eunice viridis*) flourishes among coral reefs in the Pacific; its sexual activity, when its rear end containing sperm or ova detaches and swims to the surface to release the gametes, is governed by the phases of the moon. There is a small rising in October (Vula i balolo lailai in the Fijian calendar), and a much larger one in November (Vula i balolo levu), when the islanders put to sea to collect the delicacy.

Barat
Sulawesi (Celebes) – a heavy northwest squall December-February in Manado Bay on the north coast; see Winds.

Barber
A strong wind carrying damp snow/sleet/spray that freezes upon contact with objects, especially the beard and hair; see Winds.

Barcelona
Capital of the Spanish Region of Catalonia; see Spanish Autonomous Communities.

Bartholomew Fair
An annual fair held at Smithfield (London) on St Bartholomew's Day (24 August), from 1133 to 1752, and then (after calendar reform) on 3 September until its last year: 1855. It moved from Smithfield to Islington in 1840; its successor was the Caledonian Market ('The Stones') which closed in 1939, but lives on as the New Caledonian Market in Bermondsey, South London.

Basel
Capital of the Swiss half-Canton (*qv*) of Basel-Stadt.

Baten Kaitos
A significant star in Cetus; see Astral Constellations.

Baton Rouge
State capital of Louisiana; see United States of America.

Battle Born State
Nickname of the State of Nevada; see United States of America.

Bay State
Nickname of the State of Massachusetts; see United States of America.

Bayamo
Cuba – a violent wind blowing from the land on the south coast, especially near the Bight of Bayamo; see Winds.

Bayou State
Nickname of the State of Louisiana ; see United States of America.

Bear State
Nickname of the State of Arkansas; see United States of America.

Beaver State
Nickname of the State of Oregon; see United States of America.

Beef State
Nickname of the State of Nebraska; see United States of America.

Beehive State
Nickname of the State of Utah; see United States of America.

Bellatrix
A significant star in Orion; see Astral Constellations.

Bellinzona
Capital of the Swiss Canton (*qv*) of Ticino.

Below the line
1   In adagencyspeak, marketing methods that are less visible, such as gifts and loyalty cards.
2   In accountancyspeak, money used for capital expenditure (*cf* Above the line).

Bentu de Soli
Sardinia – an east wind on the coast; see Winds.

Berg
1   A South African mountain or large hill, often of historical importance.
2   South Africa – a hot, dry wind; see Winds.

Beringia
The historical Bering (or Siberian) Land Bridge to Alaska, now submerged under the Bering Strait.

Berkshire Hills (Berkshires)
(*pron* Burke-shears) In the US, in West Massachusetts, a southern extension of the Green Mountains of Vermont. The highest point is Mount Greylock (3,491ft).

Bern (Berne)
Swiss Canton (*qv*) and its capital.

Betelgeuse
Alpha star in Orion; see Astral Constellations.

Beverly Hills
A town that has become home to many of America's leading film stars and other media celebrities, found in south west California, close to Los Angeles. Couch tours take tourists around the area to view the grand houses belonging to their favourite screen stars. Douglas Fairbanks was the first movie star to live there, renting a 36-room mansion in 1919. During the years of 1922 and 1930 the population rose two-and-a-half-thousand-fold.

Bible Belt
In the US, the rural South and Midwest of America, home of fundamentalism, especially before WW2.

Big Apple, The
New York City, on and off since the 1920s, perhaps because it's the core of activity, where it's all at, man.

Big Easy
A nickname for the city of New Orleans, Louisiana.

Big Sea Day
Old-time custom in New Jersey when, on the second Saturday in August, the farmers and their families drive to the sea-shore to picnic and to bathe in their everyday clothes.

Big Triangle
In the days of sailing ships, the route from Britain to New South Wales; then with a load of coal to South America, and back to Britain with a cargo of nitrates.

Biggin Hill
London Biggin Hill Airport, on a site opened in 1917, later RAF Biggin Hill in the London Borough of Bromley, was one of the command bases for the defence of London in WW2, with squadrons of Hurricanes and Spitfires; it played a crucial part in the Battle of Britain (10 July–31 October 1940).

Bise, Bize
Switzerland – a cold dry northerly wind mainly prevalent in Spring; see Winds.

Bismarck
State capital of North Dakota; see United States of America.

Bivvy
Short for bivouac, a temporary encampment where, for example, a groundsheet hung from a string might form a primitive shelter.

Blaast
A frigid wind of the north; see Winds.

Black Belt
In the US, a crescent-shaped and highly fertile prairie region of about 5,000 square miles along the valley of the Alabama River in Alabama and NE Mississippi, Carolina.

Bleak House
The ninth Charles Dickens novel begun in 1851 and published in parts between March 1852 and September 1853; it deals with the vexations of the Court of Chancery in the interminable case of Jarndyce –v– Jarndyce.

Blefuscu
In Swift's *Gulliver's Travels* (1726), an island separated from Lilliput (*qv*) by a narrow channel, whose navy was put out of action by Gulliver; the story is a satire on the relationship between England and France.

Blighty
Particularly in WW1, Blighty referred to Britain, as well as a wound severe enough to get one sent home. Hindi *bilayati* = foreign land.

Blizzard
A strong, bitterly cold wind that whips falling snow into a frenzy; see Winds.

Bloomsday
16 June 1904, the day on which Stephen Dedalus and Leopold Bloom wander round Dublin and finally meet, in James Joyce's *Ulysses* (1918). It was the very day on which Joyce and Nora Barnacle (later Mrs Joyce) first walked out together.

Blue Grass State
Nickname of the State of Kentucky; see United States of America.

Blue Norther
See Norther.

Boise City
State capital of Idaho; see United States of America.

Bolivia
South American country named after Simón Bolivar (1783–1830). Nicknamed The Liberator he liberated Columbia, Ecuador, Peru and Venezuela from Spanish rule, but failed to unite them. In his honour, Upper Peru was named Bolivia in 1825.

Bollywood
See Hollywood.

Bombay
See Mumbai.

Boötes
The Herdsman; see Astral Constellations.

Bora
West coast of the Adriatic – a violent cold North wind that blows (usually in the winter) from the Hungarian basin; see Fall wind.

Borasco
Mediterranean – a thunderstorm or violent squall; see Winds.

Border(s), The
1   The area on either side of the England-Scotland boundary.
2   In South Africa, the Cape Province region around East London.

Borders Region
A local government region dating from 1975 of about 1,800 square miles (4,700 km^2) in the south of Scotland, incorporating Berwick, part of Midlothian, Peebles, Roxburgh, and Selkirk; its administrative centre is Newton St Boswells.

Boreas, Borras
A Classical name for north winds; may be the origin of Bora; see Winds.

Boston Stump
The familiar name of the stumpy octagonal tower 272ft (83m) in height of the church of St Botolph, a familiar landmark in the town of Boston, Lincs for travellers both on land and on sea.

Boston Tea-Party
In Boston MA in 1773 a group of Americans dressed as Indians, who sought to protest against British rule and the import of cheap tea, dumped a cargo of tea into the harbor. With the sound of a thousand speakers blaring: 'No taxation without representation', the tourist may yet be photographed casting a putative bale of tea into the water (hiding the rope provided for its retrieval).

Boston
State capital of Massachusetts; see United States of America.

Botein
A significant star in Aries; see Astral Constellations.

Brickfielder
S Australia – a hot dry wind; similar to the Harmattan; see Winds.

Brigadoon
According to the Lerner and Lowe musical (1947), and the film of 1954, a Scottish village that appears out of the mist for a day every 100 years; the strength of his love with Brigadoonian Cyd Charisse enables Gene Kelly (in the film) to leave the real world and become part of the mystical village.

Brisa, Briza
S America – a northeast coastal wind; Puerto Rico – an east wind during the Trade Wind season; Philippines – the north East Monsoon; see Winds.

Brisote
Cuba – the strongest northeast trade winds; see Winds.

Boxer Rebellion

The Boxers (properly Fists of Righteous Harmony) were a secret society in China in the late C19 with two aims: the overthrow of the Imperial Qing or Ch'ing dynasty, and the expulsion of foreigners. At that time, several European countries – Austria, France, Germany, Great Britain, Italy, as well as Japan and Russia, had forced China to accept humiliating and unwelcome trading concessions. The USA was also trying to acquire trading rights in the country. In 1898 the Dowager Empress Isu Hsi managed to turn the Boxers' revolutionary tendencies to violent attacks on foreign religious and trade missions, and the uprising culminated in mid-June 1900 with the Boxers besieging the foreign legations' compound outside the Forbidden City in Beijing (Peking), the capital of China. 45,000 foreign troops, from all the besieged nations as well as the USA, fully equipped with the most modern weapons, invaded China and raised the siege on 14 August. They went on to sack the Forbidden City, forcing the court to flee. The Dowager Empress was humiliated further when the foreign nations then enforced an 'open door' trading policy, giving them huge trading concessions.

Broad, The

The Oxford penchant for shortening street names results in Broad Street becoming The Broad, High Street becoming The High, Turl Street becoming The Turl, St Ebbe's Street becoming St Ebbs, and so on.

Brobdingnag

See Gulliver's Travels.

Brookside Close

The fictional setting for the Liverpudlean soap Brookside, so-named because a brook runs alongside the close. The show was axed 4 November 2003 due to low ratings, yet rumours are rife that the programme will start up again November 2004. Brookside was devised by Phil Redmond, who was also responsible for Grange Hill (a soap based on a secondary school) and Hollyoaks (qv).

Brownfield site

A piece of land on which building is proposed which has already been developed at some time; cf greenfield site.

Brubu

East Indies – a squall; see Winds.

Buckeye State
Nickname of the State of Ohio; see United States of America.

Bull's Eye Squall
S Africa – one forming off the coast in fair weather, so called because of the small isolated cloud marking the top of the invisible vortex of the storm; see Winds.

Bundu
The South African bush, or wild country.

Bura, Buran
Central Asia – a blizzard blowing from the North, or a summer wind from the North raising dust storms; see Winds.

Buster
SE Australian coast – a sudden violent cold wind; see Winds.

Butte
An isolated hill with steep sides and a smaller top than a mesa.

Byzantium
Ancient Greek city on the Bosphorous, founded c660BCE; it became Constantinople in 330CE, and Istanbul in 1930.

Caelum
The Chisel; see Astral Constellations.

Caledonian Canal
Engineered by Thomas Telford, a system of lakes and canals about 60 miles (100km) long, in Scotland that links the North Sea with the Irish Sea, via the Great Glen. It was opened to navigation on 1822, and today is used mainly by small craft.

Caledonian Market
See Bartholomew Fair.

California
An American State; see United States of America.

Camelopardalis
The Giraffe; see Astral Constellations.

Cancer
The Crab; see Astral Constellations.

Canes Venatici
The Hunting Dogs; see Astral Constellations.

Canis Major
The Great Dog; see Astral Constellations.

Canis Minor
The Little Dog; see Astral Constellations.

Cannes Film Festival
Regarded as the most important in Europe, this international film festival attracts the jet set, the world's press and many leading figures of the cinema industry each year in May at Cannes, South France.

Canopus
Alpha star in Carina; see Astral Constellations.

Cape Cod
A long, sandy peninsula in South-East Massachusetts with Cape Cod Bay to the west and the Atlantic Ocean to the east. The small seaside resort is the setting for the action of *Jaws* (1975) – Stephen Spielberg's horror film about a great white shark, based on the book written by Peter Benchley. The film culminates in a battle between the shark and the hunter (played by Robert Shaw), with the help of the chief-of-police (Roy Scheider) and the marine biologist Matt Hooper (Richard Dreyfuss).

Cape Doctor, The Doctor
South Africa – a strong southeast wind that blows on the coast; see Winds.

Cape Horn
The rocky southern tip of South America (belonging to Chile), named after his native northern Dutch home town of Hoorn in 1616 by Willem Schouten (c1580–1625).

Cape of Good Hope
Originally the Cape of Storms, the southernmost point of South-West Africa; named by Bartholemew Diaz (c1450–1500) in 1486; renamed by the less pessimistic John II of Portugal (1455–95).

Cape Peninsula
A well-named feature in South-West South Africa, on which stand Cape Town and many of its suburbs.

Capella
Alpha star in Auriga; see Astral Constellations.

Caph
A significant star in Cassiopeia; see Astral Constellations.

Cappela
A significant star in Taurus; see Astral Constellations.

Capricornus
The Goat; see Astral Constellations.

Carabinera
Spain – a squall; see Winds.

Carey Street
A street off Chancery Lane in the City of London, where is to be found the Bankruptcy Court; hence to be in (or on one's way to) Carey Street may be a description of one's financial position; *cf* Queer Street.

Carina
The Keel; see Astral Constellations.

Carlow
A county in the Republic of Ireland (Province of Leinster).

Carson City
State capital of Nevada; see United States of America.

Carthage
Having bought 'as much land as could be covered with a bull's hide', Dido then cut the hide into thin strips, enclosing enough land to build Byrsa ('bull's hide), the citadel of Carthage (*cf* Yakutsk).

Casablanca
A port, and the largest city in Morocco, the setting for the classic romantic film (1942) starring Humphrey Bogart and Ingrid Bergman as one-time lovers who meet again, and part on a misty airstrip; the film does not contain the line 'Play it again, Sam'.

Cascadia
In the US, the Cascade Mountains and the surrounding area.

Cassiopeia
The Cassiopeia; see Astral Constellations.

Castor
Alpha star in Gemini; see Astral Constellations.

Cat's Paw
US – a breeze just strong enough to ripple the surface of water; see Winds.

Cavalier State
Nickname of the State of Virginia; see United States of America.

Cavan
A county in the Republic of Ireland (Province of Ulster).

Caver, Kaver
Hebrides – a gentle breeze; see Winds.

Centaurus
The Centaur; see Astral Constellations.

Centennial State
Nickname of the State of Colorado; see United States of America.

Central Park
See New York.

Cephei
A significant star in Cepheus; see Astral Constellations.

Cepheus
See Astral Constellations.

Cetus
The Whale; see Astral Constellations.

Ceuta
Spanish Region and its capital; see Spanish Autonomous Communities.

Ceylon
1   Film location for *The Bridge on the River Kwai,* David Lean's war epic (1957). The story is set in a WW2 Burmese prisoner-of-war camp, and recounts the building of the Siam Railway.
2   See *Sri Lanka.*

Chamaeleon
See Astral Constellations.

Charleston
State capital of West Virginia; see United States of America.

Chelm
(Pronounced 'Khelm'); in Jewish folklore, a mythical city inhabited by loveable morons. In 1967, a Yiddish musical by Monty Norman and C P Taylor *Who's Pinkus – Where's Chelm,* starring Bernard Bresslaw, ran for 10 performances at the Jeanetta Cochrane Theatre, and sank without trace.

Cheyenne
State capital of Wyoming; see United States of America.

Chi'ing Fung
China – a gentle breeze; see Winds.

Chili
Tunisia – the Sirocco; see Winds.

Chinook State
Nickname of the State of Washington; see United States of America.

Chinook, Snow Eater
1   Rocky Mountains – a warm dry wind that descends the eastern slopes and may raise the temperature by up to 40°F in minutes.
2   NW Coast of US – a warm, moist southwest wind; Southern California – the Santa Ana. The Native American Chinook means 'snow eater'; it is a foehn wind; see Winds.

Chocolatero
Mexico Gulf Coast – a hot sandy squall, coloured brown by dust.

Chomolungma
See Everest.

Chort
A significant star in Leo; see Astral Constellations.

Chubasco
West coast of Central America – a violent rainy-season squall with thunder and lightning; see Winds.

Chur
Capital of the Swiss Canton (qv) of Grabünden.

Churada
Mariana Islands – a severe rain squall during the northeast monsoon, from November through April or May, especially from January through March; see Winds.

Churchill Falls
Renamed (1965) Grand Falls in South-West Labrador, East Canada, on the Churchill (formerly Hamilton) River; one of the world's greatest hydroelectric schemes.

Churchill River
1   In East Canada, flowing towards the Atlantic Ocean; about 600 miles (1,000 km) in length.
2   Also in Canada, in north-west Saskatchewan, flowing east to Hudson Bay at the town of Churchill 1,000 miles (1,600 km) in length.

Cierzo
See Mistral.

Circinus
The Compasses; see Astral Constellations.

Cirrhosis-by-the-Sea
Hollywood house shared by David Niven and Errol Flynn.

Cinque Ports

Although cinque is French for five, this confederation of five English ports – Dover, Hythe, Romney and Sandwich in Kent, and Hastings in Sussex – is pronounced 'sink' not 'sank'. The five created an informal confederation in C11 to regulate the wealth-producing herring fairs, but since they sit strategically on the south-east coast overlooking the English Channel, the Medieval kings found it expedient to gain the ports' support. In 1260 the first known formal charter was issued acknowledging their joint rights over the herring fairs and giving the ports freedom from taxes and the right to raise their own local taxes. In return the ports supplied ships for the Royal fleet, both for war and for general transport of the monarch. Rye and Winchelsea later joined the list, as did a number of others on the same coast. The post of Lord Warden of the Cinque Ports has been filled by the Duke of Wellington, Sir Winston Churchill, and Queen Elizabeth, the Queen Mother.

City of Brotherly Love
Nickname for the city of Philadelphia, PA.

City of Dreaming Spires
Oxford, England, so described in 1866 by Matthew Arnold (1822–88) in his poem *Thyrsis* (1866).

Civil War (US)
See Confederate States.

Clare
A county in the Republic of Ireland (Province of Munster).

Cleckheckmondsedge
An area in South Yorkshire between Halifax and Dewsbury, comprising Cleckheaton, Liversedge and Heckmondwike.

Clitheroe
Described as half in Lancashire and half in Fairyland.

Cloud Cuckoo-land
The inhabitants of which, often identified by their political opponents, put forward hare-brained schemes; originally the city *Nephelokokygia* built in the air by the birds (to separate humans and gods) in the play *The Birds* by Aristophanes (*c* 450–*c*385BCE).

Coat hangar, The
Sydney Harbour Bridge (AS).

COBRA
Cabinet Office Briefing Room A is at 10 Downing Street, London.

Colorado
An American State; see United States of America.

Columba, the Dove
See Astral Constellations.

Columbia
State capital of South Carolina; see United States of America.

Columbus
State capital of Ohio; see United States of America.

Coma Berenices, Berenice's Hair
See Astral Constellations.

Comstock Lode
In the US, a gold- and silver-bearing vein of rock on the eastern slope of the Sierra Nevada Mountains near Carson City, named after prospector Henry Comstock; the site of a gold rush from 1859 to 1880.

Concord
State capital of New Hampshire; see United States of America.

Confederate States

Also known as Dixie or The South – in the US comprise Alabama, Arkansas, Florida, Georgia, Louisiana, Mississippi, North and South Carolina, Tennessee, Texas, and Virginia, that seceded from the Union in 1861, resulting in the American Civil War (1861–5). The conflict was between the agricultural, slave-owning South and the industrialised North, precipitated by the election of the anti-slavery president Abraham Lincoln in 1860.

Connecticut
An American State; see United States of America.

Constantinople
Byzantium became Constantinople (after Constantine the Great) in 330 and Constantinople became Istanbul in 1930.

Constitution State
Nickname of the State of Connecticut; see United States of America.

Contiguous States
(Conterminous or the Lower 48 States) are those which border one with another; Alaska and Hawaii are not Contiguous.

Contrastes
West Mediterranean – Spring and Autumn winds a short distance apart blowing from opposite quadrants; see Winds.

Conundrum Castle
The name given by Sir Walter Scott to Abbotsford, a country estate on Tweedside, Scotland. Scott's poem *The Lady of the Lake* was set on nearby Loch Katrine.

Copyright Libraries
In the British Isles, there are six libraries who must, by law, each be offered a copy of every published work; they are The British Library (formerly The British Museum Library); The Cambridge University Library; The Bodleian Library, Oxford; The National Library of Scotland; The National Library of Wales; Trinity College Library, Dublin.

Cor Caroli
Alpha star in Canes Venatici; see Astral Constellations.

Cordonazo
West coast of Mexico – southerly hurricane winds; the 'Lash of St Francis'. associated with tropical cyclones in the Pacific Ocean. The Cordonazo may occur from May through November, with particular fury about the Feast of St Francis – 4 October; see Winds.

Cork
A county in the Republic of Ireland (Province of Munster).

Cornhusker State
Nickname of the State of Nebraska; see United States of America.

Coromell
La Paz, Gulf of California – a night land breeze prevailing from November through May; see Winds.

Corona Australis
The Southern Crown; see Astral Constellations.

Corona Borealis
The Northern Crown; see Astral Constellations.

Coronation Street
The setting for an ITV soap of that name, centring on the pub, the Rover's Return.

Corvus, the Crow
See Astral Constellations.

Coterminous States
See Contiguous States.

Cotton State
Nickname of the State of Alabama; see United States of America.

Court of St James's
The British court to which foreign ambassadors are accredited.

Coyote State
Nickname of the State of South Dakota; see United States of America.

Crab Nebula
An expanding mass of gas about 6,000 light years away in Taurus; the remains of a supernova noted in 1054CE, so-called from its shape. The Crab Pulsar resulted from the supernova, and has a period of 0.033s.

Crater, the Cup
See Astral Constellations.

Creole State
Nickname of the State of Louisiana; see United States of America.

Creole
1 A language developed by interaction between two native language from which a third language develops.
2 A name given to native-born inhabitants of French ancestry living in Louisiana and other nearby States.
3 Other peoples speaking creole languages.

Crescent City
New Orleans, LA.

Crivetz
Romania – a cold northeasterly blizzard wind; see Winds.

Cross Benches
Those in the British House of Commons or House of Lords whereon neutral or independent members sit.

Crossing the Line
An opportunity for maritime high jinks when those who haven't before sailed across the equator are subjected to some buffoonery (such as being 'shaved' with an enormous wooden 'razor') at the hands of 'King Neptune'. A similar ceremony may take place when crossing the Arctic Circle or other chosen line.

Crossroads of the Pacific
Honolulu, so called from its position with relation to shipping lanes and air routes.

Crown of the East
Antioch, the ancient capital of Syria.

Crux
The Southern Cross; see Astral Constellations.

Culloden
In 1746, Bonnie Prince Charlie and the Highland clans were defeated at Culloden Moor, near Inverness; it was the end of Scottish independence and Stuart claims to the throne.

Cumbre Vieja
A volcano on the Canary Island La Palma from which, it is feared, an enormous chunk might fall, sending off a 500-ft tsunami which would reach the coast of West Africa in five hours, and the US coast in 12 hours, hitting New York, Boston, Washington and Miami with 60 ft waves.

Cupboard
That under the Stairs at 4 Privet Drive, Little Whinging, Surrey; in the stories, the address of Harry Potter before he starts his life at Hogwarts. His parents died when he was young, and so he was taken into care by his Aunt Petunia and Uncle Vernon Dursley with their son Dudley, where he lived in a cupboard under the stairs.

Custer's Last Stand
At Little Big Horn, Montana, in 1876 (25 June), when General George Custer (b1839) and 200 men were massacred by a Red Indian (now Native American) force some ten times as large under the Sioux Chief Sitting Bull (Tatanka Iyotake (c1831–90)).

Cyclone
Indian Ocean and Bay of Bengal – a severe tropical storm (winds 64 knots); see also Hurricane and Typhoon. Closed circulations in the mid-latitudes and small-scale circulations such as tornadoes may also be termed Cyclones; see Winds.

Cygnus
The Swan; see Astral Constellations.

Deanery
See hundred.

Death Valley
The lowest, hottest and driest spot in America, in East California and West Nevada; the lowest point is 282 ft (86 m) below sea level, and the extent of the Valley is some 1,500 square miles (3,900 km^2).

Deep South
The South-East states of the US, comprising Alabama, Georgia, Louisiana, Mississippi, and South Carolina.

Delaware
An American State; see United States of America.

Delémont
Capital of the Swiss Canton (*qv*) of Jura.

Delphinus
The Dolphin; see Astral Constellations.

Delt
A significant star in Cepheus; see Astral Constellations.

Deneb Kaitos
A significant star in Cetus; see Astral Constellations.

Deneb
Alpha star in Cygnus; see Astral Constellations.

Denebola
A significant star in Leo; see Astral Constellations.

Denver
State capital of Colorado; see United States of America.

Des Moines
State capital of Iowa; see United States of America.

Deschubba
A significant star in Scorpius; see Astral Constellations.

Devils Dyke
1   A military fortification in Cambridgeshire, England extending from the village of Reach to the village of Woodditton.
2   A ravine in the South Downs north-west of Brighton, East Sussex.

Diablo
Northern California – Chinook or Santa Ana winds blowing below canyons in Diablo range (East Bay) hills; may exceed 60 mph. The Diabolo develops when the pressure over Nevada is higher than that over the central California coast; see Winds.

Diadem
Alpha star in Coma Berenices; see Astral Constellations.

Diagon Alley
In the stories of Harry Potter, a small cobbled street, packed full of shops, such as Eelops Owl Emporium, Quality Quidditch Supplies, Flourish and Blotts, Ollivanders Fine Wands, and Florean Fortescue's Ice Cream Parlour, for every wizard's needs. To get to Diagon Alley Harry has to go through the pub, The Leaky Cauldron, into the small courtyard behind where he must tap the bricks of the brick wall in the

right order so as to reveal the archway leading to Diagon Alley – 'Three up, Two Across...'

Diamond State
Nickname of the State of Delaware; see United States of America.

Dixie
See Confederate States.

Docklands
An area of east London once a thriving port, but now reduced to commercial and residential use.

Doctor
Tropics – a cooling sea breeze; South Africa – the Cape Doctor; West Australia – the Fremantle Doctor; the Harmattan; see Winds.

Dogger Bank
A large submerged sandbank in the North Sea, between the North of England and Denmark.

Doinionn
An Irish wind; see Winds.

Donegal
A county in the Republic of Ireland (Province of Ulster).

Donga
A South African dry watercourse or gully.

Dorado
The Swordfish; see Astral Constellations.

Dordogneshire
Area of the Dordogne favoured by the British.

Dorp
Afrikaans = a village.

Dotheboys Hall
In Charles Dickens's *Nicholas Nickleby* (1838–9), a dreadful boys' school in Yorkshire (designed to expose such real-life establishments of the time) presided over by the brutal, rapacious and ignorant Mr Whackford Squeers.

Dover
State capital of Delaware; see United States of America.

Down Train
That which travels away from London; *cf* up train.

Down
A county of Northern Ireland.

Downing Street
1   A short street leading off Whitehall where the British Prime Minister officially lives at No 10, next to the Chancellor of the Exchequer at No 11; the Government Whip's office is at No 12; it is named after Sir George Downing (1623–84) who once owned property there.
2   An epithet for the government in power ('Downing Street denies all knowledge of the claim').

Draco
The Dragon; see Astral Constellations.

Dragon('s) Hill

According to legend, the hill in Berkshire, England, where St George slew the dragon; other contenders for the site of the dracocide are Silene in Libya, or Berytus (Beyrut). Another Dragon Hill possibility is the West Saxon hero Cedric (+ 5,000 men) slaying Naud the pendragon.

Dream Factory, The
Hollywood.

Drift
A South African ford over a stream or river; *eg* Rourke's Drift.

Driftless Region
In the US, Northwestern Illinois, northeastern Iowa, southeastern Minnesota and southwestern Wisconsin. This area was not subject to glaciation in the most recent ice age and is therefore relatively hilly. When the ice sheets covering adjacent areas melted they left a deposit of rock and soil called glacier drift; the Driftless Region derives its name from its lack of this drift.

Drove
That which is driven, as a track or watercourse.

Dubhe
Alpha star in Ursa Major; see Astral Constellations.

Dublin
A county in the Republic of Ireland (Province of Leinster).

Dudman and Ramhead

Dudman and Ramhead are two forelands 23 sea miles apart; the phrase 'when Dudman and Ramhead meet' therefore refers to something which will never happen.

Ealing Studios

Known for the Ealing Comedies, a series of frivolous comedies made in the 1940s and 50s, such as Alexander Mackendrick's *The Ladykillers* (1955) and Charles Crichton's *Titfield Thunderbolt* (1952). This small British studio complex built in London, and costing £140,000, opened in 1931. Despite low budgets, production standards were high, and the films produced often concentrated on characterisation, plotting and scripts rather than the action and glamorous settings. Ealing studios were closed in 1956 and were sold to the BBC – the last film to be made was *The Long Arm* (1956). However Ealing films continued to be made at the Elstree studios in Borehamwood for a further three years until the assets were sold to Associated British.

Earl's Court

A district of west London where there is a great exhibition complex; it is also a magnet for Australians, hence its nickname Kangaroo Valley.

Edge Hill

A station originally on the London and North West Railway; the last stop before Liverpool Lime Street; hence 'getting out at Edge Hill' refers to *coitus interruptus*; in Glasgow, they get off at Paisley; a Cambridge equivalent might be 'getting out at Barnwell Junction', for Oxford 'at Kidlington', and so on.

Edgehill

A ridge in South Warwickshire where the first (indecisive) battle of the English Civil War took place in 1642.

Edinburgh

Since C15 the capital of Scotland, on the south side of the Firth of Forth across which stride that monument of Victorian engineering the cantilever railway bridge (1890) and the suspension road bridge (1964). As the commercial and cultural centre of Scotland, Edinburgh has been hosting a summer Festival for half a century. Its features include the castle on top of the 443ft Castle Rock, Palace of Holyroodhouse, the Scott Monument and the Royal Mile.

Egremont Crab Fair

Held in Egremont, Cumbria on the third Saturday in September; crab apples, now represented by apples, are distributed, and all manner of high jinks take place, particularly gurning (making hideous faces) through a braffin (horse-collar).

Elephanta

Malabar Coast, India – a strong southerly or southeasterly wind blowing during September and October; it marks the end of the south-west monsoon; see Winds.

Elnath

A significant star in Auriga; see Astral Constellations.

Eltanin

A significant star in Cygnus; see Astral Constellations.

Emmerdale

A fictional area of Yorkshire, England, where is set an ITV soap centring on *The Woolpack*; the original name of the soap was *Emmerdale Farm*.

Empire State of the South

Nickname of the State of Georgia; see United States of America.

Empire State

Nickname of the State of New York; see United States of America.

England

The 'Land of the Angles', named after Angeln, the home of the C5 Germanic invaders of the land conquered by the Normans in 1066, east of Wales (with which it was united in 1536); and south of Scotland (with which it was united in 1707); in C18 the world's leading colonial power in an age of colonialism, and seat of the developments that became identified as the Industrial Revolution.

Equality State

Nickname of the State of Wyoming; see United States of America.

Equator

The great circle of the Earth whose latitude is 0°, equidistant from the poles. The equator divides the Earth into Northern and Southern Hemispheres.

Equuleus

The Little Horse; see Astral Constellations.

Eridanus

See Astral Constellations.

Erinsborough

The fictional area in which *Neighbours*, an Australian soap is set. The lives of the characters centre on various locations in the area, such as Harold's Coffee Shop, Lassiter's Hotel, Lou's Place and the street on which all the neighbours live: Ramsey Street.

Ermine Street

A Roman road from Pevensey (invasion point) to London to Lincoln to York.

Errai

A significant star in Cepheus; see Astral Constellations.

Etesian

Eastern Mediterranean; Aegean Sea – NW winds of the summer months; see Winds.

Euroclydon

See Gregale.

Euros, Eurus

In Greek mythology, the rainy, stormy SE wind; see Winds.

Everest

The world's highest mountain, in the Himalaya, was named in 1865 after Sir George Everest (1790–1866), Surveyor General of India from 1830, knighted in 1861; properly pronounced Eve-Rest; it has now reverted to its PC name: in Nepal Sagarmatha (means mother goddess of the sky) and in Tibet Chomolungma (means mother goddess of the universe).

Evergreen State

Nickname of the State of Washington; see United States of America.

Fall wind

A large-scale katabatic wind (air currents descending the lee side of a mountain) that remains cold as it flows. Examples are the Adriatic Bora, the S French Mistral and the extremely cold winds along the coasts of Antarctica; see Winds.

Fangorn Forest

In *The Lord of the Rings,* the forest in Eriador, inhabited by Treebeard and the Ents, in which Merry and Pippin escape from the enemy Orcs.

Far East

The countries of East Asia; China, Japan, North and South Korea, East Siberia and the like.

Far North

The Arctic and sub-Arctic regions.

Fault plane

The surface of a fault fracture along which the rocks have been displaced.

Fault

A fracture in the earth's crust resulting in the relative displacement and loss of continuity of the rocks on either side of it.

Fawlty Towers

A BBC Comedy based on a real-life hotel and manager – the Gleneagles Hotel in the English seaside resort of Torquay run by a Mr Sinclair – where John Cleese and the team stayed whilst filming Monty Python. Basil Fawlty, played by John Cleese, is the hotel manager, with overbearing Sybil (Prunella Scales) his wife, the patient Polly (Connie Booth, who co-wrote the series with Cleese) and the piteous waiter Manuel (Andrew Sachs) from Barcelona. Famous for the catchphrase 'Don't mention the war' and the sign that changes at the beginning of each episode – the letters of Fawlty Towers rearrange (more or less) to create alternative names – such as Watery Fowls, Farty Towels and Fatty Owls. Popular worldwide, it has been shown in more than 60 countries – from Tonga to Bosnia, from China to Pakistan and from Latvia to Malta. Only 12 episodes were ever made.

Fermanagh

A county of Northern Ireland.

Fingals' Cave

An impressive basaltic cavern on the Isle of Staffa, supposed to have been the home of the legendary Gaelic hero Fingal, and inspiration for Mendelssohn's *Hebrides* Overture (1830).

First State

Nickname of the State of Delaware; see United States of America.

Firth of Forth

In Scotland, an inlet of the North Sea north of Edinburgh (*qv*).

Firth or Frith

A narrow sea inlet, especially in Scotland; *cf* fjord.

Fitzrovia

Area of London encompassing Fitzroy Square and Belgravia.

Five Towns, The

In the novels of Arnold Bennett, the pottery towns of Tunstall (represented as Turnhill), Burslem (Bursley), Hanley (Hanbridge), Stoke on Trent (Knype) and Longton (Longshaw). When challenged, Bennett admitted that he had overlooked Fenton.

Flatland

'A Romance in Many Dimensions' by 'A. Square', *ie* the mathematician Dr Edwin A. Abbott, first published in 1884, and running to several editions. In his introduction, the mathematician William Garnett wrote: 'To many... Dr Abbott's ... Flatland points the way to the clearest imagery of the fourth dimension they are likely to attain.'

Flickertail State

Nickname of the State of North Dakota; see United States of America.

Florida

An American State; see United States of America.

Foehn, Föhn

Alpine valleys – a warm dry katabatic wind whose temperature increases by adiabatic compression as it descends the lee side of a mountain range. Other Foehns include the Chinook and the Santa Ana; see Winds.

Fomalhaut

Alpha star in Piscis Austrinus (or Australis); see Astral Constellations.

Food capital of Australia, The

Melbourne.

Fogo

A volcanic island in the Cape Verde Islands group, discovered by the Portuguese at the end of C15. Fogo erupts from time to time, most recently in 1951 and 1995. An anonymous poet referred to the eruptions in a curious verse set by the madrigalist Thomas Weelkes (?1575–1623):

> Thule, the period of cosmography,
>   Doth vaunt of Hecla, whose sulphureous fire
> Doth melt the frozen clime and thaw the sky;
>   Trinacrean Etna's flames ascend not higher:
> These things seem wondrous, yet more wondrous I,
> Whose heart with fear doth freeze, with love doth fry.
>
> The Andalusian merchant that returns
>   Laden with cochineal and china dishes
> Reports in Spain how strangely Fogo burns
>   Amidst an ocean full of flying fishes:
> These things seem wondrous, yet more wondrous I,
> Whose heart with fear doth freeze, with love doth fry.

Foot of Our Stairs, The
Destination signifying surprise: 'Well! I'll go to the foot of our stairs!'

Footprint
1   An impression made by a foot.
2   The area that something affects or occupies, whether it be a computer on a desk or the sound of a sonic boom.

Formentera
One of the Balearic Islands; see Spanish Autonomous Communities.

Formosa
Now Taiwan, an island in South-East Asia between the East and the South China Seas; in 1703 there appeared in London one George Psalmanazar (c1679–1763) who purported to be Formosan and published an account of the island, complete with a grammar, all a complete fabrication that took in the London literary world until he was exposed by missionaries who knew Formosa, whereat he confessed all and turned over a new leaf. Apart from the fact that he was French, nothing about his origins is known – not even his real name.

Fornax
The Furnace; see Astral Constellations.

Fort Knox
In North Kentucky, the site of the US depository of gold reserves; hence a generic name for any tightly secured premises.

Fort Lamy
Became Ndjamena in 1973.

Fort Lauderdale
City in South-East Florida, on the Atlantic coast.

Fort Sumter
Guards Charleston Harbour in South-East South Carolina; the Fort saw the opening of the American Civil War when it was captured by Confederate forces (1861).

Fort Wayne
US city in North-East Indiana.

Fort William
1   Scottish town at the head of Loch Linnhe, named for the now-demolished fort built in 1655, named for William III in 1690, and razed in 1866.
2   Part of the Canadian city and port on Lake Superior, the other part being Port Arthur, the two now forming Thunder Bay (1970).

Fort Worth

City on North Texas on the confluence of the Clear and West forks of the Trinity River.

Forth

Scottish river 65 miles (104 km) long flowing into the Firth of Forth (*qv*) north of Edinburgh.

Forty-Ninth Parallel

The line of latitude, part of which forms a long section of the border between the USA and Canada in the west.

Forum Romanum

The great forum of ancient Rome between the Capitoline and Palatine Hills.

Frankfort

State capital of Kentucky; see United States of America.

Frauenfeld

Capital of the Swiss Canton (*qv*) of Thurgau.

Free State

Nickname of the State of Maryland; see United States of America.

Fremantle Doctor

West Australia – a cooling sea breeze, often noted during hot summer-time cricket matches; see Doctor; see Winds.

Freo

Fremantle WA.

Fribourg

Swiss Canton (*qv*) and its capital.

Fuerteventura

One of the Canary Islands; see Spanish Autonomous Communities.

Fuggaras

Moroccan underground water galleries.

Gad's Hill

In Kent, upon which stood the house that the young Charles Dickens decided that he would one day own – and did; a well-known picture 'The Empty Chair at Gad's Hill' shows Dickens's study after the master's death. Gad = Vagabond.

Gaea or Gaia

1   A Greek goddess personifying the earth, hence.

2   A name given to the concept of the earth and all things upon it as one enormous system, so arranged that its elements interact for the good of the whole.

Galway
A county in the Republic of Ireland (Province of Connacht).

Ganges or Ganga
The Ganga is a major river in Indian, associated in myth and reality with the land and people of India as well as neighbouring countries such as Bangladesh. The source of the river is the Gangotri Glacier, a vast expanse of ice five miles by fifteen, at the foothills of the Himalayas (14000 ft) in North Uttar Pradesh, which joins with Alaknanda to form Ganga at the craggy canyon-carved town of Devprayag.

Gaora
The land where (according to the traveller Richard Hakluyt) the people had no heads, eyes in their shoulders and mouths in their breasts. They are sometimes thus illustrated on old maps (*cf* René Magritte *Le Viol*)

Garden of Eden
The paradise, or place of pleasure, into which God introduced his pinnacle of creation, Adam; it is generally supposed to be in the fertile land of Mesopotamia.

Garden of Gethsemane
In Jerusalem, the scene of the betrayal the night before the crucifixion, and hence the cradle of Christianity.

Garden State
Nickname of the State of New Jersey; see United States of America.

Gassi
A flat open area between Arabian desert dunes in the desert, and often found as part of the name of a place.

Gasteiz
See Vitoria.

Gem of the Mountains
Nickname of the State of Idaho ; see United States of America.

Gem State
Nickname of the State of Idaho; see United States of America.

Gemini
The Twins; see Astral Constellations.

Geneva (Genève)
Swiss Canton (*qv*) and its capital.

Geyser

A geyser is a hot spring that periodically erupts, throwing water into the air; they are rare, as there are only 1,000 or so active geysers on earth. Four components must be present for geysers to exist: an abundant supply of water; an intense source of heat, (often from volcanic activity); unique plumbing (which must be pressure-tight; according to scientists the volcanic rock rhyolite is particularly effective at hosting geysers, as it is high in silica which can deposit a water-tight seal along the walls of the geyser plumbing.) and remoteness. Over one-half of the world's geysers are located within the boundaries of Yellowstone National Park in NW Wyoming, S Montana and E Idaho, including Old Faithful, the geyser that erupts at approximately hourly intervals.

Georgia
An American State; see United States of America.

Ghibli
Libya – the Scirocco (qv).

Giant's Causeway
'Worth seeing, but not worth going to see' said Dr Johnson, a sentiment that applies to so much in this world. The Causeway is a pavement of some 40,000 hexagonal basalt columns reaching out into the sea from the coast of County Antrim.

Glarus
Swiss Canton (qv) and its capital.

Glastonbury
A town in south-west England, in Somerset, home of a rock-music festival, but for much longer the site of what may be the oldest Benedictine Abbey (now ruined) in England, and reputedly the burial place of King Arthur.

Golden Rivet
A nautical leg-pull where the uninitiate is persuaded that every ship has one rivet of solid gold, and is sent to find it.

Golden State
Nickname of the State of California; see United States of America.

Gopher State
Nickname of the State of Minnesota; see United States of America.

Gower, The
A peninsula in West Glamorgan, Wales, west of Swansea, whereon are to be found The Mumbles and Worms Head.

Graceland
Elvis Preseley's house, now a shrine and museum.

Graffias
A significant star in Scorpius; see **Astral Constellations**.

Grafham Water
A 1,500 acre reservoir in the one-time county of Huntingdonshire formed by drowning the village of Grafham, and opened in 1966 for water supply. It became the premier trout lake in the country. Following its success, Anglian Water has since opened other reservoirs, including Rutland Water and many smaller waters for leisure pursuits.

Gran Canaria
One of the Canary Islands; see **Spanish Autonomous Communities**.

Grand Canyon State
Nickname of the State of Arizona; see **United States of America**.

Grand Canyon
In North Arizona, a gorge eroded by the Colorado River in its journey from the Little Colorado River to Lake Mead; it varies in width from 4 to 18 miles (6 to 29 km), and its greatest depth is 1 mile (1.5 km).

Grand Central Station
Not just a tourist attraction, it is one of the world's busiest railway stations – over 150,000 commuters use it every day. What is referred to as Grand Central Station is actually a terminus, serving the line Metro-North, which goes to nearby suburbs in Westchester and Conneticut via the underground route along Park Avenue. A marvellous façade with statues of Hercules, Minerva and Mercury surrounds a thirteen-foot clock, designed by architect Whitney Warren in 1913. The interior is extraordinary – 120 feet wide, 375 feet long and 125 feet high, the ceiling lavishly decorated like an evening sky with gilded stars and constellations, allowing New Yorkers something they never get to see – a night-time sky above the Big Apple!

Grand Coulee
A canyon in central Washington State on the Columbia River, at the north end of which stands the Grand Coulee Dam (1942) 550 ft (168 m) high, and 4,300 ft (1,310 m) wide.

Grand Rapids
City on the Grand River in west-central Michigan.

Grand Junction Railway

Established in 1833, and opened for passengers, parcels and light goods on 4 July 1837. Built after the success of the Liverpool and Manchester Railway the Grand Junction Railway was over eighty-two miles long, linking Birmingham with the Liverpool and Manchester line, passing through Wolverhampton, Stafford, Crewe and Warrington before reaching the Newton Junction, including 100 underbridges, 50 overbridges, 5 viaducts, 2 tunnels and 2 aqueducts. The chairman of the company was John Moss and he recruited George Stephenson and Joseph Locke as engineers. Locke had worked under Stephenson at the Stockton and Darlington Railway and the Liverpool and Manchester Railway. Stephenson did not find it easy to share power with his former pupil, and decided to leave the project in 1835. Sixteen days later the London to Birmingham line was opened, which meant that the four major cities in England – London, Birmingham, Manchester and Liverpool – were now linked by rail.

Grand Union Canal

An undertaking to connect various English canals, comprising the main length from London to Birmingham (137 miles with 166 locks) and an arm from Braunston to the Trent and Mersey (66 miles and 59 locks).

Granicus

An ancient river in NW Asia Minor; here it was that Alexander the Great, king of Macedon and founder of Alexandria, fought the Persians and won (334BCE).

Granite City, The

Aberdeen, so called from its fine granite buildings. Other names include The Flower of Scotland, The Silver City by the Golden Sands, The City of Opportunity and The City of Flowers, it having won the 'Britain in Bloom' competition several times.

Granite State

Nickname of the State of New Hampshire; see United States of America.

Great Australian Bight

The wide bay on the south coast of Australia from SE Western Australia to SW South Australia.

Great Circle

A circle, or arc thereof, on the surface of a sphere whose centre is contiguous with that of the sphere; the shortest distance between two points on the surface of a sphere.

Great Fire of London

A Frenchman, Robert Hubert was hanged at Tyburn for setting fire to Master Farryner's bakehouse in Pudding Lane, Thames Street in the early hours of Sunday 2 September 1666. In five days it laid waste 450 acres (0–7 sq mile) of London including St Paul's Cathedral, 87 other churches, and over 13,000 houses; it was finally halted by blowing up properties in its path to form a fire break.

Great Lakes, The

Superior, Michigan, Huron, Erie and Ontario, that form much of the eastern border between Canada and the US.

Great North Woods

In the US, forested regions of northern Vermont, New Hampshire and Maine; not to be confused with North Woods.

Great Plains

In the US, the Plains States are those located in the Great Plains region, between the Mississippi and the Rockies; the area known as the Mid-West lies to the east of the Great Plains.

Great Rift Valley

An extensive rift valley about 4000 miles (6400km) long in the Middle East and East Africa extending from the Jordan Valley in Syria along the Red Sea into Ethiopia and through Kenya, Tanzania, and Malawi into Mozambique. Marked by a chain of lakes; Turkana (formerly Rudolf) and Natron, and by volcano Mount Kilima-Njaro.

Great Wall of China

Extending some 4,000 miles (6,400 km) westwards from the Yellow Sea, the Great Wall was begun some 2,500 years ago in order to keep the Mongolian hordes at bay. Generally, it is about 30 ft (9 m) high, with 40 ft (12 m) towers every 1,000 yards (914 m). Compare this with Hadrian's Wall, where the milecastles are a Roman mile (540 yards) apart; perhaps the intervals have something to do with the distance for audible shouting. The Great Wall is a popular tourist attraction; it is also said to be the only man-made terrestrial object visible from the moon.

Great Trek, The
The Abolition of Slavery Act 1833 resulted in the following years in the exodus of many of the Boer farmers from Cape Colony to the Transvaal and Orange Free State.

Great Victoria Desert
In SE Western Australia and W South Australia; its area is 125,000 square miles (324,000km^2).

Great Wen
London, according to William Cobbett in *Rural Rides* (1830). Medically, a wen is a sebaceous cyst, particularly on the scalp. Perhaps Prince Charles had this metaphor in mind when he referred to the proposed extension to the National Gallery as 'like a monstrous carbuncle on the face of a much-loved and elegant friend'.

Green Belt
Sacrosanct land around a settlement where development is forbidden (unless it suits those who so designate it).

Green Mountain State
Nickname of the State of Vermont; see **United States of America**.

Greenfield site
An untouched, supposedly grassy, piece of land on which it is proposed to build, *cf* brownfield site.

Greenwich
A borough in the south east of Greater London, on the south bank of the River Thames. It has important royal and maritime connections; the Greenwich Royal Hospital, designed by Wren, became the Royal Naval College in 1873, and Wren's original Royal Greenwich Observatory is also here.

Greenwich Meridian
0° latitude, passing through the Royal Greenwich observatory.

Greenwich Village
A residential section of New York City, in Manhattan, it became a favourite bohemian haunt of authors and artists in early C20. It is the site of the main campus of New York University.

Gregale
Central and West Mediterranean – a strong, cold northeast winter wind; may be identified with the Euroclydon wind that sank St. Paul's ship; see **Winds**.

Grid North
The notional direction of north indicated by a grid of parallel lines superimposed on a map or chart; logic decrees that there is an infinite

number of grid norths, but this is acceptable only for a small area. The map will also give the grid variation or grivation: the angle between grid north and magnetic north for that map, and the rate at which it changes.

Grid Variation
See grivation.

Gringotts
In the stories of Harry Potter, a wizards' bank, run by goblins and guarded by dragons, located hundreds of miles under London, beneath the Underground. The only way of getting down to the vaults is to ride the magic mine cart – Harry's vault is #687, and Voldemort's is #713.

Grivation
Short for grid variation; on a navigation chart, the angle between grid north and magnetic north at any point.

Grub Street
Before 1830, the name of Milton Street in the London ward of Cripplegate Without, of which Dr Johnson said in his dictionary: 'Much inhabited by writers of small histories, dictionaries, and temporary poems; whence any mean production is called *grub street*'.

Grus
The Crane; see Astral Constellations.

Gulliver's Travels

Jonathan Swift (1667–1745) published this book in 1726. Ship's surgeon Lemuel Gulliver is first shipwrecked on the island of Lilliput, whose inhabitants are but six inches high; the island's goings-on satirise the politics and religious differences of Swift's time. Gulliver is then left in the country of Brobdingnag, whose inhabitants are as large as Lilliput's are small; the king's comments on Gulliver's account of Europe show Swift's views in no uncertain terms. Gulliver's third visit (that written last) is to the flying island of Laputa, where Swift lampoons philosophy, science, and particularly the 'projectors' of great plans and the speculators who support them. Gulliver's final visit is to the land of the Houyhnhnms (*pron* whinnims), gentle, cultured horses, who are contrasted with their co-dwellers, the rough and filthy Yahoos, whose qualities turn Gulliver against civilisation when he returns home. It is little wonder that children's versions of *Gulliver's Travels* concentrate on Lilliput and Brobdingnag, and omit the home truths.

Haboob

Northern and Central Sudan, especially around Khartum – a strong wind and sand- or dust-storm, followed by rain, occurring some 24 times each year (Arabic *habb* = wind); see Winds.

Hacienda

1   A large estate or ranch.
2   The main building thereon.

Hadar

A significant star in Centaurus; see Astral Constellations.

Hades

According to ancient Greek myth, the underworld where dwelt the souls of the dead, having been ferried thence across the River Styx by Charon, in return for the obeli left in their mouths.

Hadj or Hajj

1   The pilgrimage to Mecca.
2   Those who have completed it.

Hadrian's Wall

Built across England on the orders of the Roman Emperor Hadrian (76–138; emperor 117–138) in about 120ce, stretching from the Solway Firth in the east to Wallsend in the West to keep out the North Britons. Excavations in recent years have yielded an enormous amount of information about the Roman occupation.

Hamal

Alpha star in Aries; see Astral Constellations.

Hanging Gardens of Babylon

A stepped area some 400 feet square, arranged so that the planting cascaded down the terraces. It was one of the Seven Wonders of the ancient world. Some idea of the area may be gained from the official size of a football pitch, which may be between 150 and 300 feet wide, and between 600 and 780 feet long. At 3.67 acres, the Hanging Gardens occupied about the same area as an average football pitch based on the above figures.

Harem

1   The secluded part of a Moslem household where women live separately.
2   The inhabitants thereof.

Harmattan

West African Coast – a dry dusty wind blowing from the Sahara Desert across the Gulf of Guinea and the Cape Verde Islands; sometimes called the Doctor; see Winds.

Harrisburg
State capital of Pennsylvania; see United States of America.

Hartford
State capital of Connecticut; see United States of America.

Hawaii
An American State; see United States of America.

Hawkeye State
Nickname of the State of Iowa; see United States of America.

Hayate
Japan – a gale; see Winds.

Headlong Hall
A Welsh country house in the satire on the culture of his times of that name by Thomas Love Peacock (1785–1866) published in 1816. The cast of character includes the optimist Mr Forster, the pessimist Mr Escot, the status-quo-ite Mr Jenkinson, the gluttonous cleric Dr Gaster and particularly the landscape gardener Mr Milestone (a parody of Humphrey Repton (1752–1818) who succeeded Lancelot 'Capability' Brown, and indeed coined the term 'landscape gardening') who blows up part of the grounds of Headlong Hall to achieve a Reptonian effect.

Heart of Dixie
Nickname of the State of Alabama; see United States of America.

Heartbeat
Police soap, ITV family viewing, featuring the North Yorkshire Moors railway (Pickering-Grosmont) and the village of Goathland.

Heaviside Layer
An ionised, gaseous layer in the upper atmosphere predicted in 1902 by the English physicist Oliver Heaviside (1850–1925).

Heights of Abraham
See Plains of Abraham.

Hejaz
An area along the Red Sea and Gulf of Aqaba which united with Njed in 1932 to form the Kingdom of Saudi Arabia; area about 134,600 square miles (348,600 km^2).

Helena
State capital of Montana; see United States of America.

Hercules
See Astral Constellations.

Herisau

Capital of the Swiss half-Canton (*qv*) of AppenzellAusser-Rhoden.

Hide

In feudal England the amount of land sufficient to support a family, usually varying between 60 and 120 acres (24–49ha) according to the locality and quality of the land. A hide of good land was smaller than one of the poorer quality. It was long used as the basis for assessing taxes.

High, The

See Broad.

Hithe (Hythe)

Found in a place name, signifies a landing place.

Hogsnorton

Fictitious seat of Lord Marshmallow, according to the English music-hall comedian Gillie Potter ('Good evening, England, this is Gillie Potter speaking to you in English') in his comic monologue which remained virtually unchanged for many years.

Hogwarts School of Witchcraft and Wizardry

In the stories of Harry Potter, the school which Harry Potter and others attend. It is divided into four houses: Gryffindor, Hufflepuff, Ravenclaw, and the notorious Slytherin.

Holby City Hospital

Setting for the BBC1 medisoap *Holby City*, wherein all medical disciplines are practised on one floor in so far as they do not interfere with the chaotic amours of the staff, not to mention the complex beliefs and domestic dramas of the patients.

Holy Grail

The cup used by Christ at the Last Supper. Sought by many and the subject of medieval legend, romance and allegory. It was supposedly brought to England by Joseph of Arimethea and was blessed by the blood of the Saviour. The knights of the Round Table spent much of their adventures on a quest for the Holy Grail. Legend tells that the Grail disappears when approached by anyone of imperfect purity, though whether or not they are allowed to glimpse it before it vanishes we are not told; if they are not, they'll never know. Conversely, anyone who drinks of the chalice (and is therefore of perfect purity) will receive immortal life.

Hollyoaks

A TV Channel 4 teen drama series set in Chester, in the fictional borough Hollyoaks, centring mainly on the lives of the students of the college and university in that area. The first episode was broadcast 23 October 1995; since then, the show has gone from one episode a week to five episodes a week.

Hollywood

A NW suburb of Los Angeles CA, centre of American film industry because of its favourable climate; hence Bollywood, the centre of the Indian film industry based in Bombay (now Mumbai), but also a word descriptive of Indian films in general; also Nollywood, the Nigerian film industry based in Surulere.

Home Counties

Those nearest to London: Surrey, Kent, Essex and Middlesex (now no more), with sometimes Hertfordshire, Buckinghamshire and Berkshire added, and Sussex if it suit the case.

Homestake Lode

In the US, the vein of gold-bearing rock in the Black Hills of South Dakota.

Honolulu

State capital of Hawaii; see **United States of America**.

Hooghly

A river in NE India wherethrough the Ganges flows into the Bay of Bengal.

Horologium

The Clock; see **Astral Constellations**.

Horse Head Nebula

B-33; a dust cloud in the shape of a horse's head, below the first of the three stars that form Orion's Belt.

House of Keys

With the Legislative Council, a body constituting the Tynwald, or governing body of the Isle of Man.

Hundred

An ancient division of a country in England, Ireland, and parts of the US. It may still have some ecclesiastical significance, for example the outer boundary of parishes of a deanery (those under the wing of a named dean) may coincide with the boundary of a hundred.

Hundred-acre Wood

In the children's books *Winnie-the-Pooh* (1926) and *The House at Pooh Corner* (1928), A(lan) A(lexander) Milne (1882–1956) recounts the adventures of Christopher Robin (based on his son, who never forgave him) and his friends Winnie-the-Pooh (a bear of very little brain), Piglet, Kanga and Baby Roo, Eeyore, Tigger and the rest who live in Hundred-acre Wood. The Wood is based on the area in which Milne lived – Cotchford Farm in Ashdown Forest, Sussex.

Hurricane
Atlantic, Caribbean, Gulf of Mexico and Eastern Pacific – a severe tropical storm; the Caribbean Indian storm god is named Huracan; see Winds.

Hwang He (Ho)
China: the Yellow River.

Hyades
A significant star in Taurus; see Astral Constellations.

Hydra
The Sea Serpent; see Astral Constellations.

Hydrus
The Water Snake; see Astral Constellations.

Ibiza
One of the Balearic Islands; see Spanish Autonomous Communities.

Idaho
An American State; see United States of America.

IJssel
Distributary of the Rhine that flows into the IJsselmeer in northern Holland; 72 miles (116 km) in length.

Illinois
An American State; see United States of America.

Inns of Court

The collective name of the four legal societies in London that have the exclusive right of admission to the bar – Lincoln's Inn, Gray's Inn, the Inner Temple, and the Middle Temple – dating from before C14. The Inns take their name from the buildings where originally schools of law were held, apprentice lawyers gathering to learn from masters of law, much as in guild training. Today the societies are more like clubs, although they still control admission to the bar. The Inns of Chancery were lesser societies (preparatory colleges for law), dependent on the Inns of Court; their importance declined in the C18, and they disappeared in the C19.

Indianapolis
State capital of Indiana; see United States of America.

Indus
The Indian; see Astral Constellations.

Intermountain States
In the US, those between the Rocky Mountains (to the east) and the Sierras (to the west in the south) and the Cascades (to the west in the north).

International Date Line
The imaginary great semicircle running from the North Pole to the South Pole that represents the end of one day and the beginning of another. The line of longitude defined as the Greenwich meridian is the line of 0°; the date line is for the most part accordingly the line of 180°. Suppose it to be 12 noon on Sunday at Greenwich. Then just to the *west* of the date line it is 12 midnight at the *end of Sunday*, almost the first thing Monday morning. And just to the *east* of the date line it is 12 midnight at the *end of Saturday*, almost the first thing Sunday morning.

Ionosphere
A region of the earth's atmosphere, 60–1,000 km up, where there is a high concentration of charged particles (free electrons) owing to the ionising radiation from space.

Ionosphere
A region of the upper atmosphere that reflects short radio waves, enabling transmissions to be made around the curved surface of the earth. The gases in the ionosphere are ionised by absorption of radiation from the sun.

Iowa
An American State; see United States of America

Istanbul
Modern name for Constantinople (*qv*).

Isthmus
A narrow neck of land with water on each side which joins two larger areas of land, for example, the Isthmus of Panama, which connects the two Americas.

Izar
A significant star in Boötes; see Astral Constellations.

Jackson
State capital of Mississippi; see United States of America.

Jamaica Inn

The title of a 1936 novel by Dame Daphne du Maurier (1907–89) who spent much of her life in the West Country; a tourist attraction at Bolventor, Cornwall, on the A30, lately remarkable for Mr Potter's Museum of Curiosities which was so shamefully dispersed in 2003. However, it appears that the extraordinary Collectors World of Eric St John Foti, just west of Downham Market in Norfolk, may be a worthy successor.

Jayhawk State

Nickname of the State of Kansas; see **United States of America**.

Jebel

North African hill or mountain.

Jefferson City

State capital of Missouri; see **United States of America**.

Jericho

A village in Jordan near the north end of the Dead Sea, 825ft (251m) *below* sea level. On the site of an ancient city, the first place to be taken by the Israelites under Joshua after entering the Promised Land (C6BCE).

John O'Groats

A village at the northwesternmost tip of the Scottish mainland, generally thought of as the most northerly point of the UK. That honour, if so it be, belongs to Dunnet Head, as any map will show. John O'Groats, however, is the furthermost point on a main road from Land's End – hence 'Land's End to John O'Groats' is the longest journey in the UK (874 miles, 1,406 km), beloved of those making an identifiable journey to raise money for a good cause.

Juneau

Original state capital of Alaska; see **United States of America**.

Jungle Surfing

An adventure holiday whose participants move along wires from one platform to another in the jungle canopy.

Jurassic Park

A Stephen Spielberg blockbuster movie (1993), based on a novel by Michael Crichton (1991); the most commercially successful film of all time, costing $58.7 million, and taking nearly $1 billion at the box office. Richard Attenborough plays the role of a wealthy entrepreneur who clones live dinosaurs from fossilized DNA, and sets up a dinosaur park – with predictable results.

Kadja
Bali – a steady breeze off the sea; see Winds.

Kakadu
Wilderness in Northern Territory, Australia.

Kale yard
Where cabbages etc are grown.

Kamseen, Kamsin, Khamseen, Khamsin
Egypt – the Sirocco (*qv*).

Kansas
An American State; see United States of America.

Karoo, Karroo
Dry or semi-desert tableland of southern Africa.

Kasar
Moroccan fortified town or village.

Kaus Australis
A significant star in Sagittarius; see Astral Constellations.

Kaus Borealis
A significant star in Sagittarius; see Astral Constellations.

Kaus Medius
A significant star in Sagittarius; see Astral Constellations.

Kaver
See Caver.

Kentucky
An American State; see United States of America.

Kerry
A county in the Republic of Ireland (Province of Munster).

Keystone State
Nickname of the State of Pennsylvania; see United States of America.

Kiel canal
Connects the North Sea and the Baltic.

Kiel
Port and shipbuilding centre in NW Germany, capital of Schleswig-Holstein, joined the Hanseatic League in 1284, became part of Denmark in 1773, then of Prussia in 1866.

Kildare
A county in the Republic of Ireland (Province of Leinster).

Kilkenny
A county in the Republic of Ireland (Province of Leinster).

Kiritimati
Former name of the 52mile^2 Christmas Island SW of Java in the Indian Ocean that became a territory of the Commonwealth of Australia in 1958.

Kitalpha
Alpha star in Equuleus; see Astral Constellations.

Klondike
A region of NW Canada in the Yukon in the basin of the Klondike River (that flows c90 miles (145km) west into the Yukon River) where rich gold deposits were discovered in 1896; they were all but worked out by 1910.

Kloof
Afrikaans = a steep, narrow gully.

Knik
Palmer, Alaska – a strong southeast winter wind; see Winds.

Knockaloe
Site of a WW1 internment camp just south of Peel on the Isle of Man described in *The Woman of Knockaloe* by (Sir Thomas Henry) Hall Caine.

Knockturn Alley
In the stories of Harry Potter, a small alleyway with shops for the Dark Arts, located just off Diagon Alley near Gringotts Bank.

Kohilo
Hawaii – a gentle breeze; see Winds.

Kolawaik
Argentina – the southerly wind of the Gran Chaco; see Winds.

Kona Storm
Hawaii – a storm over the islands, characterized by strong southerly or southwesterly winds and heavy rains; see Winds.

Kop
Afrikaans = a South African hill; *eg* Spion Kop.

Kopje, Koppie
Afrikaans = a small South African hill.

Koshava
A wind that brings Russian snows to the plains of the former Yugo-slavia; see Winds.

Kotal
An Afghani mountain pass.

Kraal
1   South African native village enclosed by a wall.
2   An animal pen.

Krakatoa
A volcanic island in Indonesia in the Sunda Strait, famous for its erup-
tion in 1883 – one of the greatest ever recorded – when 36,000 people
were killed, many from the tsunamis (tidal waves) that hit the coasts
of Java and Sumatra. Dust in the atmosphere coloured sunsets for
years afterwards. The island today lies uninhabited.

Kubang
Java – a Chinook or Foehn (*qv*).

La Palma
One of the Canary Islands; see Spanish Autonomous Communities.

Laager
A South African camp with wagons circled for defence.

Lacerta
The Lizard Constellations.

Ladi
A significant star in Taurus; see Astral Constellations.

Lake Wobegon
Fictional mid-west US setting for Garrison Keillor's wryly humorous
observations on life.

Lakshadweep
An area of 12 square miles, comprising 27 islands in the Indian Ocean,
186 miles (300km) west of Kerala – a Union Territory of India. Britain
ruled it from 1792, but handed it over to India in 1956, to be administered by Kavaratti Island. It depends economically on bananas, coco-
nuts, fish, grains, and vegetables.

Lambeth Palace
London residence of the Archbishop of Canterbury; epithet symbol-
ising the governance of the Church of England ('Lambeth Palace has
yet to comment').

Land of Enchantment
Nickname of the State of New Mexico; see United States of America.

Land of Opportunity
Nickname of the State of Arkansas; see United States of America.

Land of the Midnight Sun
Nickname of the State of Alaska; see United States of America.

Land of the White Eagle
Poland, so called from the crowned eagle on the country's armorial bearings.

Land
A division of Germany; plural Länder.

Landlash
Scotland – a gale; see Winds.

Land's End
The westernmost point of England, on the Cornish coast; see also John O'Groats.

Lansing
State capital of Michigan; see United States of America.

Lanzarote
One of the Canary Islands; see Spanish Autonomous Communities.

Laois
A county in the Republic of Ireland (Province of Leinster).

Laputa
See Gulliver's Travels.

Las Palmas
Joint capital of the Canary Islands; see Spanish Autonomous Communities.

Lathe
At one time, an administrative division of the country of Kent.

Latitude
The latitude of a point on the Earth's surface is the angle between a line through that point to the Earth's centre and the diametral plane through the equator (latitude 0°).

Lausanne
Capital of the Swiss Canton (*qv*) of Vaud.

Leinster Gardens
Numbers 23 and 24 are two façades in the Bayswater area of London (W2), left intact to avoid an unsightly gap in the terrace when the Metropolitan Railway built its Euston–Paddington stretch in 1867.

Leitrim
A county in the Republic of Ireland (Province of Connacht).

Leo Minor
The Smaller Lion; see Astral Constellations.

Leo
The Lion Constellations.

Lepus
The Hare Constellations.

Lesbos
Greek island in the East Aegean Sea, near Turkey; settled by Aeolians in about 1000BCE it became the dwelling of Alcaeus and Sappho, and hence a centre of development of Greek lyric poetry. Sappho's poetry was written particularly for her admirers on the island, whence the term 'lesbian' arose – although she was reputed to have been married and borne a child.

Leste
Madeira and Canary Islands – a hot, dry, easterly wind; see Winds.

Levadas
Portuguese agricultural terraces with flowing irrigation streams.

Levanter
West Mediterranean and the Straits of Gibraltar – a strong easterly attended by cloudy, foggy, and sometimes rainy weather, especially in winter; see Winds.

Levantera
Adriatic – a persistent east wind usually accompanied by cloudy weather; see Winds.

Levanto
Canary Islands – a hot south-easterly wind; see Winds.

Leveche
Spain – a Foehn or hot southerly wind; a Sirocco; see Winds.

Libecchio, Libeccio
West coast of Corsica – a strong westerly (or south-westerly) wind off the sea; see Winds.

Libra
The Scales Constellations.

Liestal
Capital of the Swiss half-Canton (qv) of Basel-Landschaft.

Lilliput
See Gulliver's Travels.

Limerick
A county in the Republic of Ireland (Province of Munster).

Limpopo
(aka Crocodile River) flows from South Africa to the Indian Ocean; 1,100 miles (1,770km) in length; immortalised by Kipling in *The Elephant's Child* as the 'great grey-green greasy Limpopo River'.

Lincoln
State capital of Nebraska; see United States of America.

Line, The
The equator; see Crossing the line.

Little Egypt
In the US, informal name given to the southernmost part of Illinois, at the confluence of the Ohio and Mississippi rivers. The area bears some resemblance to the Nile delta
hence the town called Cairo.

Little Rhody
Nickname of the State of Rhode Island; see United States of America.

Little Rock
State capital of Arkansas; see United States of America.

Llanfairpwllgwyngyllgogerychwyrndrobwllllantysiliogogogoch
A fabricated name for an attention-seeking village in north-west Wales, in south-west Anglesey, translated as 'St Mary's church in the hollow of the white hazel trees, near the rapid whirlpool, by the red cave of the Church of St Tysilio'. It is generally referred to as Llanfairpwllgwyngyll, Llanfairpwll, or Llanfair PG.

Llano Estacado
Spanish = staked plain; a flat, dry but fertile area covering eastern New Mexico and western Texas where, it is said, the early Spanish explorers planted stakes in the ground in order to find their way.

Lleyn Peninsula
A Welsh peninsula south of Anglesey, between Cardigan Bay and Caernarvon Bay.

Logroño
Capital of the Spanish Region of La Rioja; see Spanish Autonomous Communities.

Londonderry
A county of Northern Ireland.

Lone Star State
Nickname of the State of Texas; see United States of America.

Long Drop
1　The gallows.
2　A field latrine; a plank with holes over a trench sometimes disinfected with paraffin or petrol which could cause severe and painful burns if a cigarette-end were disposed of down the hole.

Long Meg and Her Daughters
Six miles (9.7km) north-east of Penrith, Cumbria. Long Meg is a standing stone 18ft (5.5m) high, south of a Bronze Age stone circle containing 59 shorter stones. Some of these reach 10ft (3m) high and are called Her Daughters. Legend says that the stones were witches before a spell was cast, turning them to rock.

Longford
A county in the Republic of Ireland (Province of Leinster).

Longitude
'How far round' the earth from the Greenwich meridian a place is. Latitude (*qv*) can be found by taking readings of the sun, but longitude requires that the navigator knows accurately what time it is, having set the chronometer by a known standard – hence the C18 emphasis on accurate timekeeping in rough conditions.

Lorien
In *The Lord of the Rings*, is said to be the most beautiful place in the whole of Middle-Earth. Lorien is home to Celebrant, the Lady Galadriel and the many elves that live in the tree tops. Also known as Lothlorien; meaning blossoming dream-garden, inspired by the golden-yellow blossoms of the Mallorn trees found there.

Louisiana
An American State; see United States of America.

Louth
The smallest county in the Republic of Ireland (Province of Leinster).

Lower Forty-Eight States
See Contiguous State.

Lowther Arcade
In Victorian London, an arcade of shops built early C19, listed in a contemporary gazetteer under 'Bazaars', noted for its 'toys, etc;' it ran between Adelaide Street and The Strand, in the triangle formed by these two roads and King William Street (now William IV Street). The Arcade was three storeys high and Corinthian in style.

Lucerne (Luzern)
Swiss Canton (*qv*) and its capital.

Lupus
The Wolf Constellations.

Lynx
See Astral Constellations.

Lyra
The Harp Constellations.

Madison
State capital of Wisconsin; see United States of America.

Madrid
Spanish Region and its capital; see Spanish Autonomous Communities.

Maestro
Coasts of Corsica and Sardinia, and the Adriatic – a northwesterly wind with fine weather, especially in summer; see Winds.

Maginot Line
Built by France before WW2 to protect her border with Germany. Named after its begetter André Maginot (1877–1932), it proved singularly ineffective when put to the test; see Siegfried Line.

Magnetic Pole
A wandering point on the surface of the Earth to which a compass needle points, in the direction of magnetic north; detailed maps should show in what direction it lies for the area they depict, at what date, and how far it wanders.

Magnolia State
Nickname of the State of Mississippi; see United States of America.

Maiden Castle
The best surviving Iron Age fortification in Britain; south west of Dorchester in Dorset, it occupies 120 acres (48.5ha).

Maine
An American State; see United States of America.

Mallah
An area of a kasar occupied by Jews.

Mallorca
One of the Balearic Islands; see Spanish Autonomous Communities.

Mamatele
Malta – a hot northwesterly wind; see Winds.

Manderley

The somewhat sinister house on the Cornish coast where the second Mrs de Winter is oppressed by the first, Rebecca, in the 1938 novel of that name by Dame Daphne du Maurier (1907–89).

Maria

A fictional wind appearing in the book *Storm* by George R Stewart, and taken up in *Paint Your Wagon* (Lerner and Lowe, 1951) and by the Kingston Trio (1959); see Winds.

Maritime Provinces

The most eastern provinces of Canada, on the Atlantic coast and the Gulf of St Lawrence; also known as the Atlantic Provinces, they consist of New Brunswick, Nova Scotia, Prince Edward Island, and usually Newfoundland.

Markab

Alpha star in Pegasus; see Astral Constellations.

Marshalsea, The

An infamous prison that stood originally near Mermaid Court, Southwark, wherein were confined those convicted of maritime crimes; by C18 it was so dilapidated that it was closed and another prison of the same name built nearby; it was here that Charles Dickens's father was imprisoned for debt in 1824, an event that informed the author's writing in *David Copperfield* and *Little Dorrit*. The Marshalsea closed at the end of C19 and was demolished, but there are yet reminders of it in the London district where it stood – Dorrit Street, Marshalsea Road, Quilp Street, and Lant Street where the 12-year-old Charles lodged when he worked in the bootblack factory when his father was in The Marshalsea.

Mary (not Marie) Celeste

An American brigantine found between the Azores and Portugal on 5 December 1872, minus its boat, sextant, chronometer, log and crew, but with everything else, including set sails, in place. The crew was never found; the mystery has never been solved.

Maryland

An American State; see United States of America.

Mason-Dixon line

A line drawn to settle the conflict over borders between Pennsylvania and Maryland in 1767 by two surveyors, Charles Mason and Jeremiah

Dixon. It also represented the division between southern pro-slavery and northern free states up until the Civil War, and has remained a symbolic boundary between the North and South ever since.

Massachusetts
An American State; see United States of America.

Matanuska Wind
Palmer, Alaska – a strong, gusty, northeast winter wind; see Winds.

Mato Wamniyomi
Dakota – Native American for whirlwind, dust devil or tornado; see Winds.

Mauna Kea
At 13,796 ft (4,206m) the highest island mountain in the world, being an extinct volcano on N central Hawaii Island.

Mauna Loa
An active volcano on S central Hawaii Island 13,680 ft (4,171m).

Mayo
A county in the Republic of Ireland (Province of Connacht).

Mearthim
A significant star in Aries; see Astral Constellations.

Meath
A county in the Republic of Ireland (Province of Leinster).

Megraz
A significant star in Ursa Major; see Astral Constellations.

Mekbuda
A significant star in Gemini; see Astral Constellations.

Melilla
Spanish Region and its capital; see Spanish Autonomous Communities.

Men
Alpha star in Lupus; see Astral Constellations.

Menkalinan
A significant star in Auriga; see Astral Constellations.

Menkar
Alpha star in Cetus; see Astral Constellations.

Mensa
The Table Constellations.

Merak
A significant star in Ursa Major; see Astral Constellations.

Mercia
A kingdom of Anglo-Saxon England south of the River Humber, bounded by Wales to the west and East Anglia to the east. Mercia flourished under Penda (c634–55) and reached its peak under Offa (757–96), after which it declined and joined Wessex to become part of the united England.

Mérida
Capital of the Spanish Region of Extremadura; see Spanish Autonomous Communities.

Mesa
Spanish = a table; an isolated flat-topped hill.

Mesopotamia
Greek = between two rivers; the fertile alluvial land bounded by the Euphrates and the Tigris rivers where the Sumerians settled some 6,000 years ago, founding city states such as Kish, Ur and Uruk.

Michigan
An American State; see United States of America.

Microscopium
The Microscope; see Astral Constellations.

Mid-Atlantic States
In the US, those states in the middle part of the Eastern Seaboard: Delaware, Maryland, New Jersey, New York State, Pennsylvania and Virginia.

Middle East
The area comprising Iran and the countries of the Arabian peninsula and the Mediterranean seaboard. Sometimes called the Cradle of Civilisation, the Middle East has seen the emergence of Judaism, Christianity and Islam and their associated cultures. It is perhaps contrary to its stability that the area contributes nearly half of the world's oil production.

Middle-Earth
In *The Lord of the Rings*, the name given to the land described.

Midlands, The
The central counties of England, embracing Derbyshire, Herefordshire, Leicestershire, Northamptonshire, Nottinghamshire, Staffordshire, Warwickshire, Worcestershire and particularly that great industrial conurbation centred on Birmingham.

Mid-West, The
An area of the north central US bounded by the Great Plains to the west, Lake Erie to the east, and the Ohio River to the south. Its fertile soil makes it an important producer of corn and wheat.

Mile High City
Nickname for the city of Denver, Colorado reflecting its altitude in relation to sea level.

Milky Way
The diffuse band of light visible in the (especially moonless) night sky, composed of perhaps 100,000,000,000 stars of the spiral galaxy that lies in the plane of our universe; see Watling Street of the Sky.

Mimosa
A significant star in Crux; see Astral Constellations.

Minas Tirith
In *The Lord of the Rings*, also known as the Tower of the Guard, the principal city of Gondor. It has seven circular walls with gates that connect each level to the next. In the centre of these seven layers is Citadel, and in Citadel is the Hall of the Kings where the throne of Gondor stands, and the huge White Tower of Ecthelion which towers over the rest of the stronghold.

Mines of Moria
In *The Lord of the Rings*, the excavations beneath the Misty Mountains, inhabited by the Moria Orcs and a Cave Troll.

Minnesota
An American State; see United States of America.

Minorca
One of the Balearic Islands; see Spanish Autonomous Communities.

Mintaka
A significant star in Orion; see Astral Constellations.

Mira
A significant star in Cetus; see Astral Constellations.

Mirach
A significant star in Andromeda; see Astral Constellations.

Mirfak
Alpha star in Perseus; see Astral Constellations.

Mississippi
An American State; see United States of America.

Missouri
An American State; see United States of America.

Mistral
Mediterranean; Gulf of Lions – a strong cold dry north-east wind that blows from the Rhone valley; a Fall Wind also called Cierzo; see Winds.

Mizar
A significant star in Ursa Major; see Astral Constellations.

Monaghan
A county in the Republic of Ireland (Province of Ulster).

Moncao
Portugal – a northeasterly trade wind (*qv*).

Monoceros
The Unicorn Constellations.

Monroe, Marilyn
The 'subway air-vent sequence' – her billowing skirt in *The Seven-Year Itch* (1955) – was shot in New York City on E61st Street (between 3rd and Lexington) but was later re-shot in Hollywood.

Montana
An American State; see United States of America.

Montgomery
State capital of Alabama; see United States of America.

Montpelier
State capital of Vermont; see United States of America.

Moosier State
Nickname of the State of Indiana; see United States of America.

Mordor
In *The Lord of the Rings*, the land of dread where shadows lie, between the Ash Mountains and Mountains of Shadow, home of the enemy Sauron and his minions the Easterlings, Orcs, Ringwraiths and Trolls. Frodo and Sam took on the quest of getting to Mordor, to throw the One Ring into the Crack of Doom so as to break the power of Sauron, the enemy and forger of the ring.

Mormon State
Nickname of the State of Utah; see United States of America.

Mosi-oa-Tunya
The Victoria Falls (PC) on the Zambesi River between Zimbabwe and Zambia.

Motor City; Motown
Nickname for the city Detroit, Michigan, the centre of US car manufacturing.

Moulin Rouge
Montmartre, Paris; the famous theatre and dance hall opened in 1889 and has a model of a red windmill over the entrance. When the sails turned, the figures of a miller and his wife turned and waved to each other from different windows. The theatre was (and still is) famous for its cancan dancers.

Mountain State
Nickname of the State of West Virginia; see United States of America.

Mow Cop
A village on the Cheshire-Staffordshire border where the Primitive Methodist sect was founded in 1810.

Much-Binding-in-the-Marsh
A fictitious RAF station on wartime wireless weekly whose CO was Kenneth Horne and adjutant Richard Murdoch, supported in the usual format of the time by Sam Costa and Maurice Denham (Dudley Davenport at your service). The nearest station was Spagthorpe Junction.

Mumbai
Current preferred name for Bombay; however, it should be pronounced to rhyme with dum-bye (rather than doom-bye, which Indians find more offensive than Bombay).

Murcia
Spanish Region and its capital; see Spanish Autonomous Communities.

Musca
The Fly Constellations.

Myatel
A North Russian wind; see Winds.

Naantali
Finnish town where the harvest festival begins with Sleepyhead Day, when anyone who has provided a particular service is honoured by being thrown into the Baltic Sea. It must be a great incentive to doing good.

Narnia

An imaginary world with a strong Christian moral flavour created by the Oxford don and novelist C(live) S(taples) 'Jack' Lewis (1898–1963). Narnia first appeared in *The Lion, The Witch and The Wardrobe* (1950), and in six following books.

Nashi, N'aschi

Iranian coast of the Persian Gulf and the Makran coast – a northeast winter wind similar to but less severe than the Bora; it may be associated with an outflow from the central Asiatic anticyclone that extends over the high land of Iran; see Winds.

Nashira

A significant star in Capricornus; see Astral Constellations.

Nashville

State capital of Tennessee; see United States of America.

Navajo Trail

That connecting the dispersed settlements of the native American Navajo peoples in New Mexico, Arizona and Utah; they are now the most numerous of the tribes, and live quite happily with little central authority.

Nebraska

An American State; see United States of America.

Nebulosa del Granchio

A significant star in Taurus; see Astral Constellations.

Ness, Loch

A lake in the Great Glen, Scotland, 22.5 miles (36km) long and 754ft (229m) wherein, legend has it, dwells a monster. Some say it is a plesiosaur left over from Jurassic and Cretaceous times, which makes it 100,000,000 years old (give or take a few) and thus (presumably) possessed of the secret of eternal life. Others postulate a breeding pair that has managed to limit the population of its species while evading detection (let alone capture) by the world's most advanced instruments. Two things are certain: the Loch Ness Monster is a great money spinner, and a triumph of hope over experience.

Neuchâtel

Swiss Canton (*qv*) and its capital.

Nevada

An American State; see United States of America.

Never-never Land

1   In J M Barrie's *Peter Pan* (1904), the dwelling place of the Lost Boys and Red Indians, where the Pirates sailed up the lake; originally the

Never Land, as in that ace mover Michael Jackson's fairground-ranch.

2   In Australia, once the whole of the outback; since the publication of Jeannie Gunn's *We of the Never-Never* (1908), NT only.

3   A land where everything is 'on the never-never', or hire purchase.

New Dorley
Original name (1963) for the new town of Telford, Shropshire.

New Hampshire
An American State; see United States of America.

New Jersey
An American State; see United States of America.

New Mexico
A normal American state, not a separate country, nor part of the country of Mexico which is outwith the USA.

New Mexico
An American State; see United States of America.

New York City
Largest US city, situated on New York Bay at the mouth of the Hudson River. It is in five boroughs: Manhattan, Brooklyn, the Bronx, Queens and Staten Island, noted *(inter alia)* for its skyscrapers, the Statue of Liberty (152 feet (46m) high, presented to the US by France in 1884 to commemorate their revolutions) and Central Park, the first landscaped public park in the US, authorised in 1853 (843 acres).

New York State
In the North-East of the US, and to be distinguished from *New York City*.

New York
An American State; see United States of America.

New York
Both a city, and one of the United States; hence qualify your intent by suffixing 'City' or 'State'.

Njed
See Hejaz.

Nollywood
See Hollywood.

No-Man's-Land
A piece of land belonging to nobody, notably the area between opposing trenches in WW1, whereon teams from the opposing English and German forces played football on Christmas Day 1914.

Niagara Falls

The falls of the River Niagara, a name derived from the Iroquois Indian word 'Onguiaahra' meaning 'the strait', on the Canadian-United States International Border – both in the Province of Ontario and the State of New York, attracting more than 12 million tourists yearly. Niagara is the second largest fall in the world, second only to Mosi-oa-Tunya (Victoria Falls) in southern Africa. Approximately 500 years ago the river encountered an obstacle that caused it to split into two channels, thus Goat Island was formed, named after John Stedman whose goat herds froze to death in the winter of 1780. Divided by Goat Island are the American Falls, 167ft (50m) high with a volume of about 150,000 US Gallons per second of water flowing over it, and the Canadian/Horseshoe Falls, 158ft (47m) high, with a volume of about 600,000 US gallons per second of water. The water flow on the American side is much less in strength because of Goat Island, whereas Horseshoe Falls has no obstruction to divert it. There is a third, much narrower, falls – over the years called at different times Luna Falls, Iris Falls and currently Bridal Veil Falls. Many attempts have been made to go over or cross the falls; the first to go over the falls in a barrel and survive was a 63-year-old female schoolteacher. High wire tightrope acts used to be performed across the river, most notably by Blondin (Jean François Gravelet (1824–97) in 1859, who crossed with a wheelbarrow, and then carried his manager across on his back, stopping midway to rest.

Nor'easter, Northeaster
New England coast – a strong north-east wind presaging a gale or storm; see Winds.

Norma
The Carpenter's Square; see Astral Constellations.

Norte
Mexico and the Gulf of Mexico – a strong cold northeasterly wind resulting from an outbreak of cold air from the north; the Mexican extension of a Norther (*qv*).

North Carolina
An American State; see United States of America.

North Dakota
An American State; see United States of America.

North Start State
Nickname of the State of Minnesota; see United States of America.

North Woods
In the US, the forested region of northern Minnesota, Wisconsin and Michigan; not to be confused with Great North Woods.

Norther, Blue Norther
Southern United States, particularly Texas – a cold winter wind that blows from the north resulting in a drastic drop in air temperatures; a fall of 50°F in a few hours has been noted; see Winds.

Northumbria
Land north of the Humber, but south of Scotland.

Nor'wester
The province of Canterbury, New Zealand, especially in the city of Christchurch. It is a very warm wind which may blow for days on end; it comes in from the Tasman Sea, dries as it rises over the Southern Alps, and heats as it descends; see Winds.

Notus
A Classical south wind; see Winds.

Nullarbor Plain
In South Australia, a low plateau of 100,000 square miles (260,000km^2) from the Great Australian Bight to the Great Victorian Desert; it has no trees (hence null-arbor) and no surface water; see Tea and Sugar.

Nunki
A significant star in Sagittarius; see Astral Constellations.

Nutmeg State
Nickname of the State of Connecticut; see United States of America.

Nutwood
Place where Rupert Bear and his friends Algy, Pong-Ping *et al* have lived and had their adventures since the mid–1930s.

Octans
The Octant; see Astral Constellations.

Offaly
A county in the Republic of Ireland (Province of Leinster).

Offa's Dyke
An earthwork fortification built by King Offa of Mercia (reign: 757–796) to separate his kingdom from Wales; it runs from the River Wye near Monmouth to near Prestatyn.

Ohio
An American State; see United States of America.

Oklahoma City
State capital of Oklahoma; see United States of America.

Oklahoma
An American State; see United States of America.

Old Colony State
Nickname of the State of Massachusetts; see United States of America.

Old Lady of Threadneedle Street, The
The Bank of England, so named – and depicted – in a cartoon by James Gilray dated 22 May 1797 on the occasion of the introduction of the £1 note by William Pitt the Younger (1759–1806).

Old Line State
Nickname of the State of Maryland; see United States of America.

Old North State
Nickname of the State of North Carolina; see United States of America.

Olympia
State capital of Washington; see United States of America.

Olympia
1 A valley in Elis, Peloponnesus, named after the games held there every four years.
2 An exhibition complex in West London.

Olympus, Mount
The home of the ancient Greek gods; it stands 9,550 ft (2,895 m) high on the borders of Macedonia and Thessaly.

Oodnagallabi
Imaginary place in Australia; the epitome of remote backwardness.

Ootacamund
See Udagamandalam.

Ophiuchus
The Serpent Bearer; see Astral Constellations.

Oregon
An American State; see United States of America.

Orion
See Astral Constellations.

Orion's Belt
In the heavenly constellation, three bright stars imagined as forming the belt of the mighty hunter Orion; a great deal more plausible than some other fanciful dot-joinings.

Osage Plains
In the US, plains covering western Missouri, eastern Kansas, the central part of Oklahoma, and south into central Texas.

Osgiliath
In *The Lord of the Rings,* on the banks of the great River Anduin in Ithilien, inhabited by the people of Gondor. Sam, Frodo and Gollum are brought forth here by Faramir, in the hope that the Ring will protect Gondor from the forces of the enemy Sauron.

Ostria
Bulgarian coast – a warm southerly wind, considered a precursor of bad weather; see Winds.

Over the Hills and Far Away
1   A distant, carefree land of nursery-rhyme fame.
2   The home of the Tellytubbies, a lingually-challenged BBC children's TV quartet of beings with television screens in their abdominal walls: Dipsy (green with a vertical aerial on its head), Laa Laa (yellow with a pig's tail aerial), Po (pink with a circular aerial) and Tinky Winky (purple with an inverted triangular aerial).
3   'Over the hill' is the supposed phase of life when a person has passed his or her prime, and is now coasting...

Oviedo
Capital of the Spanish Region of Asturias; see Spanish Autonomous Communities.

Oz
1   A name for Auztralia (from its pronunciation).
2   A fictional land much documented by L Frank Baum (1856–1919), who wrote *The Wizard of Oz* in 1900, followed by 13 sequels. (Throughout his career, Baum wrote about 60 books, mainly for children.) The movie *The Wizard of Oz* came out in 1938. 'In the land of Oz, we are all small children walking down a road of yellow brick in a crazy, outlandish, ozzy sort of world,' wrote Baum. Oz is roughly rectangular, surrounded by a desert, and divided into four triangles with Emerald City in the centre. The north triangle is inhabited by the Gillikins (who favour purple), east by Munchkins (blue), south by Quadlins (red) and west by Winkies (yellow).

Pacific Northwest

In the US, an area including Oregon and Washington State, and sometimes Idaho and British Columbia.

Pacific Ocean

The world's largest and deepest ocean, bounded by the Americas its eastern coast, Antarctica in the south, and Asia and Australia in the west. Its area is about 64 million square miles (166 Mkm^2), and its average depth is 14,000 feet (4,220m), though the Challenger Deep in the Mariana Trench has a depth of 37,000ft (11,000m), getting on for 6.5 miles.

Pacific rim countries

Those on the western shores of the Pacific Ocean, a description relating particularly to their commercial activities.

Padstein

A local name for Padstow, Cornwall, which the restaurateur Rick Stein has made into a gourmet centre.

Padstow

Cornish town where there is a Christmastide custom – Darkie Day – when fishermen and their wives black up and sing plantation songs to raise money for charity; an obvious target for those who believe in Political Correctness.

Pais Vasco (Basque Country)

See Spanish Autonomous Communities.

Pali

Pali Pass, Honolulu – local name for the strong winds that blow through it; see Winds.

Palm Court

A feature to be found in the better hotels where tea was served to the sound of a small orchestra; the image became widely impressed from WW2 with the broadcasts by the violinist Albert Sandler 'and the Palm Court Orchestra' (somewhere in England) contriving to give an air of normality to a troubled populace.

Palma de Mallorca

Capital of the Balearic Islands; see Spanish Autonomous Communities.

Palmetto State

Nickname of the State of South Carolina; see United States of America.

Pampero
Southern Argentina – a strong cold wind from the south or south-west that blows across the Pampas; see Winds.

Pamplona
Capital of the Spanish Region of Navarre; see Spanish Autonomous Communities.

Pandalon
Hell in Hindu mythology.

Panhandle State
Nickname of the State of West Virginia; see United States of America.

Papagayo
Pacific coast of Nicaragua and Guatemala – a violent north-easterly fall wind (qv); the cold air mass of a Norte (qv) which has overridden the mountains of Central America; see Tehuantepecer and Winds.

Papagayos
Costa Rica – a cool wind from the north; see Winds.

Park Bench
Telegraphic address of the Algonquin humorists Robert Benchley and Dorothy Parker.

Patagonia
An arid plateau in South America rising to the Andes, part of Argentina and Chile from south of the River Colorado to the Strait of Magellan.

Pavo
The Peacock; see Astral Constellations.

Peacock
Alpha star in Pavo; see Astral Constellations.

Pegasus
The Winged Horse Constellations.

Pelican State
Nickname of the State of Louisiana ; see United States of America.

Peninsula State
Nickname of the State of Florida ; see United States of America.

Pennsylvania
An American State; see United States of America.

Perseus
See Astral Constellations.

Phact
Alpha star in Columba; see Astral Constellations.

Phecda
Significant star in Ursa Major; see Astral Constellations.

Philadelphia
Originally the capital of America (1783–9), before Washington DC.

Phoenix Alley
In London, the alley leading to the Phoenix theatre, now called Drury Lane.

Phoenix Park
In Dublin, named by corruption of the Gaelic Fion-uise = fair water, so called from the health-giving spring that once attracted many visitors.

Phoenix
See Astral Constellations.

Phoenix
State capital of Arizona; see United States of America.

Pictor
The Easel Constellations.

Piedmont or Piedmont Plateau
In the US, an area lying between the coastal plain and the Appalachian Mountains in the southeastern, extending in an arc from Alabama through Georgia, South Carolina, North Carolina, Virginia, Maryland and Pennsylvania to New Jersey.

Pierre
State capital of South Dakota; see United States of America.

Pilgrim's Way
An ancient track from Winchester to Canterbury, named after its later use by pilgrims visiting the shrine of Thomas à Becket.

Pine Tree State
Nickname of the State of Maine; see United States of America.

Pisces
The Fishes; see Astral Constellations.

Piscis Austrinus (or Australis)
The Southern Fish; see Astral Constellations.

Pittarak
Greenland – a wind from the north west; see Winds.

> ## Plains of Abraham
>
> (aka Heights of Abraham) the ground above the bluffs of the St Lawrence river, west of Quebec city, Canada, named after an earlier owner Martin Abraham (1589–1664). Here in 1759 General James Wolfe (British) vanquished Louis Montcalm (French) in a decisive battle (in which both lost their lives) that ended French power in North America.

Platform 9¾

In the stories of Harry Potter, a hidden platform at London King's Cross Railway Station. The only way of getting on to the platform is to walk straight into the barrier between platforms nine and ten. From here the students take the Hogwarts Express to Hogwarts School of Witchcraft and Wizardry.

Pleiades

Significant stars in Taurus; see Astral Constellations.

Pokesdown

Former name for East Boscombe, Hants, changed because the residents thought it sounded better.

Polaris

Alpha star in Ursa Minor; see Astral Constellations.

Pollux

A significant star in Gemini; see Astral Constellations.

Pooh Corner

Site of a house made famous in children's literature (1928) by A A Milne (1882–1956), see Hundred-acre Wood.

Porridge Island

A C18 area of London, in St Martin's Churchyard, so called from the concentration of cookshops there.

Prairie State

Nickname of the State of Illinois; see United States of America.

Procyon

Alpha star in Canis Minor; see Astral Constellations.

Providence

State capital of Rhode Island; see United States of America.

Pudding Lane

See Great Fire of London.

Puna
Andes – probably the harshest cold wind; see Winds.

Puppis
The Stern (of a ship); see Astral Constellations.

Purdah
The practice of shielding women from the world by segregating them, or not allowing them out without being 'covered', with only a slit in the veil for them to see through or even a gauze allowing them to see without their eyes being seen.

Purgas
A Siberian wind; see Winds.

Pyxis
The Compass; see Astral Constellations.

Quarry Bank Mill
A textile mill near Styal village south of Altrincham in Cheshire, built by Samuel Greg in 1784. Five generations of the Greg family ran Quarry Bank, until they handed it over to the National Trust in 1939; production ceased in 1959. The Mill is now an important home to spinning and weaving machinery which is demonstrated to visitors. The original driving force was a large waterwheel, still in working order, supplemented by a steam engine.

Queen of Long-distance Roads
See Appian Way.

Queer Street
Traditionally, the location of financially dodgy customers; *cf* Carey Street.

Quexalcoatl
Aztec – a wind from the west; see Winds.

Rainbow's End
Where there is supposed to be a crock of gold; however, locating exactly where the rainbow ends is uncertain, even with a distant observer directing the seeker.

Raleigh
State capital of North Carolina; see United States of America.

Ras al Mothallah
Alpha star in Triangulum; see Astral Constellations.

Ras elasted australis, borealis
Significant stars in Leo; see Astral Constellations.

Rasalgethi
Alpha star in Hercules; see Astral Constellations.

Rasalhague
Alpha star in Ophiuchus; see Astral Constellations.

Raven's Eye
A pool that never dries up associated with The Wrekin.

Regolo
A significant star in Leo; see Astral Constellations.

Regulus
Alpha star in Leo; see Astral Constellations.

Reservoirs
Lakes, either natural or artificial, in which water is trapped and stored for a range of uses: irrigation, to supply water for municipal needs, to provide hydroelectric power, or to control water flow. Dams are placed across suitable land formations so as to create a lake, invaluable in areas in which rainfall is low, or unpredictable. However, the water flowing into a reservoir must not contain too much sediment, as this can diminish the capacity of the reservoir.

Reticulum
The Net; see Astral Constellations.

Rhode Island
An American State; see United States of America.

Richmond
State capital of Virginia; see United States of America.

Ridgeway, The
Britain's oldest track, 85miles (137km) in length, running from Ivinghoe Beacon NE of Aylesbury to Overton Hill E of Avebury.

Rigel
A significant star in Orion; see Astral Constellations.

Rigil Kentaurus (*aka* Alpha Centauri)
Alpha star in Centaurus; see Astral Constellations.

Rivers of the Underworld
Styx (the river of hate, flowing nine times round the infernal regions), Acheron (across which the dead were to be ferried by Charon, in return for an obelus in the mouth), Lethe (whose waters the dead must taste to erase their memories of life), Phlegethon (the river of liquid fire flowing into the Acheron (seemingly more long-lasting than the millennium fiasco)), Cocytus (along whose banks the unburied were

doomed to wander for 100 years), and Avernus (with its sulphurous exhalations).

Rohan

In *The Lord of the Rings,* the far stretches of rolling grassland where horses roam, known as the Kingdom of the Rohirrim; the horse-lords, ruled by King Theoden from his Golden Hall in Edoras. The Rohirrim are known for their horses, and the skill with which they train them. The fastest of the horses is Shadowfax, tamed by Gandalf.

Room

The auction room; when the auctioneer says that bidding is 'in the room' it means that the assembled company is bidding, as opposed to bids not meeting the reserve, or not yet exceeding any bids placed 'on the book' in advance.

Ropewalk

Barristers' term for an Old Bailey practice, in the days when criminals were liable to be hanged. Technically, a rope walk is a long narrow shed in which ropes are laid (manufactured).

Roscommon

A county in the Republic of Ireland (Province of Connacht).

Roseland Peninsula

In Cornwall, south of Truro, where are to be found St Just in Roseland, St Mawes, and other villages.

Rose-red City half as old as Time, A

Petra, according to J W Burgon's Newdigate Prize-winning poem of 1845.

Route 66

Santa Monica CA via Arizona, North Mexico, Texas, Oklahoma, Kansas, Missouri to Chicago IL.

Rubicon

A small river dividing Italy and Cisalpine Gaul. When Julius Caesar crossed the Rubicon in 49BCE, he became an invader, and there was no reversal of the act; a meaning nowadays attributed to the phrase 'crossing the Rubicon'.

Ruchbah

A significant star in Cassiopeia; see Astral Constellations.

Rukbat

Alpha star in Sagittarius; see Astral Constellations.

Sabik

A significant star in Scorpius; see Astral Constellations.

Sacramento
State capital of California; see United States of America.

Sadachbia
A significant star in Aquarius; see Astral Constellations.

Sadal Melik
Alpha star in Aquarius; see Astral Constellations.

Sadal Sund
A significant star in Aquarius; see Astral Constellations.

Sadr
A significant star in; see Astral Constellations.

Sagarmatha
See Everest.

Sagebrush State
Nickname of the State of Nevada; see United States of America.

Sagitta
The Arrow; see Astral Constellations.

Sagittarius
The Archer; see Astral Constellations.

Saiph
A significant star in Orion; see Astral Constellations.

Salem
State capital of Oregon; see United States of America.

Salt Lake City
State capital of Utah; see United States of America.

Samiel
Arabian and North African deserts; Turkey – a hot, dry sand-laden wind, also known as Simoom or Simoon (*qv*).

San Andreas Fault, California

In the US, the line running from Point Arena (north of San Francisco, south of Fort Bragg) to Imperial Valley (southeast of Los Angeles) along which the North American and Pacific tectonic plates meet. The movement of the plates along the fault is the source of frequent minor and occasional major earthquakes.

Santa Ana
Santa Ana Pass, California – a Chinook (*qv*) from the Californian desert; see Winds.

Santa Cruz de Tenerife
Joint capital of the Canary Islands; see Spanish Autonomous Communities.

Santa Fé
State capital of New Mexico; see United States of America.

Santander
Capital of the Spanish Region of Cantabria; see Spanish Autonomous Communities.

Santiago de Compostela
Capital of the Spanish Region of Galicia; see Spanish Autonomous Communities.

Sargas
A significant star in Scorpius; see Astral Constellations.

Sargasso Sea
A calm area of the Atlantic Ocean between the West Indies and the Azores characterised by the profusion of *Sargassum*, a floating seaweed.

Sarnen
Capital of the Swiss half-Canton (*qv*) of Obwalden.

Sastrudi
Rough ice surface at the pole.

Satis House
In *Great Expectations* (Charles Dickens, 1860–1), the derelict home of Miss Havisham, the jilted bride, and the adopted Estella (with whom Pip was in love). It was inspired by Restoration House in Rochester (Kent); another house in the same town inspired the name (Latin = enough).

Schaffhausen
Swiss Canton (*qv*) and its capital.

Schedar
Alpha star in Cassiopeia; see Astral Constellations.

Scheiddih
A significant star in Capricornus; see Astral Constellations.

Scheveningen

The most popular Dutch seaside resort, a major fishing port of Den Haage. The name is reputed to be difficult to pronounce, and hence was (said to be) used in WW2 to unmask those seeking to pass themselves off as Dutch.

Schwyz

Swiss Canton (*qv*) and its capital.

Scirocco, Sirocco

North Africa and the North Mediterranean coastline – a hot, dry, dusty wind, either a foehn or a hot southerly wind in advance of a low pressure area moving from the Sahara or Arabian deserts; in Spain, Leveche; see Winds.

Scorpius (Scorpio)

The Scorpion; see Astral Constellations.

Scotch Corner

Where the A66 joins the A1, 10 miles south west of Darlington. The A66 goes to Brough, Penrith, Keswick and the Lake District.

Scotland Yard

Originally the London residence of visiting kings of Scotland, Great Scotland Yard was the first home of the Metropolitan Police until 1890; the HQ then moved to New Scotland Yard, and the name went with the HQ when it moved to Broadway, Westminster in 1967. The slowly turning triangular sign is iconic of the organisation.

Sculptor

See Astral Constellations.

Scutum

The Shield; see Astral Constellations.

Serpens

The Serpent; see Astral Constellations.

Seven Wonders of the World

In the Ancient World, they are as follows: the Pyramids of Egypt; the Hanging Gardens of Babylon (*qv*); the Tomb of Mausolos (Mausoleum); the Temple of Diana at Ephesus; the Colossus of Rhodes; the Statue of Zeus by Phidias; the Pharos of Alexandria. Later wonders include: the Colosseum of Rome; the Catacombs of Alexandria; the Great Wall of China; Stonehenge; the Leaning Tower of Pisa; the Porcelain Tower of Nanking; the Mosque of San Sophia at Constantinople (Istanbul).

Seven Hills of Rome
The Aventine, Caelian, Capitoline, Colline (or Quirinal – now Monte Cavallo), Esquiline, Palatine, and Viminal.

Seville
Capital of the Spanish Region of Andalusia; see Spanish Autonomous Communities.

Sextans
The Sextant; see Astral Constellations.

Shaitan
Middle East – a dust storm; see Winds.

Shamal
Iraq and the Persian Gulf – a summer northwesterly wind often stronger during the day than the night; see Winds.

Shangri La
An imaginary valley in the Himalaya, set by James Hilton in his novel *Lost Horizon* (1933).

Sharki
Persian Gulf – an occasional southeasterly wind; see Winds.

Shauka, Shaula
Significant stars in Scorpius; see Astral Constellations.

Shawondasee
Hudson Bay – the Algonquin lazy wind that blows from the south in the late summer; see Winds.

Sheliak
A significant star in Lyra; see Astral Constellations.

Shelob's lair
In *The Lord of the Rings*, the lair belonging to Shelob, a giant spider-like monster. Frodo and Sam must travel through Shelob's cave to get to the Crack of Doom so as to dispose of the One Ring, which would break the power of the enemy, Sauron.

Sheol
Hebrew = abode of the dead (rather than 'Hell' as it is sometimes rendered).

Sheratan
A significant star in Aries; see Astral Constellations.

Sherwood Forest
33,000 acres (13.3 kha) of Nottinghamshire, one of the sites renowned for housing Robin Hood and his Merry Men (Alan a'Dale,

Little John, Will Scarlett Friar Tuck *et al*) who robbed from the rich and gave to the poor, a group in which they were no doubt included; the untouchable love interest was provided by Maid Marian.

Shieling
A circular settlement in the Scottish highlands.

Show Me State
Nickname of the State of Missouri; see United States of America.

Siegfried Line
Built by Germany to parallel the French Maginot Line (*qv*) before and during WW2; it gave rise to the song: *We're going to hang out the washing on the Siegfried Line, Have you any dirty washing mother dear ...* (Jimmy Kennedy and Michael Carr, 1939). A great tune for whistling and marching to; however, since the Maginot Line proved ineffective, and the military traffic was all from East to West, the song soon fell into embarrassed disfavour.

Silicon Fen
An establishing name for the area around Cambridge, England where there is a concentration of high-tech companies, described in 1985 as the *Cambridge Phenomenon* (in a report by Nick Segal of Segal, Quince and Partners). The received wisdom is that the companies 'grew out of' Cambridge University, but this is not strictly true. The first identified is the Cambridge Instrument Co (1881), followed by the numerous Pye companies (starting 1896), Aero Research (1934), and so on. New companies have spun off from existing ones, and there is generally more rivalry than co-operation. The name Silicon Fen is modelled on Silicon Glen (*qv*) though, in the light of the Cambridge Phenomenon, Silicon Phen might be more appropriate.

Silicon Glen
The area of central Scotland where there is a high concentration of high-tech companies in all stages of development from local start-ups to international. Its name is modelled on that of Silicon Valley (*qv*); a glen being a Scottish valley.

Silicon Valley
A name bestowed in 1971 on the land leased to high-tech companies by Stanford University (Palo-Alto. CA), the same year the Intel produced the first microprocessor chip. There are now some 4,000 IT and allied companies in the area – in spite of the threat posed by the

San Andreas Fault (750 miles, 1,200km in length) that runs through California and whose movement was the cause of the San Francisco earthquake in 1906.

Silver State
Nickname of the State of Nevada; see United States of America.

Sion
Capital of the Swiss Canton (*qv*) of Valais.

Sioux State
Nickname of the State of North Dakota; see United States of America.

Sirius
Alpha star in Canis Major; see Astral Constellations.

Skat
A significant star in Aquarius; see Astral Constellations.

Sligo
A county in the Republic of Ireland (Province of Connacht).

Sludge Hall
Fictitious mansion in the county of Loamshire, occupied by Baron Mire.

Smoke, The
London, especially in the days when coal was the preferred fuel, *cf* Auld Reckie.

Solano
Andalusia, Northern Spain – a hot, dry, often sand-laden south-easterly wind that brings suffocating weather; see Winds.

Solar system, edge of
Where the solar wind meets the incoming plasma.

Solothurn
Swiss Canton (*qv*) and its capital.

Sooner State
Nickname of the State of Oklahoma; see United States of America.

South Carolina
An American State; see United States of America.

South Dakota
An American State; see United States of America.

Souther
A south gale; see Winds.

Spagthorpe Junction
The railhead for Much-Binding in the Marsh (*qv*).

Spica
Alpha star in Virgo; see Astral Constellations.

Springfield
State capital of Illinois; see United States of America.

Squamish
The fjords of British Columbia – a strong and often violent wind; Squamishes occur in those fjords oriented such that cold polar air can be funneled westward. They are notable in Jervis, Toba, and Bute inlets and in Dean Channel and Portland Canal. They lose their strength when free of the confining fjords, and are not noticeable 15 to 20 miles offshore; see Winds.

Squeezegut Alley
Whitstable, Kent.

Sri Lanka
(= Replendent Island), a republic on the island off the east coast of India once know as Ceylon, occupied since 550BCE, host to Portuguese settlements from early C16, controlled by the Dutch East India Company 1658–1796, a British colony from 1802 to 1948, and a republic within the British Commonwealth from 1792.

St Gallen (Sankt Gallen)
Swiss Canton (*qv*) and its capital.

St Paul
State capital of Minnesota; see United States of America.

St Trinian's
Fictional anarchic, corrupt and decayed girls' school created by the artist Ronald Searle in the 1940s and inspiration for four successful films in the 50s and 60s starring Alistair Sim as the headmistress.

Stamford
One of the finest medieval towns in Europe; a market town in Lincolnshire which a century and a half ago had the chance of a station on what is now the East Coast Main Line from London to Edinburgh and later Inverness. The councillors rejected the chance, with the result that Peterborough became the bustling interchange that it is today. A wise decision.

Stans
Capital of the Swiss Canton (*qv*) of Nidwalden.

Steppenwind
A wind of the Russian Steppes; see Winds.

Stockbridge
In the US, a town in the area of the Berkshires (*qv*); the location of Arlo Guthrie's *Alice's Restaurant*.

Stones, The
See Bartholomew Fair.

Streatham Place
The house of Henry and Hester Thrale (née Salusbury; later Piozzi (1741–1821)) where Dr Johnson made his second home between 1764 and 1783.

Stromboli
One of the Lipari Islands, off the north coast of Sicily, whereon is found the active volcano of that name 3040ft (927m) high.

Sualocin
Alpha star in Delphinus; see Astral Constellations.

Suestada
Uruguay and Argentina – a strong, rainy gale; see Winds.

Suestado
The coasts of Argentina, southern Brazil and Uruguay – a winter storm with southeast gales, caused by intense cyclonic activity; see Winds.

Sugar State
Nickname of the State of Louisiana; see United States of America.

Sukhovey
Mongolia – a warm, easterly dust storm wind in the Gobi Desert; see Winds.

Sulafat
A significant star in Lyra; see Astral Constellations.

Sumatra
Straits of Malacca – a brief but violent nocturnal squall that emanates from Sumatra especially during the southwest monsoon; see Winds.

Sundowner
Southern California coast in the vicinity of Santa Barbara – warm downslope winds; the name refers to their typical occurrence in the late afternoon or early evening, though they may occur at any time of the day. Wind speeds may exceed gale force, with temperatures in excess of 100°F; see Winds. ·

Sunflower State
Nickname of the State of Kansas; see United States of America.

Sunset Boulevard
Also known as *The Strip,* once the centre of the movie colony, yet still the best known street in Los Angeles, and immortalised by Billy Wilder's Hollywood drama *Sunset Boulevard* (1950). It runs 20 miles east-west from Dodger Stadium, through Hollywood and Beverly Hills, before meeting the ocean at Topanga Beach. It was along Sunset Boulevard that the first film studio in Hollywood was established; the Nester Film Company, in 1911.

Sunshine State
Nickname of the State of Florida; see United States of America.

Sunshine State
Nickname of the State of New Mexico; see United States of America.

Sunshine State
Nickname of the State of South Dakota; see United States of America.

Supercontinent

In prehistoric times, the two enormous landmasses now called Laurasia and Gondwanaland that together comprised virtually all the present-day continents of the world. Before that, there was an single, even greater, landmass known as Pangaea or Pangea. Laurasia eventually divided to become Asia (without India), Europe, Greenland, and North America; Gondwanaland separated into Africa (and Madagascar), Antarctica, Australasia, India, and South America.

Table Mountain
In South Africa, a mesa overlooking Cape Town and Table Bay; takes its name from its flat top and steep sides; 3,570 ft (1,087m) high.

Taku Wind
Juneau, Alaska – a strong, gusty, east-northeast wind, blowing between October and March; at the mouth of the Taku River, after which the wind is named, it sometimes attains hurricane force; see Winds.

Tallahassee
State capital of Florida; see United States of America.

Tar Heel State
Nickname of the State of North Carolina; see United States of America.

Taurus
The Bull; see Astral Constellations.

Tea and Sugar, The
The weekly train across the Nullarbor (*qv*) from Cook SA to Parkeston WA (and back).

Tegmeni
A significant star in Cancer; see Astral Constellations.

Tehuantepecer
In the Gulf of Tehuantepec (south of southern Mexico) – a violent squally winter wind from the north or north-northeast, originating in the Gulf of Mexico as a Norther that crosses the isthmus and blows through the gap between the Mexican and Guatamalan mountains. It may be felt up to 100 miles out to sea; see also Papagayos; see Winds.

Tejat poster
A significant star in Gemini; see Astral Constellations.

Tejat prior
A significant star in Gemini; see Astral Constellations.

Telescopium
The Telescope; see Astral Constellations.

Tellytubbies
See Over the Hills.

Tenerife
One of the Canary Islands; see Spanish Autonomous Communities.

Tennessee
An American State; see United States of America.

Texas
An American State; see United States of America.

The Dagorlad Plain
In *The Lord of the Rings*, an uninhabited area of land north of the Black Gates of Mordor, on which the Battle of the Last Alliance takes place.

The Lake District
Area of England now called Cumbria, characterised by mountains and lakes including Windermere, Grasmere, Derwentwater and Ullswater.

The Last Frontier
Nickname of the State of Alaska; see United States of America.

The Leaky Cauldron

In the stories of Harry Potter, a small pub with rooms available to stay in, located just off Charing Cross Road and run by the bald and tooth-less landlord Tom. In order to get to Diagon Alley, Harry has to go through the pub, into the courtyard where he must tap the bricks of the brick wall in the right order so as to reveal the magic archway – 'Three up, Two Across...'

The Old Dominion

Nickname of the State of Virginia; see United States of America.

The Shire

In *The Lord of the Rings*, a rural region in the west of Eriador, populated by friendly folk, the Hobbits. Divided into four Farthings; Eastfarthing, Southfarthing, Westfarthing and Northfarthing. The home of Frodo and Bilbo Baggins is situated in Northfarthing, in a small village called Hobbiton.

The Sickle

A significant star in Leo; see Astral Constellations.

The South

See Confederate States.

The White Mountains

In *The Lord of the Rings*, a mighty range dividing Rohan and Gondor, where the fortress of Helm's Deep stands, ruled by King Theoden and the Rohirrim.

Thrushcross Grange

See Wuthering Heights.

Thuban

Alpha star in Draco; see Astral Constellations.

Thule

1 The most remote northern land known to the ancients (also called Ultima Thule); Pytheas, the Greek navigator, says 'it is six days' sail from Britain', and its climate is 'a mixture of earth, air and sea'. Ptolemy says it is 63° north, which would suggest Iceland, though others have suggested Norway and Shetland. See Fogo.
2 An Inuit settlement and Danish trading post in North-West Greenland (1910) and US Air Force base.

Tierra del Fuego

(Land of Storms) An archipelago separated from the southern most tip of South America by the Strait of Magellan. The West and South islands (chief town Punta Arenas) belong to Chile, and the Eastern islands (chief town Ilshuaia) belong to Argentina; other islands are in dispute.

Timbuctu

1   A town in Central Mali on the River Niger at the end of a trans-Saharan caravan route.

2   A generic name used to imply some far-flung exotic destination.

Time ball

Knowing the 'exact' time at sea is necessary for fixing one's position. Armed with a sextant and a chronometer set to the time at the home port, the navigator can work out the position of the vessel. Chronometers of the necessary accuracy were developed from the end of the 18th century, but how to fix the time at one's home port? To avoid ships' timekeepers having to go ashore, a visible time signal was needed, and the first was the 'time ball' which, set on high, drops at a known time each day. This device was proposed by Captain Robert Wauchope of the British Royal Navy in 1824. A manually operated device was first set up at the Royal Observatory, Greenwich in 1833. In due course, time balls were erected in London and in many ports and, in 1862, time balls in The Strand and Cornhill in London, and at the ports of Deal and Liverpool, were dropped by telegraph signals from Greenwich to inaugurate Greenwich Mean Time. In the United States, the Naval Observatory was set up at Washington in 1845; one of its tasks was to provide a national time service, and it first sent out automatic time signals in 1880.

Tinseltown

Another name for Hollywood, connoting the glittering world of the stars and lack of reality; see Hollywood.

Tipperary

A county in the Republic of Ireland (Province of Munster). Made famous by the song 'It's a long way to Tipperary' (1912) words Harry J Williams, music Jack Judge, which has come to evoke WW1. By some stroke of genius, Tipperary Ward (men's orthopedic) was on the fourth floor of Old Addenbrooke's Hospital, Cambridge.

Tiruchchirappalli

Updated name for the Tamil Nadu town Trichinopoly, though most locals still call it Tricky.

Toad Hall

The residence of Mr Toad, the antisocial pioneer motorist, in the 1908 children's book *The Wind in the Willows* (Kenneth Grahame 1859–1932); the book dramatised in 1929 by A A Milne (1882–1956) as *Toad of Toad Hall*.

Tokalau

Fiji – a wind from the northeast; see Winds.

Toledo

Capital of the Spanish Region of Castile-La Mancha; see Spanish Autonomous Communities.

Topeka

State capital of Kansas; see United States of America.

Topside(s)

That part of a marine structure above sea level.

Towers of Silence

Whereon Parsees and Zoroastrians place their dead, much to the delight of the resident vultures who can pick a skeleton clean in a day.

Toyshop of Europe

Edmund Burke's epithet for Birmingham.

Trade Winds

Equator ±30° – blowing generally from the north east in the Northern hemisphere, and from the south east in the Southern hemisphere, they are noted for their constancy of direction and speed, and therefore helpful to sailing ships plying their trade; see Winds.

Trafalgar Day

21 October 1805, when the British Fleet under Admiral Lord Nelson on HMS *Victory* defeated the French off Cape Trafalgar (between Cape Càdiz and Gibraltar), using the daring tactic of attacking the French longitudinally rather than broadside, thus establishing British naval supremacy for over a century. Nelson (*b*1758) was mortally wounded in the battle.

Tramontana

Italy – a cold northeasterly or north wind of the fine weather mistral type off the west coast; see Winds.

Treasure Island

In about 1880, Robert Louis Stevenson (1850–94) and his stepson Lloyd Osbourne whiled away a Scottish holiday inventing an island which RLS turned into a series for *Young Folks* (July 1881–June 1882) as *The Sea Cook or Treasure Island*. The book, with its memorable cast

of characters (Long John Silver, Jim Hawkins (arrrgh, Jim lad), Blind
Pew and the rest) was published in 1883.

Treasure State
Nickname of the State of Montana; see United States of America.

Tree Planter's State
Nickname of the State of Nebraska; see United States of America.

Trenches, The
Those dug by the opposing forces in the WW1, facing one another
across No-Man's-Land (qv), the scene of one of the most wasteful and
pointless exercises mankind has ever seen.

Trenton
State capital of New Jersey; see United States of America.

Trevose Head
Promontory on the North coast of Cornwall, whose representation on
the map seems to provide an apt description of feelings the morning
after: 'I'm suffering from Trevose Head'.

Triangulum Australe
The Southern Triangle; see Astral Constellations.

Triangulum
The Triangle; see Astral Constellations.

Trichinopoly
See Tiruchchirappalli.

Trinacria
Latin name for Sicily; see Fogo.

Tucana
The Toucan; see Astral Constellations.

Twister
A tornado; see Winds.

Two Cities
London and Paris in *A Tale of Two Cities* (Charles Dickens, 1859), a story
of the French Revolution and its horrors.

Tyburn
A tributary of the River Thames on which was situated the district of
London once famous for its public executions (hanging from Tyburn
tree) until 1783; the site of the gallows is now marked in the pavement
where Edgware Road meets Bayswater Road.

Tynwald
See House of Keys.

Typhon
> A whirlwind; see Winds.

Typhoon
> Western Pacific – a severe tropical storm; perhaps from the Chinese *ty fung*; see Winds.

Tyrone
> A county of Northern Ireland.

Udagamandalam
> Updated name of the Indian hill-station Ootacamund, though most Indians still call it Ooty.

Ultima Thule
> The northern extent of civilisation; see Thule.

Uluru

Formerly known as Ayers Rock – a large rock formation more than 986 feet (318m) high and 5 miles (8km) around, and extending 1.5 miles into the ground (2.5km) in the Northern Territory of central Australia, located in Uluru-Kata Tjuta National Park, close to the small town Yulara, and not far from Kata Tjuta. Made of sandstone infused with minerals such as feldspar (Arkosic sandstone) which give the effect of a red glow at sunset and sunrise, the rust colour is due to oxidation. The name Ayers Rock was given to it by European settlers, after the Premier of South Australia, Henry Ayers. Since the 1980s Uluru, the Aboriginal name, has been officially preferred, although many still call it Ayers Rock. The rock is sacred to Aborigines, and has been the feature of many rock caves and ancient paintings. The Australian Government returned ownership of Uluru to the local Aboriginal people, the Anangu, who then leased it back for 99 years as a National Park of Australia.

Unuck al Hai
> Alpha star in Serpens; see Astral Constellations.

Up the Creek
> Generally without a paddle, a metaphor for being in an awkward position; has led to the further saying: 'Up Jacob's Creek without a corkscrew'.

Up train
> That which travels towards London; *cf* down train.

Ur
An ancient Sumerian city, located on a former channel of the Euphrates.

Ursa Major
The Great Bear; see Astral Constellations.

Ursa Minor
The Little Bear; see Astral Constellations.

Utah
An American State; see United States of America.

Utopia
(Greek = no place), an island of perfection portrayed by Sir Thomas More in his political romance of the same name.

Vale of Tears
A somewhat pessimistic name for the world we inhabit.

Valencia
Spanish Region and its capital; see Spanish Autonomous Communities.

Valhalla
In Scandinavian mythology, the hall where heroes of battle were taken by the Valkyries after death. The souls of the slain spent eternity in joy and feasting (valr, 'slain warriors' + höll, 'hall').

Valladolid
Capital of the Spanish Region of Castile and León; see Spanish Autonomous Communities.

Valley of the Kings
A site in Egypt, north west of Thebes, where the tombs of the Kings of the New Kingdom were or are located. The best known resident is Tutankhamun (formerly Tutenkhamen) whose tomb was excavated by Howard Cartier in 1922–3.

Van Allen belt
Discovered by the US physicist James Van Allen in 1954, two belts of particles charged by cosmic rays and trapped by the earth's magnetic field. The inner belt is between 2,400 and 5,600km above the earth's surface, and the outer belt from 13,00 to 19,000km.

Vardar, Vardarac
The Vardar Valley, Greece to the Gulf of Salonica – a cold fall wind blowing from the northwest that often occurs in winter when atmospheric pressure over eastern Europe is higher than that over the Aegean Sea; see Winds.

Vatican Hill
In Ancient Rome, the home of the vaticinatores (soothsayers), which gave its name to the Vatican City State (1929), home of the Pope and his offices, occupying about 1 square mile ($2.6km^2$).

Vectis
Roman name for the Isle of Wight, perpetuated in the transport system: Southern Vectis.

Vega
Alpha star in Lyra; see Astral Constellations.

Vela
The Sails; see Astral Constellations.

Venice of the East
Krung Thep (Bangkok) capital of Thailand.

Venice of the North
Stockholm (Sweden) or Amsterdam (Holland).

Venice of the West
Glasgow.

Vermont
An American State; see United States of America.

Victoria Falls
See Mosi-oa-Tunya.

Vind Gnyr
Ancient Ireland – a blustery thunderstorm downdraft, described in the Norse Sagas; see Winds.

Vind-Blaer
Icelandic Sagas – a breeze; see Winds.

Vindemiatrix
A significant star in Virgo; see Astral Constellations.

Vinland
An area of what is now designated North America discovered by the Norseman Leif Ericsson (son of Eric the Red) about 1,000 years ago. The identification of 'The Vinland Map' (found in 1957) as a fake does not detract from the Ericsson story.

Virginia and West Virginia
During the Civil War, the inhabitants of West Virginia were loyal to the Union and formed a separate state when the rest of Virginia became part of the Confederacy.

Virginia
An American State; see United States of America.

Virgo
The Virgin; see Astral Constellations.

Virugas
A Siberian wind; see Winds.

Vitoria (Gasteiz)
Capital of the Spanish Basque Region; see Spanish Autonomous Communities.

Volans
The Flying Fish; see Astral Constellations.

Volk's Electric Railway
Built by Victorian engineer Magnus Volk, the electric railway was the first on mainland Britain, running a mile along Brighton (originally Brighthelmstone) beach from Palace Pier to the Marina. It opened in 1883, and may still be experienced between March and September.

Volunteer State
Nickname of the State of Tennessee; see United States of America.

Vulpecula
The Fox; see Astral Constellations.

Wall Street
The street on which the New York Stock Exchange is situated, in the center of the financial district.

Walmington-on-Sea
Town on the South coast of England where *Dad's Army*, the boys of the Home Guard – CO Capt Mainwaring (Arthur Lowe), Sgt Wilson (John Le Mesurier) *et al* – have the task of repelling any invasion from across the channel; much of the filming was on location at Thetford, Norfolk.

Warm Braw
The Schouten Islands north of New Guinea – a foehn wind; see Winds.

Wasat
A significant star in Gemini; see Astral Constellations.

Washington
An American State; see United States of America.

Washington
1   The capital of the USA, situated in the district of Columbia on the east coast and known as Washington DC as distinct from.

2   Washington State, which is on the opposite side of the US, to the north west.

Waterford
A county in the Republic of Ireland (Province of Munster).

Watling Street of the Sky
The Milky Way.

Wessex
Old English kingdom of the West Saxons, founded by Cerdic in C6 on the present-day Berkshire and Hampshire, but later spreading from Cornwall in the west to Essex and Kent in the east. Its most famous ruler was Alfred the Great.

West Flanders
The agricultural province of Belgium.

West Virginia
An American State; see United States of America.

Western Samoa
Since 1962, an independent state in the South Pacific archipelago of the Samoan Islands comprising nine islands, four inhabited.

Westmeath
A county in the Republic of Ireland (Province of Leinster).

Wexford
A county in the Republic of Ireland (Province of Leinster).

Whispering Gallery
A circular gallery in a stone building whose acoustic properties are such that two people diametrically opposite can communicate by whispering to the wall; perhaps the most famous is that in St Paul's Church in London.

White Squall
In the tropics, a sudden and unexpected strong gust of wind, signed by whitecaps or white, broken water; in clear weather, usually seen as a whirlwind; see Winds.

Whittle
England – a gust of wind gust so named when Captain Whittle's coffin was upset; see Winds.

Wicklow
A county in the Republic of Ireland (Province of Leinster).

Whitehall, Dials at

How King Charles II's timekeeper, set up in 1669, worked, is not clear. Britten writes: 'This curious erection had no covering; exposure to the elements and other destroying influences led to its speedy decay and subsequent demolition.' However, it is elsewhere reported that this fancy construction of glass globes became the focus of the well-known rake John Wilmot, 2nd Earl of Rochester, and his companions as they returned from some drunken gathering. Stung by the impudence of the multiphallic construction ('What? Dost thou stand here to f*ck time?'), they laid about it with their sticks and smashed it to smithereens. The king was not amused.

Wildfell Hall

In the novel *The Tenant of Wildfell Hall* by Anne Brontë (1820–49) published the year before her death, the tenant is a 'widow' (who is actually fleeing from her hateful husband) and her son, and her landlord turns out to be her brother.

Williwaw, Williwau, Willy Waw

Straits of Magellan or the Aleutian Islands – a strong gust of cold wind blowing seawards from a mountainous coast; see Winds.

Willow South (orig Juneau)

State capital of Alaska; see United States of America.

Will's Mother's

See All round.

Willy-willy

Australia (especially SW) – a tropical cyclone (33 knots); a dust-devil; see Winds.

Windermere, Lake

In England's Lake District; the largest lake in the country at 10.5 miles (17km) long.

Windy City, The

Chicago IL, so-called not because of the steady breeze off Lake Michigan, but because of the inhabitants' gift of the gab.

Wisconsin

An American State; see United States of America.

Witch City
Salem MA, where the notorious witchcraft trials took place in 1692, seemingly as the result of alleged satanic possession, itself the result of mass hysteria.

Wizard of Menlo Park, The
Thomas Alva Edison (1847–1931), American patentee of the phonograph, incandescent lamp, microphone and a thousand other things.

Wizard of Oz
See Oz.

Wolverine State
Nickname of the State of Michigan; see United States of America.

Wonder State
Nickname of the State of Arkansas; see United States of America.

Wonderland
1   A fictional setting for experiencing wonderful things, as by Alice (Lewis Carrol) or Mr Tompkins (George Gamow).
2   A real presentation of so-dubbed wonders, *eg* Christmas decorations in a garden centre.

Wooden Hill
The stairs, in an attempt to add glamour to the domestic structure when trying to persuade children it's bedtime.

Worcester
1   An English cathedral city on the River Severn; Cromwell defeated Charles II at the Battle of Worcester.
2   A US textile-manufacturing city in Massachusetts on the Blackstone River, settled in 1673.

Worms
SW German city on the Rhine, C5 capital of Burgundy. The well-known Diet (assembly) of Worms was an ecclesiastical assembly held in 1521, at which Martin Luther refused to recant those views others saw as heretical.

Wrekin, The
A 1,300ft hill in mid-Shropshire of volcanic rock, close to the dormant Church Stretton fault; 'All round the Wrekin': going the long way round, or not explaining something clearly and directly.

Wuthering Heights
In the novel by Emily Brontë (1818–48), published the year before her death, the home of the Earnshaw family who rescue the waif Heathcliff from Liverpool; he turns out to be a thoroughly unpleasant character, though redeemed in his final years, when he expresses the

hope that the families of Wuthering Heights and Thrushcross Grange (the seat of the Lintons) will be united in the next generation.

Wyoming
An American State; see United States of America.

Xanadu
City in Coleridge's *Kubla Khan*, a poem whose idea is drawn from Purchas's *Pilgrimmage* (1613) where X is called Xamdu.

Xlokk
Malta – a hot, dry wind; see Winds.

Yakutsk
In Siberia, where the strangers bought as much land as they could encompass with a cow-hide, cutting it into thin strips so as to enclose enough land to build a city (*cf* Carthage).

Yamo
Uganda – a whirlwind; see Winds.

Yathreb
The ancient name of Medina.

Yellow Brick Road
See Oz.

Yellow River
1   The Tiber, whose waters are coloured with yellow sand.
2   The Yellow River of China, Hwang He (or Ho).

Yggdrasil

In Norse mythology, the evergreen ash tree that grows from the surface of the world, whose branches and leaves form the sky and whose roots embrace the subterranean worlds: Asgard, Jotunheim and Nilfheim. Its existence is threatened by the serpent Nidhögg who chews its buds. However, it is kept alive by the Norns (Fates) who water it from one of the three wells or fountains: Mímisbrunnr (the Well of Wisdom), Urdarbrunnr (the Well of Fate – particularly associated with the Norns) and Hvergelmir (the Roaring Kettle, source of many rivers). The branches of Yggdrasil drop honey which nourishes the squirrel Ratatosk and the tree snake Vidofnir, as well as the golden cockerel that sits on the topmost bough, and the four stags. Yggdrasil represents space and time, life and knowledge. The Norns, in their capacity as Fates, represent also past, present and future (time was, is and will be).

Yellowhammer State
Nickname of the State of Alabama; see United States of America.

Zaragoza
Capital of the Spanish Region of Aragón; see Spanish Autonomous Communities.

Zephyr
Italy – a mild breeze bringing pleasant weather; see Winds.

Zephyros
Ancient Greek – the West wind; see Winds.

Zonda
Argentina – a hot, humid air that blows from the north across the plains; an Andes Chinook; see Winds.

Zozma
A significant star in Leo; see Astral Constellations.

Zuben Elakrab
A significant star in Libra; see Astral Constellations.

Zuben Elgenubi
Alpha star in Libra; see Astral Constellations.

Zuben Elkaribi
A significant star in Libra; see Astral Constellations.

Zuben Elschemali
A significant star in Libra; see Astral Constellations.

Zug
Swiss Canton (*qv*) and its capital.

Zürich
Swiss Canton (*qv*) and its capital.

Part 2   The tables
The natural world

Land

The continents

Continent	Area miles²	km²	% of Earth's land	Lowest point	ft	m
Asia	16,988,000	43,998,000	29.9	Dead Sea	− 1312	− 400
*America	16,185,000	41,918,000	28.5	Death Valley	− 282	− 86
Africa	11,506,000	29,800,000	20.3	Lake Assal	− 512	− 156
Antarctica	5,100,000	13,209,000	9.5	Ice-covered	− 8325	− 2538
†Europe	3,745,000	9,699,000	6.6	Caspian Sea	− 92	− 28
Australia	2,941,526	7,618,493	5.2	Lake Eyre	− 52	− 16

* North and Central America has an area of 24,255,000km² (9,365,000 miles²).

† Includes 5,571,000km² (2,151,000 miles²) of former USSR territory, including the Baltic states, Belarus, Moldova, Ukraine and the part of Russia west of the Ural Mountains and Kazakhstan west of the Ural river. European Turkey (24,378km²/9,412 miles²) comprises territory to the west and north of the Bosporus (Bosphorus) and the Dardanelles.

Countries of the world; capitals, divisions etc

AFGHANISTAN   Asa (Afganistan (Pushtu), Afqanestan (Dari), Afghanistan) **Capital** Kabul. **Main cities** Heart, Jalalabad, Qandahar, Mazar-e-Sharif. **ICR** AFG. **IC** .af **ND** 19 August.

ALBANIA   Eur (Republika e Shqipërisë – Republic of Albania) **Capital** Tirana. **ICR** AL. **IC** .al **ND** 11 January.

ALGERIA   Afr   (Al-Jumhuiyya   al-Jaza'iriyyaad-Dimuqratiyya   ash-Sha'biyya – People's Democratic Republic of Algeria) **Capital** Algiers. **Main cities** Annaba, Bejaia, Blida, Constantine, Mostaganem, Oran, Setif, Sidi-Bel-Abbes, Skikda, Tizi Ouzou, Tlemcen. **ICR** DZ. **IC** .dz **ND** 1 November.

ANDORRA   Eur (Principat d'Andora – Principality of Andorra) **Capital** Andorra La Vella. **ICR** AND. **IC** .ad **ND** 8 September.

ANGOLA   Afr (Republica de Angola – Republic of Angola) **Capital** Luanda. **IC** .ao **ND** 11 November – ID.

ANGUILLA   Am **Capital** The Valley. **DoL. IC** .ai

ANTIGUA AND BARBUDA   Am (State of Antigua and Barbuda) **Capital** St John's. **Main cities** Codrington. **DoL. IC** .ag **ND** 1 November – ID.

ARGENTINA   Am (República Argentina – Argentine Republic) **Capital** Buenos Aires. **Main cities** Córdoba, La Plata, Mar del Plata, Mendoza, Rosatio, San Miguel de Tucumán. **Subdivisions** Provinces: Buenos Aires, Catamarca, Chaco, Chubut, Cordóba, Corrientes, Entre Rios, Federal Capital, Formosa, Jujuy, La Pampa, La Rioja, Mendoza, Misiones, Nequén, Rio Negro, Salta, San Juan, San Luis, Santa Cruz, Santa Fé, Santiago del Estero, Tierra del Fuego, Tucumán. **Admin capitals** La Plata, San Fernando del Valle de Catamarca, Resistencia, Rawson, Córdoba, Corrientes, Paraná, Buenos Aires, Formosa, San Slavador de Jujuy, Santa Rosa, La Rioja, Mendoza, Posadas, Nequén, Viedma, Salta, San Juan, San Luis, Rio Gallegos, Santa Fé, Santiago del Estero, Ushuaia, San Miguel de Tucumán. **ICR** RA. **IC** .ar **ND** 25 May.

ARMENIA   Eur (Hayastani Hanrapetut'yun – Republic of Armenia) **Capital** Erevan. **IC** .am **ND** 21 September – ID.

AUSTRALIA   Oce (The Commonwealth of Australia) **Capital** Canberra. **Main cities** Adelaide, Brisbane, Hobart, Melbourne, Perth, Sydney. **Subdivisions** States and Territories: Australian Capital Territory, New South Wales, Northern Territory, Queensland, South Australia, Tasmania, Victoria, Western Australia, External territories: Ashmore and Cartier Islands, Australian Antarctic Territory, Christmas Island, Cocos (Keeling) Islands, Coral Sea Islands Territory, Heard Island and McDonald Islands, Norfolk Island. **Admin capitals** Canberra, Sydney, Darwin, Brisbane, Adelaide, Hobart, Melbourne, Perth, Kingston. **ICR** AUS. **DoL. IC** .au, .cx, .cc, .hm **ND** 26 January – Australia Day.

AUSTRIA   Eur (Republik Österreich – Republic of Austria) **Capital** Vienna. **Main cities** Graz, Innsbruck, Klagenfurt, Linz, Salzburg. **Subdivisions** Provinces, Burgenland, Carinthia, Lower Austria, Salzburg, Styria, Tirol, Upper Austria, Vienna, Vorarlberg. **Admin capitals** Eisenstadt, Klagenfurt, St Pölten, Salzburg, Graz, Innsbruck, Linz, Vienna, Bregenz. **ICR** A. **IC** .at **ND** 26 October.

AZERBAIJAN Eur (Az'rbaycan Respublikasi – Azerbaijani Republic) **Capital** Baku. **Main cities** Gäncä, Sumqayit. **Subdivisions** Autonomous Republic: Naxçivan. **Admin capital** Naxçivan. **IC** .az **ND** 28 May – ID.

BAHAMAS Am (The Commonwealth of the Bahamas) **Capital** Nassau. **ICR** BS. **DoL. IC** .bs **ND** 10 July – ID.

BAHRAIN Asa (Dawlat al-Bahrayn – The Kingdom of Bahrain) **Capital** Manama. **ICR** BRN. **IC** .bh **ND** 16 December.

BANGLADESH Asa (Gan Prajatantri Bamlades – People's Republic of Bangladesh) **Capital** Dhaka. **ICR** BD. **DoL. IC** .bd **ND** 26 March – ID.

BARBADOS Am **Capital** Bridgetown. **Main cities** Holetown, Oistins, Speightstown. **ICR** BDS. **DoL. IC** .bb **ND** 30 November.

BELARUS Eur (Respublika Belarus – Republic of Belarus) **Capital** Minsk. **Main cities** Brest, Homyel', Hrodna, Mahilyow, Vitsyebsk. **ICR** SU. **IC** .by **ND** 27 July – ID.

BELGIUM Eur (Koninkrijk België/Royaume de Belgique/Königreich Belgien – Kingdom of Belgium) **Capital** Brussels. **Main cities** Antwerp, Bruges, Charleroi, Ghent, Liège, Leuven, Mons, Namur. **Subdivisions** Regions and Provinces: Brussels, Flanders: Antwerp, East Flanders, Flemish Brabant, Limburg, West Flanders, Wallonia: Hainault, Liège, Luxembourg, Namur, Walloon Brabant. **Admin capitals** Brussels, Antwerp, Ghent, Leuven, Hasselt, Bruges, Mons, Liège, Arlon, Namur, Wavre. **ICR** B. **IC** .be **ND** 21 July – Accession of King Leopold I, 1831.

BELIZE Am **Capital** Belmopan. **Main cities** Belize City, Corozal, Dangriga, Orange Walk, San Ignacio. **ICR** BH. **IC** .bz **ND** 21 December – ID.

BENIN Afr (République du Benin – Republic of Benin) **Capital** Porto Novo. **Main cities** Cononou. **ICR** DY. **IC** .bj **ND** 30 November.

BHUTAN Asa (Druk Gyal Khab – Kingdom of Bhutan) **Capital** Thimphu. **DoL. IC** .bt **ND** 17 December.

BOLIVIA Am (República de Bolivia – Republic of Bolivia) **Capital** La Paz. **Main cities** Cochabamba, El Alto, Oruro, Potosi, Santa Cruz, Sucre. **IC** .bo **ND** 6 August – ID.

BOSNIA-HERCEGOVINA Eur (Republika Bosna iHercegovina – Republic of Bosnia and Hercegovina) **Capital** Sarajevo. **Main cities** Banja Luka, Mostar, Tuzla, Zenica. **Subdivisions** States: Federation of Bosnia-

Herzegovnia, Republika Srpska. **Admin capitals** Sarajevo, Pale. **ICR** BIH. **IC** .ba **ND** 1 March – Anniversary of 1992 declaration of independence.

BOTSWANA Afr (The Republic of Botswana) **Capital** Gaborone. **Main cities** Francistown, Molepolole, Selebi-Phikwe. **ICR** RB. **DoL. IC** .bw **ND** 30 September.

BRAZIL Am (República Federativa doBrasil – Federative Republic of Brazil) **Capital** Brasilia. **Main cities** Belo Horizonte, Fortaleza, Porto Alegre, Recife, Rio de Janeiro, Salvador, São Paolo. **Subdivisions** Federal Districts and States: Central West: Distrito Federal, Goiás, Mato Grosso, Mato Grosso do Sul, North: Acre, Amapá, Amazonas, Pará, Rondônia, Roraima, Tocantins, North-east: Alagoas, Bahia, Ceará, Maranhão, Paraiba, Pernambuco, Piauí, Rio Grande do Norte, Sergipe, South: Paraná, Rio Grande do Sul, Santa Catarina, South East: Espirito Santo, Minas Gerais, Rio de Janeiro, São Paulo. **Admin capitals** Brasilia, Goiânia, Cuiabá, Campo Grande, Rio Branco, Macapá, Manaus, Belém, Pôrto Velho, Boa Vista, Palmas, Maceió, Salvador, Fortaleza, São Luís, João Pessoa, Recife, Teresina, Natal, Aracajú, Curitiba, Pôrto Alegre, Florianópolis, Vitória, Belo Horizonte, Rio de Janeiro, São Paulo. **ICR** BR. **IC** .br **ND** 7 September – ID.

BRUNEI Asa (Negara Brunei Darussalam – State of Brunei Darussalam) **Capital** Bandar Seri Begawan. **ICR** BRU. **DoL. IC** .bn **ND** 23 February.

BULGARIA Eur (Republika Balgarija) **Capital** Sofia. **Main cities** Burgas, Plovdiv, Varna. **ICR** BG. **IC** .bg **ND** 3 March.

BURKINA FASO Afr (République Démocratiquedu Burkina Faso – Democratic Republic of Burkina Faso) **Capital** Ouagadougou. **Main cities** Bobo-Dioulasso, Koudougou. **IC** .bf **ND** 11 December.

BURUNDI Afr (République du Burundi – Republic of Burundi) **Capital** Bujumbura (was Usumbura). **Main cities** Kitega. **ICR** RU. **IC** .bi **ND** 1 July.

CAMBODIA Asa (Preah Réachéanachâkr Kâmpuchéa – The Kingdom of Cambodia) **Capital** Phnom Penh. **ICR** K. **IC** .kh **ND** 9 November – ID.

CAMEROON Afr (République du Cameroun – Republic of Cameroon) **Capital** Yaoundé. **Main cities** Douala. **IC** .cm **ND** 20 May.

CANADA Am **Capital** Ottawa. **Main cities** Calgary, Edmonton, Hamilton, Montreal, Québec, Toronto, Vancouver, Winnipeg. **Subdivisions** Provinces/Territories: Alberta (AB), British Columbia (BC), Manitoba (MB), New Brunswick (NB), Newfoundland and Labrador (NF), Northwest

Territories (NT), Nova Scotia (NS), Nunavut (NT) [born of Northwest Territories 1999], Ontario (ON), Prince Edward Island (PE), Québec (QC), Saskatchewan (SK), Yukon Territory (YT). **Admin capitals** Edmonton, Victoria, Winnipeg, Fredericton, St John's, Yellowknife, Halifax, Iqaluit, Toronto, Charlettetown, Québec, Regina, Whitehorse. **ICR** CDN. **IC** .ca **ND** 1 July – Canada Day.

CAPE VERDE ISLANDS   Afr (República de Cabo Verde – Republic of Cape Verde) **Capital** Praia. **IC** .cv **ND** 5 July – ID.

CENTRAL AFRICAN REPUBLIC   Afr (République Cantrafricaine/Ködrö tî Bê-Afrîka – Central African Republic) **Capital** Bangui. **ICR** RCA. **IC** .cf **ND** 1 December.

CHAD   Afr (République du Tchad – Republic of Chad) **Capital** Ndjaména. **IC** .td **ND** 13 April, 1 December.

CHILE   Am (República de Chile – Republic of Chile) **Capital** Santiago. **Main cities** Antofagasta, Concepción, Puente Alto, Valparaíso, Punta Arenas. **ICR** RCH. **IC** .cl **ND** 18 September.

CHINA   Asa (Zhonghua Renmin Gongheguo – The People's Republic of China) **Capital** Beijing (Peking). **Main cities** Chengdu, Chongqing, Dalian, Guangzhou, Harbin, Qingdo, Shanghai, Shenyang, Tianjin, Wuhan, Wuxi, Yantai, Zaozhuang. **Subdivisions** Provinces etc: Anhui, Beijing (Peking), Fujian, Gansu, Guangdong (Canton), Guangxi Zhuang, Autonomous Region: Guizhou, Hainan, Hebei, Heilongjiang, Henan, Hong Kong Special, Administrative Region: Hubei, Hunan, Jiangsu, Jiangxi, Jilin, Liaoning, Nei Mongol, Autonomous Region: Ningxia Hui, Autonomous Region: Qinghai, Shaanxi, Shandong, Shanghai, Municipal Province: Shanxi, Sichuan, Tianjin (Tientsin), Xizang (Tibet), Autonomous Region: Xinjiang Uygur (Sinkiang), Autonomous Region, Yunnan, Zhejiang. **Admin capitals** Hefei, Beijing (Peking), Fuzhou, Lanzhou, Guangzhou, Nanning, Guiyang, Haikou, Shijazhuang, Harbin, Zhengzhou, Hong Kong, Wuhan, Changsha, Nanjing, Nanchang, Changchun, Shenyang, Hohhot, Yinchuan, Xining, Xian, Jinan, Shanghai, Taiyuan, Chengdu, Tianjin, Lhasa, ürümqi, Kunming, Hangzhou. **ICR** CHI. **IC** .cn **ND** 1 October – Founding of People's Republic, HK; DoL; .hk.

COLOMBIA   Am (República de Colombia – Republic of Colombia) **Capital** Bogotá. **Main cities** Barranquilla, Buenaventura, Cali, Cartagena, Medllin. **ICR** CO. **IC** .co **ND** 20 July – ID.

COMOROS   Afr (L'Union des Comores – Union of the Comoros) **Capital** Moroni. **IC** .km **ND** 6 July – ID.

CONGO Afr (République Démocratiquedu Congo – Democratic Republic of Congo) **Capital** Kinshasa. **Main cities** Kananga, Kisangani, Likasi, Lubumbashi, Matadi, Mbandaka. **ICR** ZRE. **IC** .cd **ND** 30 June – ID.

CONGO-BRAZZAVILLE Afr (République du Congo-Brazzaville – Republic of Congo-Brazzaville) **Capital** Brazzaville. **Main cities** Kananga, Kisangani, Likasi, Lubumbashi, Matadi, Mbandaka, Pointe Noire. **ICR** RCB. **IC** .cg **ND** 15 August.

COSTA RICA Am (República de Costa Rica – Republic of Costa Rica) **Capital** San José. **Main cities** Alajuela, Cartago. **ICR** CR. **IC** .cr **ND** 15 September.

CÔTE D'IVOIRE Afr (République de la Côte d'Ivoire – Republic of Côte d'Ivoire) **Capital** Yamoussoukro. **Main cities** Abidjan. **Subdivisions** Regions: Agneby, Bafing, Bas-Sassandra, Denguele, Dix-Huit Montagnes, Fromager, Haut-Sassandra, Lacs, Lagunes, Marahoue, Moyen-Cavally, Moyen-Comoe, N'zi-Comoe, Savanes, Sud-Bandama, Sud-Comoe, Vallee duBandama, Worodougou, Zanzan. **ICR** CI. **IC** .ci **ND** 7 December, 7 August – ID.

CROATIA Eur (Republika Hrvatska – Republic of Croatia) **Capital** Zagreb. **Main cities** Osijek, Rijeka, Split. **ICR** HR. **IC** .hr **ND** 30 May – Statehood Day.

CUBA Am (República de Cuba – Republic of Cuba) **Capital** Havana. **Main cities** Camagüey, Guantánamo, Holguín, Santa Clara, Santiago. **ICR** C. **IC** .cu **ND** 1 January – Day of Liberation.

CYPRUS Eur (Kypriaka Dimokratía/Kibris Çumhuriyeti – Republic of Cyprus) **Capital** Nicosia. **Main cities** Famagusta, Larnaca, Limassol, Paphos. **ICR** CY. **DoL. IC** .cy **ND** 1 October – ID.

CZECH REPUBLIC Eur (Ceská Republika) **Capital** Prague. **Main cities** Brno, Ostrava, Plzen. **ICR** CZ. **IC** .cz **ND** 28 October.

DENMARK Eur (Kongeriget Danmark/Kingdom of Denmark) **Capital** Copenhagen. **Main cities** Ålborg, Århus, Odense. **ICR** DK. **IC** .dk **ND** 5 June – Constitution Day.

DENMARK – FÆRØE ISLANDS Eur **Capital** Tórshavn. **ICR** FO. **IC** .fo **ND** 5 June – Constitution Day.

DENMARK – GREENLAND   Eur **Capital** Godthåb (Nuuk). **IC** .gl

DJIBOUTI   Afr (Jumhuriyya Jibuti/République Djibouti – Republic of Djibouti) **Capital** Djibouti. **IC** .dj **ND** 27 June – ID.

DOMINICA   Am (The Commonwealth of Dominica) **Capital** Roseau. **ICR** WD. **DoL**. **IC** .dm **ND** 3 November – ID.

DOMINICAN REPUBLIC   Am (República Dominicana – Dominican Republic) **Capital** Santo Domingo. **Main cities** Duarte, La Vega, Puerto Plata, San Cristóbal, San Juan, Santiago de los Caballeros. **ICR** DOM. **IC** .do **ND** 27 February – ID.

EAST TIMOR (República Democrática de Timor-Leste/Republik Demokratis Timor Leste/Repúblika Demokrátika Timór-Leste – Democratic Republic of East Timor) **Capital** Dili. **Main cities** Lautem. **IC** .tp

ECUADOR   Am (República del Ecuador – Republic of Ecuador) **Capital** Quito. **Main cities** Cuenca, Guayaquil. **ICR** EC. **IC** .ec **ND** 10 August – ID.

ECUADOR – GALÁPAGOS ISLANDS   Am **Capital** Puerto Barquerizo Moreno.

EGYPT   Afr (Al-Jumhuiyya al-Misriyyaal-'Arabiyya – Arab Republic of Egypt) **Capital** Cairo. **Main cities** Alexandria, Asyut, Faiyum, Ismailia, Port Said, Suez. **ICR** ET. **IC** .eg **ND** 23 July – Anniversary of Revolution in 1952.

EL SALVADOR   Am (República de El Salvador) **Capital** San Salvador. **Main cities** San Miguel, Santa Ana. **ICR** ES. **IC** .sv **ND** 15 September.

EQUATORIAL GUINEA   Afr (República de Guinea Ecuatorial – Republic of Equatorial Guinea) **Capital** Malabo. **Main cities** Bata. **IC** .gq **ND** 12 October.

ERITREA   Afr (Hagere Eretra/al-Dawlaal-Iritra – State of Eritrea) **Capital** Asmara. **Main cities** Assab, Massawa. **IC** .er **ND** 24 May – ID.

ESTONIA   Eur (Eesti Vabariik – Republic of Estonia) **Capital** Talinn. **Main cities** Kohtla-Järve, Narva, Pärnu, Tartu. **ICR** EW. **IC** .ee **ND** 24 February – ID.

ETHIOPIA   Afr (Ya'Ityopya Federalawi Dimokrasyawi Repeblik – Federal Democratic Republic of Ethiopia) **Capital** Addis Ababa. **Main cities** Dire Dawa. **ICR** ETH. **IC** .et **ND** 28 May.

FIJI   Oce (Matanitu ko Viti – Republic of the Fiji Islands) **Capital** Suva. **ICR** FJI. **DoL**. **IC** .fj **ND** 10 October – Fiji Day.

FINLAND Eur (Suomen Tasavalta/Republiken Finland – Republic of Finland) **Capital** Helsinki (Helsingfors). **Main cities** Espoo, Oulu, Tampere, Turku, Vantaa. **Subdivisions** Autonomous Province, Åland (Ahvenanmaa). **Admin capital** Mariehamn (Maarianhamina). **ICR** FIN. **IC** .fi **ND** 6 December – ID.

FRANCE Eur (La République française – The French Republic) **Capital** Paris. **Main cities** Bordeaux, Grenoble, Lille, Lyon, Marseille, Nantes, Nice, Strasbourg, Toulon, Toulouse, Ajaccio, Bastia. **Subdivisions** Regions and Departments, Alsace: Bas-Rhin, Haut-Rhin, Aquitaine: Dordogne, Gironde, Landes, Lot-et-Garonne, Pyrénées-Atlantiques, Auvergne: Allier, Cantal, Haute-Loire, Puy-de-Dôme, Basse-Normandi (Lower Normandy): Calvados, Manche, Orne, Bourgogne (Burgundy): Côtes-d'Or, Nièvre, Saôane-et-Loire, Yonne, Bretagne (Brittany): Côtes-d'Armor, Finistère, Ille-et-Vilaine, Morbihan, Centre-Val de Loire: Cher, Eure-de-Loir, Indre, Indre-et-Loire, Loiret, Loir-et-Cher, Champagne-Ardennes: Ardennes, Aube, Haute-Marne, Marne, Corse (Corsica): Corse-du-Sud, Haute-Corse, Franche-Comté: Doubs, Haute-Saône, Jura, Territoire de Belfort, Haute-Normandie (Upper Normandy): Eure, Seine-Maritime, Île-de-France: Essonne, Hauts-de-Seine, Paris, Seine-et-Marne, Seine-Saint-Denis, Val-de-Marne, Val d'Oise, Yvelines, Languedoc-Roussillon: Aude, Gard, Hérault, Lozère, Pyrénées-Orientales, Limousin: Corrèze, Creuse, Haute-Vienne, Lorraine: Meutre-et-Moselle, Meuse, Moselle, Vosges, Midi-Pyrénées: Ariège, Aveyron, Gers, Haute-Garonne, Haute-Pyrénées, Lot, Tarn, Tarn-et-Garonne, Nord-Pas-de-Calais: Nord, Pas-de-Calais, Pays de la Loire: Loire-Atlantique, Maine-et-Loire, Mayenne, Sarthe, Vendée, Picardie (Picardy): Aisne, Oise, Somme, Poitou-Charentes: Charente, Charente-Maritime, Deux-Sèvres, Vienne, Provence-Alpes-Côte d'Azur: Alpes-de-Haute-Provence, Alpes-Maritimes, Bouches-de-Rhône, Hautes-Alpes, Var, Vaucluse, Rhône-Alpes: Ain, Ardèche, Drôme, Haute-Savoie, Isère, Loire, Rhône, Savoie, Overseas Departments: French Guiana, Guadeloupe, Martinique, Réunion, Territorial Collectives: Mayotte, St Pierre and Miquelon, Overseas Territories, French Polynesia, New Caledonia, Southern and Antarctic Territories, Wallis and Futuna Islands. **Admin capitals** Strasbourg, Strasbourg, Colmar, Bordeaux, Périgeux, Bordeaux, Mont-de-Marsan, Agen, Pau, Clemont-Ferrand, Moulins, Aurillac, Le Puy, Clermont-Ferrand, Caen, Caen, Saint Lô, Alençon, Dijon, Dijon, Nevers, Tours, Auxerre, Rennes, Saint-Brieuc, Quimper, Rennes, Vannes, Orléans, Bourges, Chartres, Châteauroux, Tours, Orléans, Blois, Reims, Charleville-Mézières, Troyes, Chaumont, Chalôns-sur-Marne, Ajaccio, Ajaccio, Bastia, Besançon, Besançon, Vesoul, Lons-le-Saunier,

Belfort, Rouen, Évreux, Rouen, Paris, Évry, Nanterre, Paris, Melun, Bobigny, Créteil, Pontoise, Versailles, Montpellier, Carcassonne, Nîmes, Montpellier, Mende, Peripignan, Limoges, Tulle, Guéret, Limoges, Nancy, Nancy, Bar-le-Duc, Metz, Épinal, Toulouse, Foix, Rodez, Auch, Toulouse, Tarbes, Cahors, Albi, Montauban, Lille, Lille, Arras, Nantes, Nantes, Angers, Laval, Le Mans, La Roche-sur-Yon, Amiens, Laon, Beauvais, Amiens, Poitiers, Angoulème, La Rochelle, Niort, Poitiers, Marseille, Digne, Nice, Marseille, Gap, Toulon, Avignon, Lyon, Bourg-en-Bresse, Privas, Valence, Annecy, Grenoble, Saint-Étienne, Lyon, Chambéry, Cayenne, Basse-Terre, Fort-de-France, St-Denis, Mamoudzou, St-Pierre, Papeete, Nouméa, Mata-Utu. **ICR** F. **IC** .fr, .gf, .gp, .mq, .pm, .pf, .tf, **ND** 14 July – Bastille Day 1789.

GABON Afr (République Gabonaise – Gabonese Republic) **Capital** Libreville. **IC** .ga **ND** 17 August.

GAMBIA Afr (The Republic of the Gambia) **Capital** Banjul. **ICR** WAG. **IC** .gm **ND** 18 February – ID.

GEORGIA Eur (Sak'art'velos Respublikis – Georgia) **Capital** Tbilisi. **Main cities** Batumi, Kutaisi, Rustavi, Sukhumi. **Subdivisions** Autonomous Republic, Akhazia, Ajaria. **Admin capitals** Sukhumi, Batumi. **ICR** GE. **IC** .ge **ND** 26 May – ID.

GERMANY Eur (Bundesrepublik Deutschland – Federal Republic of Germany) **Capital** Berlin. **Main cities** Bremen, Cologne, Dortmund, Dresden, Duisburg, Düssldorf, Essen, Frankfurt am Amin, Hamburg, Hannover, Leipzig, Munich, Nuremberg, Stuttgard. **Subdivisions** Länder (singular: Land): Baden-Württemberg, Bavaria, Berlin, Brandenburg, Bremen, Hamburg, Hesse, Lower Saxony, Mecklenburg – Western Pomerania (M-Vorpommern), North Rhine – Westphalia (Nordrhein-Westfalen), Rhineland-Palatinate (R-Pfalz), Saarland, Saxony (Sachsen), Saxony-Anhalt (Sachsen-A), Schleswig-Holstein, Thuringia (Thüringen). **Admin capitals** Stuttgart, Munich (München), Berlin, Potsdam, Bremen, Hamburg, Wiesbaden, Hannover, Schwerin, Düsseldorf, Mainz, Saarbrücken, Dresden, Magdeburg, Kiel, Erfurt. **ICR** D. **IC** .de **ND** 3 October – Anniversary of 1990 Unification.

GHANA Afr (The Republic of Ghana) **Capital** Accra. **Main cities** Kofoidua, Kumasi, Takoradi, Tamale. **ICR** GH. **IC** .gh **ND** 6 March – ID.

GREECE Eur (Elliniki Dimokratia – Hellenic Republic) **Capital** Athens. **Main cities** Iráklion, Lárisa, Pátrai, Thessaloniki, Vólos. **Subdivisions**

Autonomous Monks' Republic: Mount Athos (Ayion Oros). **Admin capital** Karyai. **ICR** GR. **IC** .gr **ND** 25 March – ID.

GRENADA   Am (The State of Grenada) **Capital** St George's. **ICR** WG. **DoL. IC** .gd **ND** 7 February.

GUAM (USA)   Oce **Capital** Agaña. **IC** .gu

GUATEMALA   (República de Guatemala – Republic of Guatemala) **Capital** Guatemala City. **Main cities** Mazatenango, Puerto Barrios, Quetzaltenango, Cobån, Escuintla. **ICR** GCA. **IC** .gt **ND** 15 September.

GUINEA   Afr (République de Guinée – Republic of Guinea) **Capital** Conakry. **Main cities** Kankan, Kindia, Labé, Mamou, N'Zérékoré, Siguiri. **IC** .gn **ND** 2 October – Anniversary of Proclamation of Independence.

GUINEA-BISSAU   Afr (Repûblica da Guiné-Bissau – Republic of Guinea-Bissau) **Capital** Bissau. **IC** .gw **ND** 24 September – ID.

GUYANA   Am (The Co-operative Republic of Guyana) **Capital** Georgetown. **Main cities** Corriverton, Linden, New Amsterdam. **ICR** GUY. **DoL. IC** .gy **ND** 26 May – ID, 23 February – Republic Day.

HAÏTI   Am (République d'Haïti – Republic of Haïti) **Capital** Port-au-Prince. **Main cities** Cap Haïtien, Carrefour, Delmas. **ICR** RH. **IC** .ht **ND** 1 January.

HONDURAS   Am (República de Honduras – Republic of Honduras) **Capital** Tegucigalpa. **Main cities** Choluteca, La Ceiba, Puerto Cortés, San Pedro Sula, Tela. **IC** .hn **ND** 15 September.

HUNGARY   Eur (Magyar Köztársaság – Republic of Hungary) **Capital** Budapest. **Main cities** Derecen, Miskolc, Pécs, Szeged. **ICR** H. **IC** .hu **ND** 15 March, 20 August, 23 October.

ICELAND   Eur (L´ydveldid Ísland – Republic of Iceland) **Capital** Reykjavik. **Main cities** Akranes, Akureyri, Egilsstadir, Harnarfjordur, Isafjordur, Kopavogur, Reykjanesbær, Siglufjordur. **ICR** IS. **IC** .is **ND** 17 June.

INDIA   Asa (The Republic of India/Bharatiya Ganarajya) **Capital** Delhi. **Main cities** Ahmedabad, Bangalore, Bombay/Mumbai, Calcutta/Kolkata, Hyderabad, Kanpur, Lucknow, Madras/Chennai, Pune. **Subdivisions** States: Andhra Pradesh, Arunachal Pradesh, Assam, Bihar, Goa, Gujarat, Hayana, Himachal Pradesh, Jammu and Kashmir, Karnataka, Kerala, Madhya Pradesh, Maharashtra, Manipur, Meghalaya, Mizoram, Nagaland, Orissa, Punjab, Rajasthan, Sikkin, Tamil Nadu, Tripura, Uttar Pradesh,

West Bengal, Union Territories, Andaman and Nicobar Islands, Chandigarh, Dara and Nagar Haveli, Daman and Diu, Delhi, Lakshadweep, Pondicherry. **Admin capitals** Hyderabad, Itanagar, Dispur, Patna, Panaji, Gandhinagar, Chandigarh, Shimla, Srinagar / Jammu, Bangalore, Trivandrum, Bhopal, Bombay, Imphal, Shillong, Aizawl, Kohima, Bhubaneswar, Chandigarh, Jaipur, Gangtok, Madras, Agartala, Lucknow, Calcutta, Port Blair, Silvassa, Kavaratti. **ICR** IND. **DoL. IC** .in **ND** 26 January – Republic Day.

INDONESIA   Asa (Republik Indonesia – Republic of Indonesia) **Capital** Jakarta. **Main cities** Bandung, Semarang, Surabaya, Banjarmasin, Pontianak, Ambon, Ujung Pandang, Medan, Palembang. **Subdivisions** Provinces: Aceh (special region), Sumatera Utara, Sumatera Barat, Riau, Jambi, Sumatera Selatan, Bengkulu, Lampung, Jakarta Raya, Jawa Barat, Jawa Tengah, Yogyakarta, Jawa Timur, Bali, Nusa Tenggara Barat, Nusa Tenggara Timur, Kalimantan Barat, Kalimantan Tengah, Kalimantan Selatan, Kalimantan Timur, Sulawesi Utara, Sulawesi Tengah, Sulawesi Selatan, Sulawesi Tenggara, Maluku, Irian Jaya. **Admin capitals** Banda Aceh, Medan, Padang, Pakanbaru, Jambi, Palembang, Bengkulu, Tanjungkarang, Jakarta, Bandung, Semarang, Yogyakarta, Surabaya, Denpasar, Mataram, Kupang, Pontianak, Palangkaraya, Bankarmasin, Samarinda, Menado, Palu, Ujung Pandang, Kendari, Amboina, Jayapura. **ICR** RI. **DoL. IC** .id **ND** 17 August – ID.

IRAN   Asa (Jomhûri-ye-Eslâmi-ye-Îrân – Islamic Republic of Iran) **Capital** Tehran. **Main cities** Ahwaz, Esfahan, Mashad, Qom, Shiraz, Tabriz. **ICR** IR. **IC** .ir **ND** 11 February.

IRAQ   Asa (Al-Jumhuriyya al-Iraqiyya – Republic of Iraq) **Capital** Baghdad. **Main cities** Al-Basra, Kirkuk, Al-Mawsil. **Admin capitals** Autonomous Region, Irbil. **ICR** IRQ. **IC** .iq **ND** 17 July – Revolution Day, 9 April – Overthrow of Ba'ath regime of Saddam Hussein.

IRELAND, REPUBLIC OF   Eur (Éire/Ireland) **Capital** Dublin. **Main cities** Cork, Galway, Limerick, Waterford. **Subdivisions** Provinces and Counties: Ulster: Cavan, Donegal, Monaghan, Leinster: Carlow, Dublin, Kildare, Kilkenny, Laoighs, Longford, Louth, Meath, Offaly, Westmeath, Wexford, Wicklow, Munster: Clare, Cork, Kerry, Limerick, Tipperary, Waterford, Connacht: Galway, Leitrim, Mayo, Roscommon, Sligo. **Admin capitals** Cavan, Lifford, Monaghan, Carlow, Dublin, Naas, Kilkenny, Portlaoise, Longford, Dundalk, Trim, Tullamore, Millingar, Wexford, Wicklow, Ennis, Cork, Tralee, Limerick, Clonmel, Waterford, Galway, Carrick-on-Shannon,

Castlebar, Roscommon, Sligo. **ICR** IRL. **DoL. IC** .ie **ND** 17 March – St Patrick's Day.

ISRAEL   Asa (Medinat Yisra'el DawlatIsra'il – State of Israel) **Capital** Tel Aviv. **Main cities** Beersheba, Haifa, Rishon Le'Zion. **ICR** IL. **IC** .il

ISRAEL – WEST BANK AND GAZASTRIP   Asa (Palestinian Autonomous Area) **Capital** Gaza City. **Main cities** Khan Yunis, Rafah, Nablus, Hebron, Jericho, Ramallah, Bethlehem. **IC** .ps

ITALY   Eur (Repubblica Italiana – Italian Republic) **Capital** Rome. **Main cities** Bologna, Florence, Genoa, Milan, Naples, Turin, Sicily, Palermo, Sardinia, Cagliari. **Subdivisions** Regions: Abruzzi, Basilicata, Calabria, Campania, Emilia-Romagna, Friuli-Venzia Guilia, Lazio, Liguria, Lombardy, Marche, Molise, Piemonte, Puglia, Sardinia, Sicily, Tuscany, Trentino-Alto Adige, Umbria, Valle d'Aosta, Venetia. **Admin capitals** L'Aquila, Potenza, Catanzaro, Naples, Bologna, Trieste, Rome, Genoa, Milan, Ancona, Campobasso, Turin, Bari, Cagkiari, Palermo, Florence, Bolzano-Bozen and Trento, Perugia, Aosta, Venice. **ICR** I. **IC** .it **ND** 2 June.

JAMAICA   Am **Capital** Kingston. **Main cities** Mandeville, May Pen, Montego Bay, Ocho Rios, Spanish Town. **ICR** JA. **DoL. IC** .jm **ND** 6 August – ID.

JAPAN   Asa (Nihon-koku – State of Japan) **Capital** Tokyo. **Main cities** Fukuoka, Kobe, Kyoto, Nagoya, Osaka, Sapporo, Yokohama. **ICR** J. **DoL. IC** .jp **ND** 23 December – Emperor'sB'day.

JORDAN   Asa (Al-Mamlaka al-Urdunniyyaal-Hashimiyya – Hashemite Kingdom of Jordan) **Capital** Amman. **Main cities** Irbid, Az-Zarqa. **ICR** HKJ. **IC** .jo **ND** 25 May – ID.

KAZAKHSTAN   Asa (Qazaqstan Respublikasy – Republic of Kazakhstan) **Capital** Astana. **Main cities** Almaty, Pavlodar, Karaganda, Shymkent. **ICR** KZ. **IC** .kz **ND** 16 December – Republic Day, 25 October – Republic Day.

KENYA   Afr (Jamhuri ya Kenya – Republic of Kenya) **Capital** Nairobi. **Main cities** Kisumu, Mombasa, Nakuru. **ICR** EAK. **DoL. IC** .ke **ND** 12 December – ID.

KIRIBATI   Oce (Ribaberikin Kiribati – Republic of Kiribati) **Capital** Tarawa. **DoL. IC** .ki **ND** 12 July – ID.

KOREA, DPR (NORTH)   Asa (Chosun Minchu-chui Inmin Kongwa-guk – Democratic People's Republic of Korea) **Capital** Pyongyang. **ICR** DVRK. **IC** .kp **ND** 8 September, 16 February – Kin Jong-il's birthday.

KOREA, REP OF (SOUTH)   Asa (Taehan Min'guk – Republic of Korea) **Capital** Seoul. **Main cities** Inchon, Pusan, Taegu. **ICR** ROK. **IC** .kr **ND** 15 August – Liberation Day.

KUWAIT   Asa (Dawlat al-Kuwayt – Stateof Kuwait) **Capital** Kuwait (city). **ICR** KWT. **IC** .kw **ND** 25 February.

KYRGYZSTAN   Asa (Kyrgyz Respublikasy – Kyrgyz Republic) **Capital** Biskek. **ICR** KS. **IC** .kg **ND** 31 August – ID.

LAOS   Asa (Satharanarath Pasathipatai Pasason Lao – Lao People's Democratic Republic) **Capital** Vientiane. **ICR** LAO. **IC** .la **ND** 2 December.

LATVIA   Eur (Latvijas Republika – Republic of Latvia) **Capital** Riga. **Main cities** Daugavpils, Jelgava, Jurmala, Liepaja, Ventspils. **ICR** LV. **IC** .lv **ND** 18 November – ID 1918.

LEBANON   Asa (Al-Jumhuriyyaal-Lubnaniyya – Republic of Lebanon) **Capital** Beirut. **Main cities** Sayda, Tarabulus, Sur. **ICR** RL. **IC** .lb **ND** 22 November.

LESOTHO   Afr (Mmuso wa Lesotho – Kingdom of Lesotho) **Capital** Maseru. **ICR** LS. **DoL. IC** .ls **ND** 4 October – ID.

LIBERIA   Afr (Republic of Liberia) **Capital** Monrovia. **Main cities** Buchanan, Greenville, Harper. **ICR** LB. **IC** .lr **ND** 26 July.

LIBYA   Afr (Al-Jamahiriyya Al-'Arabiyya Al-Libiyya Ash-Sha'biyya Al-Ishtirmakiyya – Great Socialist People's Libyan Arab Jamahiriya) **Capital** Tripoli. **Main cities** Bangazi, Misratah, Sirte. **ICR** LAR. **IC** .ly **ND** 1 September.

LIECHTENSTEIN   Eur (Fürstentum Liechtenstein – Principality of Liechtenstein) **Capital** Vaduz. **ICR** FL. **IC** .li **ND** 15 August.

LITHUANIA   Eur (Lietuvos Respublika – Republic of Lithuania) **Capital** Vilnius. **Main cities** Kuanas, Klaipeda. **ICR** LT. **IC** .lt **ND** 16 February – ID.

LUXEMBOURG   Eur (Groussherzogtom Lëtzebuerg/Grand-Duché de Luxembourg/Großherzogtum Luxembourg – Grand Duchy of Luxembourg) **Capital** Luxembourg. **ICR** L. **IC** .lu **ND** 23 June.

MACAO (PORTUGAL)   Asa **Capital** Macao. **IC** .mo

MACEDONIA   Eur (Republika Makedonija – Republic of Macedonia) **Capital** Skopje. **Main cities** Bitola, Kumanovo, Prilep. **IC** .mk

MADAGASCAR Afr (Repoblikan'i Madagasikara/République de Madagascar – Republic of Madagascar) **Capital** Antananarivo. **Main cities** Anstiranana, Fianarantsoa, Mahajanga, Toamasina. **ICR** RM. **IC** .mg **ND** 26 June – ID.

MALAWI Afr (Mfuko la Malawi/Republic of Malawi) **Capital** Lilongwe. **Main cities** Blantyre, Mzuzu, Zomba. **ICR** MW. **DoL. IC** .mw **ND** 6 July – ID.

MALAYSIA Asa **Capital** Kuala Lumpur. **Main cities** Ipoh, Johore Bharu, Petaling Jaya. **Subdivisions** States: Johore, Kedah, Kelantan, Melaka, Negri Sembilan, Pahang, Penang, Perak, Perlis, Sabah, Sarawak, Selngor, Terengganu. **Admin capitals** Johore Bahru, Alor Setar, Kota Bahru, Melaka, Seremban, Kuantan, Georgetown, Ipoh, Kangar, Kota Kinabalu, Kuching, Shah Alam, Kuala Terengganu. **ICR** MAL. **DoL. IC** .my **ND** 31 August – HariKebangsaan.

MALDIVES Asa (Divehi Rajje ge Jumhuriyya – Republic of the Maldives) **Capital** Malé. **DoL. IC** .mv **ND** 26 July.

MALI Afr (République du Mali – Republic of Mali) **Capital** Bamako. **Main cities** Gao, Kayes, Mopti, Segou, Sikasso, Timbuktu. **ICR** RMM. **IC** .ml **ND** 22 September.

MALTA Eur (Repubblika ta' Malta/Republic of Malta) **Capital** Valletta. **ICR** GBY. **DoL. IC** .mt **ND** 31 March – Freedom Day, 8 September – Our Lady of Victories, 7 June – Sette Guigno Riots, 21 September – ID, 13 December – Republic Day.

MARSHALL ISLANDS Oce (Republic of the Marshall Islands) **Capital** Majuro. **Main cities** Ebeye. **ICR** M H. **IC** .mh **ND** 21 October – Compact Day, 1 May – ID.

MAURITANIA Afr (Al-Jumhuriyyaal-Islamiyya al-Mawritaniyya – Islamic Republic of Mauritania) **Capital** Nousakschott. **ICR** RIM. **IC** .mr **ND** 28 November.

MAURITIUS Afr (Republic of Mauritius) **Capital** Port Louis. **Main cities** Beau Bassin, Curepipe, Quatre Bornes, Vacoas-Phoenix. **ICR** MS. **DoL. IC** .mu **ND** 12 March.

MAYOTTE (FRENCH) Afr **Capital** Mamoundzou. **IC** .yt

MEXICO Am (Estados Unidos Mexicanos – United Mexican States) **Capital** Mexico City. **Main cities** Cuidad Juárez, Ecatepec de Morelos, Guadalajara, León, Monterrey, Nezahualcóyotl, Puebla, Tijuana, Toluca, Torreón. **Subdivisions** States and Territories: Federal District,

Aguasclientes, Baja California, Baja California Sur, Campeche, Coahuila, Colima, Chiapas, Chihuahua, Durango, Guanajuato, Guerrero, Hidalgo, Jalisco, México, Michoacán, Morelos, Nayarit, Nuevo León, Oaxaca, Puebla, Querétao, Quintana Roo, San Luis Potosí, Sinaloa, Sonora, Tabasco, Tamaulipas, Tlaxcala, Veracruz, Yucatán, Zacatecas. **Admin capitals** Mexico City, Aguascalientes, Mexicali, La Paz, Campeche, Saltillo, Colima, Tuxtla Gutiérrez, Chihuahua, Victoria de Durango, Guanajuato, Chilpancingo, Pachuca de Soto, Guadalajara, Toluca de Lerdo, Morelia, Cuernavaca, Tepic, Monterrey, Oaxaca de Juárez, Puebla de Zaragoza, Querétaro, Chetumal, San Luis Potosi, Culiacán Rosales, Hermosillo, Villahermosa, Cuidad Victoria, Tlaxcala, Jalapa Enríquez, Mérida, Zacatecas. **ICR** MEX. **IC** .mx **ND** 16 September – Proclamation of Independence.

MICRONESIA, FED. STATES OF   Oce **Capital** Palikir. **ICR** FSM. **IC** .fm

MOLDOVA   Eur (Republica Moldova – Republic of Moldova) **Capital** Chisinau. **Subdivisions** Autonomous Republics: Gagauzia, Trannsdniestria. **Admin capitals** Komrat, Tighina. **IC** .md **ND** 27 August – ID.

MONACO   Eur (Principauté de Monaco – Principality of Monaco) **Capital** Monaco-Ville. **ICR** MC. **IC** .mc **ND** 19 November.

MONGOLIA   Asa (Mongol Uls – Mongol State) **Capital** Ulan Bator. **ICR** MGL. **IC** .mn **ND** 11 July.

MOROCCO   Afr (Al-Mamlaka Al-Maghribiyya – Kingdom of Morocco) **Capital** Rabat. **Main cities** Agadir, Casablanca, Fez, Marrakesh, Meknes, Oujda. **ICR** MA. **IC** .ma **ND** 3 March – Anniversary of the Throne, 30 July – Anniversary of the Throne.

MOROCCO – WESTERN SAHARA   Afr (Al-Jumhuriyyaal-'Arabiyya as-Sahrawiyya ad-Dimuqratiyya – Sahrawi Arab Democratic Republic) **Capital** Laayoune. **IC** .eh **ND** 3 March – Anniversary of the Throne.

MOZAMBIQUE   Afr (República de Moçambique – Republic of Mozambique) **Capital** Maputo. **Main cities** Beira, Matola, Nampula. **IC** .mz **ND** 25 June – ID.

MYANMAR (BURMA)   Asa (Pyidaungsu Myanmar Naingngandaw – Union of Mayanmar) **Capital** Yangon (Rangoon). **Main cities** Madalay, Mawlamyine/Moulmein, Pathein/Bassein. **Subdivisions** States: Chin, Kachin, Karen, Kayah, Mon, Rakhine, Shan. **Admin capitals** Hakha, Myitkyina, Pa-an, Loi-kaw, Moulmein, Sittwe, Taunggyi. **ICR** MYA. **IC** .mm **ND** 4 January.

NAMIBIA   Afr (The Republic of Namibis) **Capital** Windhoek. **Main cities** Ondangwa, Oshakati, Rehoboth, Swakopmund, Walvis Bay. **ICR** NAM. **DoL. IC** .na **ND** 21 March – ID.

NAURU   Oce (The Republic of Nauru/Naoero) **Capital** Nauru. **DoL. IC** .nr **ND** 31 January – ID.

NEPAL   Asa (Nepal Adhirajya/Kingdom of Nepal) **Capital** Kathmandu. **Main cities** Lalitpur, Biratnagar, Bhaktapur. **DoL. IC** .np **ND** 18 February – National Democracy Day, 28 December – King's Birthday.

THE NETHERLANDS   Eur (Koninkrijk der Nederlanden – Kingdom of the Netherlands) **Capital** Amsterdam. **Main cities** Eindhoven, Groningen, Haarlem, Rotterdam, Tilburg, Utrecht. **Subdivisions** Overseas Territories: Aruba, Netherlands Antilles. **Admin capitals** Oranjestad, Willemstad. **ICR** NL, NA. **IC** .nl, .aw, .an,

NEW CALEDONIA (FRENCH)   Oce **Capital** Noumea. **IC** .nc

NEW ZEALAND   Oce **Capital** Wellington. **Main cities** Auckland, Christchurch, Dunedin, Hamilton, Napier-Hastings. **Subdivisions** Islands: North Island, South Island, Chatham Islands, Stewart Island, The Kermadec Group, Campbell Island, The Three Kings, Auckland Islands, Antipodes Group, Bounty Islands, Snares Islands, Solander. **ICR** NZ. **DoL. IC** .nz

NEW ZEALAND – COOK ISLANDS   Oce **Capital** Avarua. **DoL. IC** .ck

NEW ZEALAND – NIUE   Oce **Capital** Alofi. **DoL. IC** .nu

NEW ZEALAND – ROSSDEPENDENCY   Oce.

NEW ZEALAND – TOKELAU   Oce. **IC** .tk

NICARAGUA   Am (República de Nicaragua – Republic of Nicaragua) **Capital** Managua. **Main cities** Chinandega, Granada, León, Massaya. **ICR** NIC. **IC** .ni **ND** 15 September.

NIGER   Afr (République du Niger – Republic of Niger) **Capital** Niamey. **ICR** RN. **IC** .ne **ND** 18 December.

NIGERIA   Afr (Federal Republic of Nigeria) **Capital** Abuja. **Main cities** Ibadan, Kaduna, Kano, Lagos, Ogbomosho, Port Harcourt. **Subdivisions** State: Sokoto, Zamfara, Kebbi, Niger, Kwara, Kogi, Benue, Plateau, Nassarawa, Taraba, Adamawa, Borno, Yobe, Bauchi, Gombe, Jigawa, Kano, Katsina, Kaduna, Federal Capital Territory, Oyo, Osun, Ogun, Lagos, Ondo, Ekiti, Edo, Delta, Rivers, Bayelsa, Abia, Imo, Ebonyi, Anambra,

Enugu, Cross River, Akwa Ibom. **Admin capitals** Sokoto, Gusau, Birnin-Kebbi, Minna, Ilorin, Lokoja, Makurdi, Jos, Lafia, Jalingo, Yola, Maiduguri, Damaturu, Bauchi, Gombe, Dutse, Kano, Katsina, Kaduna, Abuja, Ibadan, Oshogbo, Abeokuta, Ikeja, Akure, Ado Ekiti, Benin City, Asaba, Port-Harcourt, Yenagoa, Umuahia, Owerri, Abakaliki, Awka, Enugu, Calabar, Uyo. **ICR** WAN. **IC** .ng **ND** 1 October – ID.

NORTHERN MARIANA ISLANDS (USA) Oce **Capital** Saipan. **IC** .mp

NORWAY Eur (Kongeriket Norge – Kingdom of Norway) **Capital** Oslo. **Main cities** Bergen, Kristiansand, Stavanger, Trondheim. **Subdivisions** Territory: Svalbard and Jan Mayen Island, Antarctic Territories: Bouvet Island, Peter the First Island, Princess Ragnhild Land, Queen Maud Land. **ICR** N. **IC** .no, .sj, .bv **ND** 17 May – Constitution Day.

OMAN Asa (Saltanat 'Uman – Sultanate of Oman) **Capital** Muscat. **Main cities** Barka, Mutrah, Ruwi, Salalah, Suhar, Sur. **ICR** OM. **IC** .om **ND** 18 November.

PAKISTAN Asa (Islami Jamhuriya-e-Pakistan – Islamic Republic of Pakistan) **Capital** Islamabad. **Main cities** Faisalabad, Karachi, Lahore, Rawalpindi. **Subdivisions** Province: Baluchistan, Federal Capital Territory Islamabad, Federally Administered Tribal Areas, North-West Frontier Province, Punjab, Sind. **Admin capitals** Quetta, Peshawar, Lahore, Karachi. **ICR** PK. **DoL. IC** .pk **ND** 23 March – Pakistan Day, 14 August – ID.

PALAU (USA) Oce (Belu'u era Belau – Republic of Palau) **Capital** Koror. **IC** .pw

PANAMA Am (República de Panamá – Republic of Panama) **Capital** Panama City. **ICR** PA. **IC** .pa **ND** 3 November.

PAPUA NEW GUINEA Oce (Gau Hedinarai ai Papua-Matamata Guinea – Independent State of Papua New Guinea) **Capital** Port Moresby. **Main cities** Goroka, Lae, Madang, Mount Hagen, Rabaul, Wewak. **ICR** PNG. **DoL. IC** .pg **ND** 16 September – ID.

PARAGUAY Am (República del Paraguay – Republic of Paraguay) **Capital** Asunción. **Main cities** Cuidad del Este, San Lorenzo. **ICR** PY. **IC** .py **ND** 15 May.

PERU Am (República del Perú – Republic of Peru) **Capital** Lima. **Main cities** Arequipa, Chiclayo, Chimbote, Trujillo. **ICR** PE. **IC** .pe **ND** 28 July – Anniversary of Independence.

PHILIPPINES Asa (República ng Pilipinas – Republic of the Philippines) **Capital** Manila. **Main cities** Quezon, Cebu, Davao, Iloilo, Zamboanga. **Subdivisions** Islands: Bohol, Cebu, Leyte, Luzon, Masbate, Mindanao, Mindoro, Negros, Palawan, Panay, Samar, Filipino Autonomous Region: Muslim Mindanao. **Admin capital** Cotabato City. **ICR** RP. **IC** .ph **ND** 12 June – ID 1898.

POLAND Eur (Rzeczpospolita Polska – Republic of Poland) **Capital** Warsaw. **Main cities** Bydgoszcz, Gdansk (Danzig), Katowice, Krakow, Lódz, Poznan, Szczecin (Steltin), Wroclaw (Breslaw). **ICR** PL. **IC** .pl **ND** 3 May.

PORTUGAL Eur (República Portuguesa – Portuguese Republic) **Capital** Lisbon. **Main cities** Oporto. **Subdivisions** Autonomous Regions: Azores, Madeira. **Admin capitals** Ponta Delgada, Funchal. **ICR** P. **IC** .pt **ND** 10 June.

QATAR Asa (Dawlat Qatar – State of Qatar) **Capital** Doha. **Main cities** Ar-Rayyan, Dukhan, Mussay'id, Al-Wakrah. **ICR** Q. **IC** .qa **ND** 3 September.

RÉUNION (FRENCH) Afr **Capital** St Denis. **IC** .re

ROMANIA Eur (România) **Capital** Bucharest. **Main cities** Brasov, Constanta, Cluj-Napoca, Craiova, Galanti, Iasi, Oradea, Ploiesti, Timisoara. **ICR** RO. **IC** .ro **ND** 1 December.

RUSSIA Eur (Rossiiskaya Federatsiya – Russian Federation) **Capital** Cities of Federal Status, Moscow, St Petersburg (Petrograd 1914 – 24; Leningrad 1924 – 91). **Main cities** Chelyabinsk, Kazan, Nizhny-Novogorod/Gorky, Novosibirsk, Omsk, Perm/Molotov, Rostov-on-Don, Samara /Kuibyshev, Ufa, Yekaterinburg / Sverdlovsk. **Subdivisions** Regions (oblast): Amur, Arkhangelsk, Astrakhan, Belgorod, Bryansk, Chelyabinsk, Chita, Irkutsk, Ivanovo, Kaliningrad, Kaluga, Kamchatka, Kemerovo, Kirov, Kostroma, Kurgan, Kursk, Leningrad, Lieptsk, Magadan, Moscow, Murmansk, Nizhny Novgorod, Novgorod, Novosibirsk, Omsk, Orel, Orenburg, Penza, Perm, Pskov, Rotstov, Ryazan, Sakhalin, Samara, Saratov, Smolensk, Sverdlovsk, Tambov, Tomsk, Tula, Tver, Tyumen, Ulyanovsk, Vladimir, Volgograd, Vologda, Voronezh, Yaroslavl, Six autonomousterritories (krai): Altai, Khabarovsk, Krasnodar, Krasnoyarsk, Primorye, Stravropol, Republics: Adygeia, Bashkortostan, Buryatia, Chechnya, Chuvashia, Daghestan, Gorno-Altay, Ingushetia, Kabardino-Balkaria, Kalmykia (Lhalmg-Tangch), Karachay-Cherkessia, Karelia, Khakassia, Komi, Mari-El, Mordvinia, North Ossetia (Alania), Sakha (formerly Yakutia), Tatarstan, Tyva (formerly Tuva), Udmurtia, Autonomous areas: Aga-Buryat, Chuckchi, Evenki, Khanty-Mansi, Komi-Permyak, Koryak, Nenets, Taimyr, Ust-Orda-Buryat, Yamal-Nenets, Autonomous Jewishregion: Birobijan. **Admin capital** Maykop, Ufa, Ulan-Ude, Dzhokhar-Ghala, Cheboksary, Makhachkala, Gorno-Altaisk, Nazran, Nalchik, Elista, Cherkessk, Petrozavodsk, Abakan, Syktyvkar, Yoshkar-Ola, Saransk, Vladikavkaz, Yakutsk, Kazan, Kyzyl-Orda, Izhevsk, Birobijan. **ICR** RUS. **IC** .ru **ND** 12 June – ID.

RWANDA   Afr (Republika y'u Rwanda/République Rwandaise – Republic of Rwanda) **Capital** Kigali. **ICR** RWA. **IC** .rw **ND** 1 July.

ST CHRISTOPHER AND NEVIS   Am (The Federation of St Christopher and Nevis) **Capital** Basseterre. **Main cities** Charlestown. **DoL. IC** .kn **ND** 19 September – ID.

ST LUCIA   Am **Capital** Castries. **ICR** WL. **DoL. IC** .lc **ND** 22 February.

ST VINCENT AND THE GRENADINES   Am **Capital** Kingstown. **ICR** WV. **DoL. IC** .vc **ND** 27 October – ID.

SAMOA, AMERICA (USA)   Oce **Capital** Pago Pago. **ND** – .

SAMOA   (Ole Malo Tutoatasi oSamoa/Independent State of Samoa) **Capital** Apia. **ICR** WS. **IC** .ws **ND** 1 June – ID.

SAN MARINO   Eur (Repubblica di San Marino – Republic of San Marino) **Capital** San Marino. **ICR** RSM. **IC** .sm **ND** 3 September.

SÃO TOMÉ AND PRÍNCIPE   Afr (República Democrática deSão Tomé ePríncipe – Democratic Republic of São Tomé and Príncipe) **Capital** São Tomé. **IC** .st **ND** 12 July – ID.

SAUDI ARABIA   Asa (Al-Mamlaka al-'Arabiyyaas-Sa'udiyya – Kingdom of Saudi Arabia)· **Capital** Riyadh. **Main cities** Jiddah, Buraydah, Ad-Dammam, Al-Hofuf, Al-Makkah (Mecca), Al-Madiina, Tabuk. **IC** .sa **ND** 23 September – proclamation and unification of the Kingdom, 1932.

SENEGAL   Afr (République du Sénégal – Republic of Senegal) **Capital** Dakar. **Main cities** Rufisque, Thies, Ziguinchor. **ICR** SN. **IC** .sn **ND** 4 April.

SERBIA AND MONTENEGRO   Eur (Srbija I Crna Gora) **Capital** Belgrade. **Main cities** Kragujevac, Nis, Novi Sad, Podgorica, Pristina, Subotica. **Subdivisions** Yugoslav Republics: Montenegro, Serbia. **Admin capitals** Podgorica, Belgrade. **ICR** SCG. **ND** 27 April.

SEYCHELLES   Afr (The Republic ofSeychelles/République des Seychelles/ Repiblik Sesel) **Capital** Victoria. **ICR** SY. **DoL. IC** .sc **ND** 5 June, 18 June.

SIERRA LEONE   Afr (The Republic of Sierra Leone) **Capital** Freetown. **ICR** WAL. **IC** .sl **ND** 27 April – ID.

SINGAPORE   Asa (Repablik Singapura/Xinjiapo Gongheguo/Singapur Kutiyara'su/Republic of Singapore) **ICR** SGP. **DoL. IC** .sg **ND** 9 August.

SLOVAK REPUBLIC   Eur (Slovenská Republika – Slovak Republic) **Capital** Bratislava. **Main cities** Kosice. **ICR** SK. **IC** .sk **ND** 1 January – Establishment of Slovak Republic, 5 July – Day of Slav Missionaires, 29 August – Slovak National Uprising, 1 September – National Constitution Day.

SLOVENIA   Eur (Republika Slovenija – Republic of Slovenia) **Capital** Ljubljana. **Main cities** Maribor. **ICR** SLO. **IC** .si **ND** 25 June – Statehood Day.

SOLOMON ISLANDS   Oce **Capital** Honiara. **DoL. IC** .sb **ND** 7 July – ID.

SOMALIA   Afr (Jamhuuriyadda Dimoqraadiya Soomaaliya – Somali Democratic Republic) **Capital** Mogadishu. **Main cities** Berbera, Boroma, Buroa, Hargeysa, Kisimaayo. **DoL. IC** .so **ND** Under review.

SOUTH AFRICA   Afr (Republic of South Africa) **Capital** Pretoria and Cape Town. **Main cities** Durban, East London, Johannesburg, Pietermaritzburg, Port Elizabeth. **Subdivisions** Provinces: Eastern Cape, Free State, Gauteng, KwaZulu/Natal, Mpumalanga, Northern, Northern Cape, North-West, Western Cape. **Admin capitals** Bisho, Bloemfontein, Johannesburg, Ulundi, Nelspruit, Pietersburg, Kimberley, Mafikeng, Cape Town. **ICR** ZA. **DoL. IC** .za **ND** 27 April – Freedom Day.

SOUTH GEORGIA AND THE SOUTH SANDWICH ISLANDS (UK) **Capital** – . **IC** .gs

SPAIN   Eur (Reino de España – Kingdom of Spain) **Capital** Madrid. **Main cities** Barcelona, Valencia, Malaga, Sevilla, Zaragoza. **Subdivisions** Spanish Autonomous Communities (Regions): Andalucia, Aragon, Asturias, Balaerics, The Basque country, Canaries, Cantabria, Castilla-La Mancha, Castill-Leon, Cataluña, Cueta, Extremadura, Galicia, La Rioja, Madrid, Melilla, Murcia, Navarre, Valencia. **Admin capitals** Seville, Zaragoza, Oviedo, Palma de Mallorca, Vitoria, Santa Crus de Tenerife and Las Palmas, Santander, Toledo, Valladolid, Barcelona, Cueta, Mérida, Santiago de Compostela, Logroño, Madrid, Melilla, Murcia, Pamplona, Valencia. **ICR** E. **IC** .es **ND** 12 October.

SRI LANKA   Asa (Sri Lanka Prajatantrika Samajavadi Janarajaya/Ilankais Sananayaka Sosalisak Kutiyarasa – Democratic Socialist Republic of Sri

Lanka) **Capital** Colombo. **Main cities** Galle, Jaffna, Kandy, Trincomalee. **ICR** CL. **DoL. IC** .lk **ND** 4 February – Independence Commemoration Day.

SUDAN Afr (Al-Jumhuriyya as-Sudan – Republic of the Sudan) **Capital** Khartoum. **Main cities** Al-Ubayyid, Nyala, Port Sudan. **ICR** SUD. **IC** .sd **ND** 1 January – ID.

SURINAME Am (Republiek Suriname – Republic of Suriname) **Capital** Paramaribo. **ICR** SME. **DoL. IC** .sr **ND** 25 November.

SWAZILAND Afr (Umbuso we Swatini/Kingdom of Swaziland) **Capital** Mbabane. **Main cities** Manzini, Hlatikulu, Mhlume, Nhangano, Pigg's peak, Siteki. **ICR** SD. **DoL. IC** .sz **ND** 6 September – ID.

SWEDEN Eur (Konungariket Sverige – Kingdom of Sweden) **Capital** Stockholm. **Main cities** Gothenburg, Malmo, Uppsala. **ICR** S. **IC** .se **ND** 6 June – Day of the Swedish Flag.

SWITZERLAND Eur (Schweizerische Eidgenossenschaft/Confédération Suisse/Confederazione Svizzera/Confederaziun Svizra – Swiss Confederation) **Capital** Bern. **Main cities** Basel, Geneva, Lausanne, Lucerne, Winterthur, Zurich. **Subdivisions** Cantons: Aagau, Appenzell-Ausserrhoden, Appenzell-Innerrhoden, Basel-Landschaft, Basel-Stadt, Bern, Fribourg, Geneva, Glarus, Graubünden, Jura, Lucerne, Neuchatel, Nidwalden, Obwalden, St Gallen, Schaffhausen, Schwyz, Solothurn, Thurgau, Ticino, Uri, Valais, Vaud, Zug, Zürich. **Admin capitals** Aarau, Herisau, Appenzell, Liestal, Basel, Bern, Fribourg, Geneva, Glarus, Chur, Delémont, Lucerne, Neuchâtel, Stans, Sarnen, St Gallen, Schaffhausen, Schwyz, Solothurn, Frauenfeld, Bellinzona, Altdorf, Sion, Lausanne, Zug, Zürich. **ICR** CH. **IC** .ch **ND** 1 August.

SYRIA Asa (Al-JumhuriyyaAl-'Arabiyya as-Suriyya – Syrian Arab Republic) **Capital** Damascus. **Main cities** Halab, Hamah, Hims, Al-Ladhiqiyah. **ICR** SYR. **IC** .sy **ND** 17 April.

TAIWAN Asa (Chung-hua Min-kuo – Republic of China) **Capital** Taipei. **Main cities** Kaohsiung, Taichung, Tainan. **IC** .tw **ND** 10 October.

TAJIKISTAN Asa (Çumhurii Toçikiston – Republic of Tajikistan) **Capital** Dushanbe. **ICR** TJ. **IC** .tj **ND** 9 September – ID.

TANZANIA Afr (Jamhuri ya Muungano wa Tanzania – United Republic of Tanzania) **Capital** Dodoma. **Main cities** Dar es Salaam, Mbeya, Mwanza, Tanga. **ICR** EAT. **DoL. IC** .tz **ND** 26 April – Union Day.

THAILAND   Asa (Prathes Thai – Kingdom of Thailand) **Capital** Bangkok. **Main cities** Chiang Mai, Chon Buri, Nakhon Ratchasima, Nanthanburi, Songkhla. **ICR** T. **DoL. IC** .th **ND** 5 December – the King's Birthday.

TOGO   Afr (République Togolaise – Togolese Republic) **Capital** Lomé. **ICR** RT and TG. **IC** .tg **ND** 13 January – National Liberation Day, 27 April.

TONGA   Oce (Pule'anga Tonga /Kingdom of Tonga) **Capital** Nuku'alofa. **IC** .to **ND** 4 June – Emancipation Day.

TRINIDAD AND TOBAGO   Am (The Republic of Trinidad and Tobago) **Capital** Port of Spain. **Main cities** San Fernando, Scarborough. **ICR** TT. **DoL. IC** .tt **ND** 31 August – ID.

TUNISIA   Afr (Al-Jumhuriyyaat-Tunisiyya – Republic of Tunisia) **Capital** Tunis. **Main cities** Bizerte, Sfax, Sousse. **ICR** TN. **IC** .tn **ND** 20 March.

TURKEY   Asa (Türkiye Çumhuriyeti – Republic of Turkey) **Capital** Ankara. **Main cities** Adana, Bursa, Gaziantep, Istanbul, Izmir, Konya. **ICR** TR. **IC** .tr **ND** 29 October – Republic Day.

TURKMENISTAN   Asa (Turkmenstan Republikasy – Republic of Turkmenistan) **Capital** Ashkhabad. **Main cities** Charjou, Tashauz. **ICR** TM. **IC** .tm **ND** 27 – 28 October – ID.

TUVALU   Oce (Fakavae Aliki-MoloiTuvalu/Constitutional Monarchy of Tuvalu) **Capital** Funafuti. **DoL. IC** .tv **ND** 1 October – ID.

UGANDA   Afr (Republic of Uganda) **Capital** Kampala. **Main cities** Jinja, Masaka, Mbale. **ICR** EAU. **DoL;. IC** .ug **ND** 9 October – ID.

UKRAINE   Eur (Ukraïna) **Capital** Kiev. **Main cities** Dnipropetrovsk, Donetsk, Kharkiv, Lviv, Odesa, Zaporizhzhya. **Subdivisions** Autonomous Republic: Crimea. **Admin capital** Simferopol. **ICR** UA;. **IC** .ua **ND** 24 August – ID.

UNITED ARAB EMIRATES   Asa (Dawlat Al-AmaratAl-'Arabiyya Al-Muttahida) **Capital** Abu Dhabi. **Subdivisions** Emirates: Abu Dhabi, Ajman, Dubai, Fujairah, Ras al-Khaimah, Sharjah, Umm al-Qaiwan. **Admin capitals** Abu Dhabi, Ajman, Dubai, Fujairah, Ras al-Khaimah, Sharjah, Umm al-Qaiwan. **ICR** UAE. **IC** .ae **ND** 2 December.

UNITED KINGDOM OF GREAT BRITAIN AND NORTHERN IRELAND Eur **Capital** London. **Main cities** Birmingham, Edinburgh, Glasgow, Liverpool, Manchester. **Subdivisions** See separate table for details of individual counties of the UK. England, Northern Ireland, Scotland, Wales, Isle of Man, Channel Islands, Alderney, Guernsey, Jersey, Sark, Overseas terri-tories: Anguilla, Bermuda, British Antarctic Territory, British Indian Ocean Territory, British Virgin Islands, Cayman Islands, Falkland Islands, Gibraltar, Montserrat, Pitcairn Islands, St Helena and Dependencies, Ascension Island, Tristan da Cunha, South Georgia and the Sandwich Islands, Turks and Caicos Islands. **Admin capitals** The Valley, Hamilton Road, Town George Town, Stanley, Gibraltar, Plymouth, Jamestown, Georgetown, Edinburgh of the Seven Seas, Grand Turk. **ICR** GB, GBM, GBA, GBG, GBJ, GBZ. **DoL. IC** .gb and .uk, .im, .gg, .je, .bm, .io, .vg, .ky, .fk, .gi, .ms, .pn, .sh, .ac, .tc **ND** 23 April – St George's Day, 17 March – St Patrick's Day, 30 November – St Andrew's Day, 1 March – St David's Day.

UNITED STATES OF AMERICA   Am **Capital** Washington DC. **Main cities** Chicago, Dallas, Detroit, Houston, Los Angeles, New York, Philadelphia, Phoenix, San Antonio, San Diego. **Subdivisions** See separate table for details of the individual states. US Territories: The Commonwealth of Puerto Rico, American Samoa, Guam, Northern Mariana Islands, US Virgin Islands. **Admin capitals** San Juan, Pago Pago, Hagatna, Saipan, Charlotte Amalie. **IC** .us, &, .um **ND** USA, (.um = United States Minor Outlying Islands).

URUGUAY   Am (República Oriental del Uruguay – Eastern Republic of Uruguay) **Capital** Montevideo. **Main cities** Canelones, Melo, Mercedes, Minas, Paysandú, Punta del Este, Rivera, Salto. **ICR** ROU. **IC** .uy **ND** 25 August – Declaration of Independence.

UZBEKISTAN   Asa (Uzbekistan Zumhurijati – Republic of Uzbekistan) **Capital** Tashkent. **Main cities** Samarkand, Bukhara. **ICR** UZ. **IC** .uz **ND** 1 September – ID.

VANUATU   Oce (Ripablik blong Vanuatu/Republic of Vanuatu/ République de Vanuatu) **Capital** Port Vila. **Main cities** Luganville. **IC** .vu **ND** 30 July – ID.

VATICAN CITY STATE   Eur (Status Civitatis Vaticanae/Stato della Città del Vaticano – State of the Vatican City) **Capital** Vatican City. **ICR** V. **IC** .va **ND** 22 October – Inauguration of present Pontiff.

VENEZUELA   Am (República Bolivariana de Venezuela – Bolivarian Republic of Venezuela) **Capital** Caracas. **Main cities** Barquisimeto, Maracaibo, Maracay, Valencia. **Subdivisions** States: Amazonas, Anzoátegui, Apure, Aragua, Barinas, Bolívar, Carabobo, Cojedes, Delta Amacuro, Falcón, Guárico, Lara, Mérida, Miranda, Monagas, Nueva Esparta, Portuguesa, Sucre, Táchira, Trujillo, Yaracuy, Zulia. **Admin capitals** Puerto

Ayacucho, Barcelona, San Fernando de Apure, Maracay, Barinas, Cuidad Bolivar, Valencia, San Carlos, Tucupita, Coro, San Juan de Los Morros, Barquisimeto, Mérida, Los teques, Maturin, La Asunción, Guanare, Cumaná, San Cristóbal, Trujillo, San Felipe, Maracaibo. **ICR** YV. **IC** .ve **ND** 5 July.

VIETNAM   Asa (Công Hòo Xã Chu Ngh~ia Viêt Nam – Socialist Republic of Vietnam) **Capital** Hanoi. **Main cities** Hai Pong, Ho Chi Minh City. **ICR** VN. **IC** .vn **ND** 2 September.

WALLIS AND FUTUNA ISLANDS (FR)   Oce **Capital** Mata-Utu. **IC** .wf

WESTERN SAMOA   Oce **Capital** Apia. **ICR** WS. **ND** 1 June – ID.

YEMEN   Asa (Al-Jumhuriyya Al-Yamaniyya – Republic of Yemen) **Capital** Sana'a'. **Main cities** Aden, Al-Hudaydah, Ta'izz. **ICR** ADN. **IC** .ye **ND** 22 May.

ZAIRE   Afr **Capital** Kinshasa. **IC** .zr **ND** 24 November;.

ZAMBIA   Afr (Republic of Zambia) **Capital** Lusaka. **Main cities** Chingola, Kabwe, Kitwe, Luanshya, Mufulira, Ndola. **ICR** Z. **DoL. IC** .zm **ND** 24 October – ID.

ZIMBABWE   Afr (Republic of Zimbabwe) **Capital** Harare. **Main cities** Bulawayo, Chitungwiza. **Subdivisions** Provinces: Manicaland, Masvingo, Matabeleland North, Matabeleland South, Midlands, Mashonaland West, Mashonaland Central, Mashonaland East. **ICR** ZW. **DoL. IC** .zw **ND** 18 April – ID.

Cities and regions

Aagau   A canton of Switzerland, its admin capital is Aarau
Aarau   Admin capital of Aagau, a canton of Switzerland
Abakaliki   Admin capital of Ebonyi, a state of Nigeria
Abakan   Admin capital of Khakassia, a republic of Russia
Abeokuta   Admin capital of Ogun, a state of Nigeria
Abia   A state of Nigeria, its admin capital is Umuahia
Abidjan   One of the main cities of Côte d'Ivoire

Abruzzi   A region of Italy, its admin capital is L'Aquila
Abu Dhabi   An emirate of United Arab Emirates, its capital is of the same name
Abuja   Admin capital of Federal Capital Territory, a state of Nigeria
Abuja   Capital of Nigeria
Accra   Capital of Ghana
Aceh   A province of Indonesia, its admin capital is Banda Aceh
Acre   A state of Brazil, its admin capital is Rio Branco
Adamawa   A state of Nigeria, its admin capital is Yola
Adana   One of the main cities of Turkey
Ad-Dammam   One of the main cities of Saudi Arabia
Addis Ababa   Capital of Ethiopia
Adelaide   Admin capital of South Australia, a territory of Australia
Aden   One of the main cities of Yemen
Ado Ekiti   Admin capital of Ekiti, a state of Nigeria
Adygeia   A republic of Russia, its admin capital is Maykop
Aga-Buryat   An autonomous area of Russia
Agadir   One of the main cities of Morocco
Agaña   Capital of Guam (USA)
Agartala   Admin capital of Tripura, a state of India
Agen   Admin capital of Lot-et-Garonne, a region of Aquitaine, a department of France
Agneby   A region of Côte d'Ivoire
Aguasclientes   A state of Mexico, its admin capital is of the same name
Ahwaz   One of the main cities of Iran
Ain   A department of Rhône-Alpes, a region of France, its admin capital is Bourg-en-Bresse
Aisne   A department of Picardie, a region of France, its admin capital is Laon
Aizawl   Admin capital of Mizoram, a state of India
Ajaccio   Admin capital of Corse-du-Sud, a region of Corse, a department of France
Ajaria   An autonomous republic of Georgia, its admin capital is Batumi
Ajman   An emirate of United Arab Emirates, its admin capital is of the same name
Akhazia   An autonomous republic of Georgia, its admin capital is Sukhumi
Akranes   One of the main cities of Iceland
Akure   Admin capital of Ondo, a state of Nigeria
Akureyri   One of the main cities of Iceland
Akwa Ibom   A state of Nigeria, its admin capital is Uyo
Alagoas   A state of Brazil, its admin capital is Maceió
Alajuela   One of the main cities of Costa Rica

Åland (Ahvenanmaa)   An autonomous province of Finland, its admin capital is Mariehamn (Maarianhamina)

Alberta   A province of Canada, its admin capital is Edmonton

Albi   Admin capital of Tarn, a region of Midi-Pyrénées, a department of France

Ålborg   One of the main cities of Denmark

Alençon   Admin capital of Orne, a region of Basse-Normandi, a department of France

Alexandria   One of the main cities of Egypt

Algiers   Capital of Algeria

Al-Hofuf   One of the main cities of Saudi Arabia

Al-Hudaydah   One of the main cities of Yemen

Al-Ladhiqiyah   One of the main cities of Syria

Allier   A department of Auvergne, a region of France, its admin capital is Moulins

Al-Madiina   One of the main cities of Saudi Arabia

Al-Makkah (Mecca)   One of the main cities of Saudi Arabia

Almaty   One of the main cities of Kazakhstan

Alofi   Capital of New Zealand   Niue

Alor Setar   Admin capital of Kedah, a state of Malaysia

Alpes-de-Haute-Provence   A department of Provence-Alpes-Côte d'Azur, a region of France, its admin capital is Digne

Alpes-Maritimes   A department of Provence-Alpes-Côte d'Azur, a region of France, its admin capital is Nice

Alsace   A region of France, its admin capital is Strasbourg

Altai   An autonomous territory (krai) of Russia

Altdorf   Admin capital of Uri, a canton of Switzerland

Al-Ubayyid   One of the main cities of Sudan

Al-Wakrah   One of the main cities of Qatar

Amapá   A state of Brazil, its admin capital is Macapá

Amazonas   1. A state of Brazil, its admin capital is Manaus; 2. A state of Venezuela, its admin capital is Puerto Ayacucho

Amboina   Admin capital of Maluku, a province of Indonesia

Amiens   Admin capital of Somme, a region of Picardie, a department of France

Amman   Capital of Jordan

Amsterdam   Capital of The Netherlands

Amur   A region (oblast) of Russia

Anambra   A state of Nigeria, its admin capital is Awka

Ancona   Admin capital of Marche, a region of Italy

Andalucia   A Spanish autonomous community (region), its admin capital is Seville

Andaman and Nicobar Islands   A union territory of India, its admin capital is Port Blair

Andhra Pradesh   A state of India, its admin capital is Hyderabad
Andorra La Vella   Capital of Andorra
Angers   Admin capital of Maine-et-Loire, a region of Pays de la Loire, a department of France
Angoulême   Admin capital of Charente, a region of Poitou-Charente, a department of France
Anhui   A province of China, its admin capital is Hefei
Ankara   Capital of Turkey
Annaba   One of the main cities of Algeria
Annecy   Admin capital of Haute-Savoie, a region of Rhône-Alpes, a department of France
Anstiranana   One of the main cities of Madagascar
Antananarivo   Capital of Madagascar
Antipodes Group   One of the islands of New Zealand
Antofagasta   One of the main cities of Chile
Antwerp   A province of Belgium, its admin capital is of the same name
Anzoátegui   A state of Venezuela, its admin capital is Barcelona
Aosta   Admin capital of Valle d'Aosta, a region of Italy
Apia   Capital of Western Samoa
Appenzell   Admin capital of Appenzell-Innerhoden, a canton of Switzerland
Appenzell-Ausserrhoden   A canton of Switzerland, its admin capital is Herisau
Appenzell-Innerrhoden   A canton of Switzerland, its admin capital is Appenzell
Apure   A state of Venezuela, its admin capital is San Fernando de Apure
Aquitaine   A region of France, its admin capital is Bordeaux
Aracajú   Admin capital of Sergipe, a state of Brazil
Aragon   A Spanish autonomous community (region), its admin capital is Zaragoza
Aragua   A state of Venezuela, its admin capital is Maracay
Ardèche   A department of Rhône-Alpes, a region of France, its admin capital is Privas
Ardennes   A department of Champagne-Ardennes, a region of France, its admin capital is Charleville-Mézières
Arequipa   One of the main cities of Peru
Århus   One of the main cities of Denmark
Ariège   A department of Midi-Pyrénées, a region of France, its admin capital is Foix
Arkhangelsk   A region (oblast) of Russia
Arlon   Admin capital of Luxembourg, a province of Belgium
Arras   Admin capital of Pas-de-Calais, a region of Nord-Pas-de-Calais, a department of France

Ar-Rayyan One of the main cities of Qatar

Aruba An overseas territory of the Netherlands, its admin capital is Oranjestad

Arunachal Pradesh A state of India, its admin capital is Itanagar

Asaba Admin capital of Delta, a state of Nigeria

Ashkhabad Capital of Turkmenistan

Ashmore and Cartier Islands A territory of Australia

Asmara Capital of Eritrea

Assab One of the main cities of Eritrea

Assam A state of India, its admin capital is Dispur

Astana Capital of Kazakhstan

Astrakhan A region (oblast) of Russia

Asturias A Spanish autonomous community (region), its admin capital is Oviedo

Asunción Capital of Paraguay

Asyut One of the main cities of Egypt

Athens Capital of Greece

Aube A department of Champagne-Ardennes, a region of France, its admin capital is Troyes

Auch Admin capital of Gers, a region of Midi-Pyrénées, a department of France

Auckland Islands One of the islands of New Zealand

Aude A department of Languedoc-Roussillon, a region of France, its admin capital is Carcassonne

Aurillac Admin capital of Cantal, a region of Auvergne, a department of France

Australian Antarctic Territory A territory of Australia

Australian Capital Territory A territory of Australia, its admin capital is Canberra

Auvergne A region of France, its admin capital is Clermont-Ferrand

Auxerre Admin capital of Yonne, a region of Bourgogne, a department of France

Avarua Capital of New Zealand   Cook Islands

Aveyron A department of Midi-Pyrénées, a region of France, its admin capital is Rodez

Avignon Admin capital of Vaucluse, a region of Provence-Alpes-Côte d'Azur, a department of France

Awka Admin capital of Anambra, a state of Nigeria

Azores An autonomous region of Portugal, its admin capital is Ponta Delgada

Az-Zarqa One of the main cities of Jordan

Baden-Württemberg A Land of Germany, its admin capital is Stuttgart

Bafing A region of Côte d'Ivoire

Baghdad   Capital of Iraq
Bahia   A state of Brazil, its admin capital is Salvador
Baja California   A state of Mexico, its admin capital is Mexicali
Baja California Sur   A state of Mexico, its admin capital is La Paz
Baku   Capital of Azerbaijan
Balaerics   A Spanish autonomous community (region), its admin capital
    is Palma de Mallorca
Bali   A province of Indonesia, its admin capital is Denpasar
Baluchistan   A province of Pakistan, its admin capital is Quetta
Bamako   Capital of Mali
Banda Aceh   Admin capital of Aceh, a province of Indonesia
Bandar Seri Begawan   Capital of Brunei
Bandung   Admin capital of Jawa Barat, a province of Indonesia
Bangalore   Admin capital of Karnataka, a state of India
Bangazi   One of the main cities of Libya
Bangkok   Capital of Thailand
Bangui   Capital of Central African Republic
Banja Luka   One of the main cities of Bosnia-Hercegovina
Banjul   Capital of Gambia
Bankarmasin   Admin capital of Kalimantan Seletan, a province of Indo-
    nesia
Barcelona   1. Admin capital of Cataluña, a Spanish autonomous commu-
    nity (region); 2. Admin capital of Anzoátegui, a state of Venezuela
Bari   Admin capital of Puglia, a region of Italy
Barinas   A state of Venezuela, its admin capital is of the same name
Barka   One of the main cities of Oman
Bar-le-Duc   Admin capital of Meuse, a region of Lorraine, a department
    of France
Barquisimeto   Admin capital of Lara, a state of Venezuela
Barranquilla   One of the main cities of Colombia
Basel   Admin capital of Basel-Stadt, a canton of Switzerland
Basel-Landschaft   A canton of Switzerland, its admin capital is Liestal
Basel-Stadt   A canton of Switzerland, its admin capital is Basel
Bashkortostan   A republic of Russia, its admin capital is Ufa
Basilicata   A region of Italy, its admin capital is Potenza
Bas-Rhin   A department of Alsace, a region of France, its admin capital is
    Strasbourg
Bas-Sassandra   A region of Côte d'Ivoire
Basse-Normandi (Lower Normandy)   A region of France, its admin
    capital is Caen
Basse-Terre   Admin capital of Guadeloupe, an overseas department of
    France
Basseterre   Capital of St Christopher and Nevis

Bastia   Admin capital of Haute-Corse, a region of Corse, a department of France

Bata   One of the main cities of Equatorial Guinea

Batumi   Admin capital of Ajaria, an autonomous republic of Georgia

Bauchi   A state of Nigeria, its admin capital is of the same name

Bavaria   A Land of Germany, its admin capital is Munich (München)

Bayelsa   A state of Nigeria, its admin capital is Yenagoa

Beau Bassin   One of the main cities of Mauritius

Beauvais   Admin capital of Oise, a region of Picardie, a department of France

Beersheba   One of the main cities of Israel

Beijing (Peking)   A province of China, its admin capital – also the capital of China – is of the same name

Beira   One of the main cities of Mozambique

Beirut   Capital of Lebanon

Bejaia   One of the main cities of Algeria

Belém   Admin capital of Pará, a state of Brazil

Belfort   Admin capital of Territoire de Belfort, a region of Franche-Comté, a department of France

Belgorod   A region (oblast) of Russia

Belgrade   Capital of Serbia and Montenegro

Belize City   One of the main cities of Belize

Bellinzona   Admin capital of Ticino, a canton of Switzerland

Belmopan   Capital of Belize

Belo Horizonte   Admin capital of Minas Gerais, a state of Brazil

Bengkulu   A province of Indonesia, its admin capital is of the same name

Benin City   Admin capital of Edo, a state of Nigeria

Benue   A state of Nigeria, its admin capital is Makurdi

Berbera   One of the main cities of Somalia

Berlin   A Länd of Germany, its admin capital – and the capital of Germany – is Berlin

Bern   A canton of Switzerland, its admin capital – and the capital of Switzerland – is of the same name

Besançon   Admin capital of Doubs, a region of Franche-Comté, a department of France

Bethlehem   One of the main cities of Israel   West Bank and Gaza Strip

Bhaktapur   One of the main cities of Nepal

Bhopal   Admin capital of Madhya Pradesh, a state of India

Bhubaneswar   Admin capital of Orissa, a state of India

Bihar   A state of India, its admin capital is Patna

Biratnagar   One of the main cities of Nepal

Birnin-Kebbi   Admin capital of Kebbi, a state of Nigeria

Birobijan   An autonomous Jewish region, its admin capital is of the same name

Bisho   Admin capital of Eastern Cape, a province of South Africa

Biskek   Capital of Kyrgyzstan

Bissau   Capital of Guinea-Bissau

Bitola   One of the main cities of Macedonia

Bizerte   One of the main cities of Tunisia

Blantyre   One of the main cities of Malawi

Blida   One of the main cities of Algeria

Bloemfontein   Admin capital of Free State, a province of South Africa

Blois   Admin capital of Loiret-et-Cher, a region of Centre-Val de Loire, a department of France

Boa Vista   Admin capital of Roraima, a state of Brazil

Bobigny   Admin capital of Seine-Saint-Denis, a region of Île-de-France, a department of France

Bobo-Dioulasso   One of the main cities of Burkina Faso

Bogotá   Capital of Colombia

Bohol   One of the Philippine islands

Bolívar   A state of Venezuela, its admin capital is Cuidad Bolivar

Bologna   Admin capital of Emilia-Romagna, a region of Italy

Bolzano-Bozen and Trento   Admin capital of Trentino-Alto Adige, a region of Italy

Bombay   See **Mumbai**

Bordeaux   Admin capital of Gironde, a region of Aquitaine, a department of France

Borno   A state of Nigeria, its admin capital is Maiduguri

Boroma   One of the main cities of Somalia

Bouches-de-Rhône   A department of Provence-Alpes-Côte d'Azur, a region of France, its admin capital is Marseilles

Bounty Islands   One of the islands of New Zealand

Bourg-en-Bresse   Admin capital of Ain, a region of Rhône-Alpes, a department of France

Bourges   Admin capital of Cher, a region of Centre-Val de Loire, a department of France

Bourgogne (Burgundy)   A region of France, its admin capital is Dijon

Bouvet Island   An Antarctic territory of Norway

Brandenburg   A Land of Germany, its admin capital is Potsdam

Brasilia   Admin capital of Distrito Federal, a state of Brazil, and the capital of Brazil

Brasov   One of the main cities of Romania

Bratislava   Capital of Slovak Republic

Brazzaville   Capital of Congo-Brazzaville

Bregenz   Admin capital of Vorarlberg, a province of Austria

Bremen   A Land of Germany, its admin capital is Bremen

Brest   One of the main cities of Belarus

Bretagne (Brittany)   A region of France, its admin capital is Rennes

Bridgetown   Capital of Barbados

Brisbane   Admin capital of Queensland, a territory of Australia

British Columbia   A province of Canada, its admin capital is Victoria

Brno   One of the main cities of Czech Republic

Bruges   Admin capital of West Flanders, a province of Belgium

Brussels   A region of Belgium, its admin capital   and the capital of
   Belgium   is of the same name

Bryansk   A region (oblast) of Russia

Buchanan   One of the main cities of Liberia

Bucharest   Capital of Romania

Budapest   Capital of Hungary

Buenaventura   One of the main cities of Colombia

Buenos Aires   The Federal Capital of Argentina; also a province of
   Argentina; its admin capital is La Plata

Bujumbura (was Usumbura)   Capital of Burundi

Bukhara   One of the main cities of Uzbekistan

Buraydah   One of the main cities of Saudi Arabia

Burgas   One of the main cities of Bulgaria

Burgenland   A province of Austria, its admin capital is Eisenstadt

Buroa   1. One of the main cities of Somalia; 2. One of the main cities of
   Turkey

Buryatia   A republic of Russia, its admin capital is Ulan-Ude

Bydgoszcz   One of the main cities of Poland

Caen   Admin capital of Calvados, a region of Basse-Normandi, a department of France

Cagkiari   Admin capital of Sardinia, a region of Italy

Cahors   Admin capital of Lot, a region of Midi-Pyrénées, a department
   of France

Cairo   Capital of Egypt

Calabar   Admin capital of Cross River, a state of Nigeria

Calabria   A region of Italy, its admin capital is Catanzaro

Calcutta   Admin capital of West Bengal, a state of India

Calgary   One of the main cities of Canada

Cali   One of the main cities of Colombia

Calvados   A department of Basse-Normandi, a region of France, its
   admin capital is Caen

Camagüey   One of the main cities of Cuba

Campania   A region of Italy, its admin capital is Naples

Campbell Island   One of the islands of New Zealand

Campeche   A state of Mexico, its admin capital is of the same name

Campo Grande   Admin capital of Mato Grosso do Sul, a state of Brazil

Campobasso   Admin capital of Molise, a region of Italy

Canaries   A Spanish autonomous community (region), its admin capital
   is Santa Crus de Tenerife and Las Palmas

Canberra   Capital of Australia, also admin capital of Australian Capital Territory, a territory of Australia

Canelones   One of the main cities of Uruguay

Cantabria   A Spanish autonomous community (region), its admin capital is Santander

Cantal   A department of Auvergne, a region of France, its admin capital is Aurillac

Cap Haïtien   One of the main cities of Haïti

Cape Town   Admin capital of Western Cape, a province of South Africa

Carabobo   A state of Venezuela, its admin capital is Valencia

Caracas   Capital of Venezuela

Carcassonne   Admin capital of Aude, a region of Languedoc-Roussillon, a department of France

Carinthia   A province of Austria, its admin capital is Klagenfurt

Carlow   A county of the Republic of Ireland, its admin capital is of the same name

Carrefour   One of the main cities of Haïti

Carrick-on-Shannon   Admin capital of Leitrim, a county of the Republic of Ireland

Cartagena   One of the main cities of Colombia

Cartago   One of the main cities of Costa Rica

Casablanca   One of the main cities of Morocco

Castilla-La Mancha   A Spanish autonomous community (region), its admin capital is Toledo

Castill-Leon   A Spanish autonomous community (region), its admin capital is Valladolid

Castlebar   Admin capital of Mayo, a county of the Republic of Ireland

Castries   Capital of St Lucia

Cataluña   A Spanish autonomous community (region), its admin capital is Barcelona

Catamarca   A province of Argentina; its admin capital is San Fernando del Valle de Catamarca

Catanzaro   Admin capital of Calabria, a region of Italy

Cavan   A county of the Republic of Ireland, its admin capital is of the same name

Cayenne   Admin capital of French Guiana, an overseas department of France

Ceará   A state of Brazil, its admin capital is Fortaleza

Cebu   One of the Philippine islands

Centre-Val de Loire   A region of France, its admin capital is Orléans

Chaco   A province of Argentina; its admin capital is Resistencia

Chalôns-sur-Marne   Admin capital of Marne, a region of Champagne-Ardennes, a department of France

Chambéry   Admin capital of Savoie, a region of Rhône-Alpes, a department of France

Champagne-Ardennes   A region of France, its admin capital is Reims

Chandigarh   A union territory of India, its admin capital is Silvassa

Chandigarh   Admin capital of Hayana, and of Punjab, states of India

Changchun   Admin capital of Jilin, an administrative region of China

Changsha   Admin capital of Hunan, an administrative region of China

Charente   A department of Poitou-Charentes, a region of France, its admin capital is Angoulème

Charente-Maritime   A department of Poitou-Charentes, a region of France, its admin capital is La Rochelle

Charjou   One of the main cities of Turkmenistan

Charleroi   One of the main cities of Belgium

Charlestown   One of the main cities of St Christopher and Nevis

Charlettetown   Admin capital of Prince Edward Island, a province of Canada

Charleville-Mézières   Admin capital of Ardennes, a region of Champagne-Ardennes, a department of France

Chartres   Admin capital of Eure-de-Loir, a region of Centre-Val de Loire, a department of France

Châteauroux   Admin capital of Indre, a region of Centre-Val de Loire, a department of France

Chatham Islands   One of the islands of New Zealand

Chaumont   Admin capital of Haute-Marne, a region of Champagne-Ardennes, a department of France

Cheboksary   Admin capital of Chuvashia, a republic of Russia

Chechnya   A republic of Russia, its admin capital is Dzhokhar-Ghala

Chelyabinsk   A region (oblast) of Russia

Chengdu   Admin capital of Sichuan, an municipal province of China

Chengdu   One of the main cities of China

Cher   A department of Centre-Val de Loire, a region of France, its admin capital is Bourges

Cherkessk   Admin capital of Karachay-Cherkessia, a republic of Russia

Chetumal   Admin capital of Quintana Roo, a state of Mexico

Chiang Mai   One of the main cities of Thailand

Chiapas   A state of Mexico, its admin capital is Tuxtla Gutiérrez

Chiclayo   One of the main cities of Peru

Chihuahua   A state of Mexico, its admin capital is of the same name

Chilpancingo   Admin capital of Guerrero, a state of Mexico

Chimbote   One of the main cities of Peru

Chin   A state of Myanmar (Burma), its admin capital is Hakha

Chinandega   One of the main cities of Nicaragua

Chingola   One of the main cities of Zambia

Chisinau   Capital of Moldova

Chita A region (oblast) of Russia
Choluteca One of the main cities of Honduras
Chon Buri One of the main cities of Thailand
Chongqing One of the main cities of China
Christmas Island A territory of Australia
Chubut A province of Argentina; its admin capital is Rawson
Chuckchi An autonomous area of Russia
Chur Admin capital of Graubünden, a canton of Switzerland
Chuvashia A republic of Russia, its admin capital is Cheboksary
Clare A county of the Republic of Ireland, its admin capital is Ennis
Clermont-Ferrand Admin capital of Puy-de-Dôme, a region of Auvergne, a department of France
Clonmel Admin capital of Tipperary, a county of the Republic of Ireland
Cluj-Napoca One of the main cities of Romania
Coahuila A state of Mexico, its admin capital is Saltillo
Cobán One of the main cities of Guatemala
Cochabamba One of the main cities of Bolivia
Cocos (Keeling) Islands A territory of Australia
Codrington One of the main cities of Antigua and Barbuda
Cojedes A state of Venezuela, its admin capital is San Carlos
Colima A state of Mexico, its admin capital is of the same name
Colmar Admin capital of Haut-Rhin, a region of Alsace, a department of France
Colombo Capital of Sri Lanka
Conakry Capital of Guinea
Concepción One of the main cities of Chile
Connacht A province of the Republic of Ireland
Cononou One of the main cities of Benin
Constanta One of the main cities of Romania
Constantine One of the main cities of Algeria
Copenhagen Capital of Denmark
Coral Sea Islands Territory A territory of Australia
Córdoba One of the main cities of Argentina; admin centre of the Province of the same name
Cork A county of the Republic of Ireland, its admin capital is of the same name
Coro Admin capital of Falcón, a state of Venezuela
Corozal One of the main cities of Belize
Corrèze A department of Limousin, a region of France, its admin capital is Tulle
Corrientes An Argetinian province whose admin capital bears the same name
Corriverton One of the main cities of Guyana
Corse (Corsica) A region of France, its admin capital is Ajaccio

Corse-du-Sud A department of Corse, a region of France, its admin capital is Ajaccio

Cotabato City Admin capital of Muslim Mindanao, a Filipino autonomous region

Côtes-d'Armor A department of Bretagne, a region of France, its admin capital is Saint-Brieuc

Côtes-d'Or A department of Bourgogne, a region of France, its admin capital is Dijon

Craiova One of the main cities of Romania

Créteil Admin capital of Val-de-Marne, a region of Île-de-France, a department of France

Creuse A department of Limousin, a region of France, its admin capital is Guéret

Crimea An autonomous republic of Ukraine, its admin capital is Simferopol

Cross River A state of Nigeria, its admin capital is Calabar

Cuenca One of the main cities of Ecuador

Cuernavaca Admin capital of Morelos, a state of Mexico

Cueta A Spanish autonomous community (region), its admin capital is of the same name

Cuiabá Admin capital of Mato Grosso, a state of Brazil

Cuidad Bolivar Admin capital of Bolívar, a state of Venezuela

Cuidad del Este One of the main cities of Paraguay

Cuidad Victoria Admin capital of Tamaulipas, a state of Mexico

Culiacán Rosales Admin capital of Sinaloa, a state of Mexico

Cumaná Admin capital of Sucre, a state of Venezuela

Curepipe One of the main cities of Mauritius

Curitiba Admin capital of Paraná, a state of Brazil

Daghestan A republic of Russia, its admin capital is Makhachkala

Dakar Capital of Senegal

Dalian One of the main cities of China

Daman and Diu A union territory of India

Damascus Capital of Syria

Damaturu Admin capital of Yobe, a state of Nigeria

Dangriga One of the main cities of Belize

Dar es Salaam One of the main cities of Tanzania

Dara and Nagar Haveli A union territory of India

Darwin Admin capital of Northern Territory, a territory of Australia

Daugavpils One of the main cities of Latvia

Delémont Admin capital of Jura, a canton of Switzerland

Delhi Capital of India, also a union territory of India, its admin capital is Kavaratti

Delmas One of the main cities of Haïti

Delta A state of Nigeria, its admin capital is Asaba

Delta Amacuro   A state of Venezuela, its admin capital is Tucupita
Denguele   A region of Côte d'Ivoire
Denpasar   Admin capital of Bali, a province of Indonesia
Derecen   One of the main cities of Hungary
Deux-Sèvres   A department of Poitou-Charentes, a region of France, its admin capital is Niort
Dhaka   Capital of Bangladesh
Digne   Admin capital of Alpes-de-Haute-Provence, a region of Provence-Alpes-Côte d'Azur, a department of France
Dijon   Admin capital of Côtes-d'Or, a region of Bourgogne, a department of France
Dili   Capital of East Timor
Dire Dawa   One of the main cities of Ethiopia
Dispur   Admin capital of Assam, a state of India
Distrito Federal   A state of Brazil, its admin capital is Brasilia
Dix-Huit Montagnes   A region of Côte d'Ivoire
Djibouti   Capital of Djibouti
Dodoma   Capital of Tanzania
Doha   Capital of Qatar
Donegal   A county of the Republic of Ireland, its admin capital is Lifford
Dordogne   A department of Aquitaine, a region of France, its admin capital is Périgeux
Douala   One of the main cities of Cameroon
Doubs   A department of Franche-Comté, a region of France, its admin capital is Besançon
Dresden   Admin capital of Saxony (Sachsen), a Land of Germany
Drôme   A department of Rhône-Alpes, a region of France, its admin capital is Valence
Duarte   One of the main cities of Dominican Republic
Dubai   An emirate of United Arab Emirates, its admin capital is of the same name
Dublin   A county of the Republic of Ireland, its admin capital is of the same name
Dublin   Capital of Ireland, Republic of
Dukhan   One of the main cities of Qatar
Dundalk   Admin capital of Louth, a county of the Republic of Ireland
Durango   A state of Mexico, its admin capital is Victoria de Durango
Dushanbe   Capital of Tajikistan
Düsseldorf   Admin capital of North Rhine-Westphalia, a Land of Germany
Dutse   Admin capital of Jigawa, a state of Nigeria
Dzhokhar-Ghala   Admin capital of Chechnya, a republic of Russia
East Flanders   A province of Belgium, its admin capital is Ghent

Eastern Cape   A province of South Africa, its admin capital is Bisho
Ebeye   One of the main cities of Marshall Islands
Ebonyi   A state of Nigeria, its admin capital is Abakaliki
Edmonton   Admin capital of Alberta, a province of Canada
Edo   A state of Nigeria, its admin capital is Benin City
Egilsstadir   One of the main cities of Iceland
Eisenstadt   Admin capital of Burgenland, a province of Austria
Ekiti   A state of Nigeria, its admin capital is Ado Ekiti
El Alto   One of the main cities of Bolivia
Elista   Admin capital of Kalmykia (Lhalmg-Tangch), a republic of Russia
Emilia-Romagna   A region of Italy, its admin capital is Bologna
Ennis   Admin capital of Clare, a county of the Republic of Ireland
Entre Rios   A province of Argentina; its admin capital is Paraná
Enugu   A state of Nigeria, its admin capital is of the same name
Épinal   Admin capital of Vosges, a region of Lorraine, a department of France
Erevan   Capital of Armenia
Erfurt   Admin capital of Thuringia (Thüringen), a Land of Germany
Escuintla   One of the main cities of Guatemala
Esfahan   One of the main cities of Iran
Espirito Santo   A state of Brazil, its admin capital is Vitória
Essonne   A department of Île-de-France, a region of France, its admin capital is Évry
Eure   A department of Haute-Normandie, a region of France, its admin capital is Évreux
Eure-de-Loir   A department of Centre-Val de Loire, a region of France, its admin capital is Chartres
Evenki   An autonomous area of Russia
Évreux   Admin capital of Eure, a region of Haute-Normandie, a department of France
Évry   Admin capital of Essonne, a region of Île-de-France, a department of France
Extremadura   A Spanish autonomous community (region), its admin capital is Mérida
Faiyum   One of the main cities of Egypt
Falcón   A state of Venezuela, its admin capital is Coro
Famagusta   One of the main cities of Cyprus
Federal Capital   A province of Argentina; its admin capital is Buenos Aires
Federal Capital Territory   A state of Nigeria, its admin capital is Abuja
Federal Capital Territory Islamabad   A province of Pakistan
Federal District   A state of Mexico, its admin capital is Mexico City

Federally Administered Tribal Areas   A province of Pakistan

Federation of Bosnia-Herzegovnia   A state of Bosnia-Hercegovina, its admin capital is Sarajevo

Fez   One of the main cities of Morocco

Fianarantsoa   One of the main cities of Madagascar

Finistère   A department of Bretagne, a region of France, its admin capital is Quimper

Flanders   A region of Belgium

Flemish Brabant   A province of Belgium, its admin capital is Leuven

Florence   Admin capital of Tuscany, a region of Italy

Florianópolis   Admin capital of Santa Catarina, a state of Brazil

Foix   Admin capital of Ariège, a region of Midi-Pyrénées, a department of France

Formosa   An Argetinian province whose admin capital bears the same name

Fortaleza   Admin capital of Ceará, a state of Brazil

Fortaleza   One of the main cities of Brazil

Fort-de-France   Admin capital of Martinique, an overseas department of France

Franche-Comté   A region of France, its admin capital is Besançon

Francistown   One of the main cities of Botswana

Frauenfeld   Admin capital of Thurgau, a canton of Switzerland

Fredericton   Admin capital of New Brunswick, a province of Canada

Free State   A province of South Africa, its admin capital is Bloemfontein

Freetown   Capital of Sierra Leone

French Guiana   An overseas department of France, its admin capital is Cayenne

French Polynesia   An overseas territory of France, its admin capital is Papeete

Fribourg   A canton of Switzerland, its admin capital is of the same name

Friuli-Venzia Guilia   A region of Italy, its admin capital is Trieste

Fromager, Haut-Sassandra   A region of Côte d'Ivoire

Fujairah   An emirate of United Arab Emirates, its admin capital is of the same name

Fujairah   An emirate of United Arab Emirates, its admin capital is of the same name

Fujian   A province of China, its admin capital is Fuzhou

Fukuoka   One of the main cities of Japan

Funafuti   Capital of Tuvalu

Funchal   Admin capital of Madeira, a region of Portugal

Fuzhou   Admin capital of Fujian, a province of China

Gaborone   Capital of Botswana

Gagauzia   An autonomous republic of Moldova, its admin capital is Komrat

Galanti   One of the main cities of Romania

Galicia   A Spanish autonomous community (region), its admin capital is Santiago de Compostela

Galle   One of the main cities of Sri Lanka

Galway   A county of the Republic of Ireland, its admin capital is of the same name

Gäncä   One of the main cities of Azerbaijan

Gandhinagar   Admin capital of Gujarat, a state of India

Gangtok   Admin capital of Sikkin, a state of India

Gansu   A province of China, its admin capital is Lanzhou

Gao   One of the main cities of Mali

Gap   Admin capital of Haute-Alpes, a region of Provence-Alpes-Côte d'Azur, a department of France

Gard   A department of Languedoc-Roussillon, a region of France, its admin capital is Nîmes

Gauteng   A province of South Africa, its admin capital is Johannesburg

Gaza City   Capital of Israel   West Bank and Gaza Strip

Gaziantep   One of the main cities of Turkey

Gdansk (Danzig)   One of the main cities of Poland

Geneva   A canton of Switzerland, its admin capital is of the same name

Genoa   Admin capital of Liguria, a region of Italy

Georgetown   1. Capital of Guyana; 2. Admin capital of Penang, a state of Malaysia

Gers   A department of Midi-Pyrénées, a region of France, its admin capital is Auch

Ghent   Admin capital of East Flanders, a province of Belgium

Gironde   A department of Aquitaine, a region of France, its admin capital is Bordeaux

Glarus   A canton of Switzerland, its admin capital is of the same name

Goa   A state of India, its admin capital is Panaji

Godthåb (Nuuk)   Capital of Denmark   Greenland

Goiânia   Admin capital of Goiás, a state of Brazil

Goiás   A state of Brazil, its admin capital is Goiânia

Gombe   A state of Nigeria, its admin capital is of the same name

Gorno-Altaisk   Admin capital of Gorno-Altay, a republic of Russia

Gorno-Altay   A republic of Russia, its admin capital is Gorno-Altaisk

Goroka   One of the main cities of Papua New Guinea

Gothenburg   One of the main cities of Sweden

Granada   One of the main cities of Nicaragua

Graubünden   A canton of Switzerland, its admin capital is Chur

Graz   Admin capital of Styria, a province of Austria

Graz   One of the main cities of Austria

Greenville   One of the main cities of Liberia
Grenoble   Admin capital of Isère, a region of Rhône-Alpes, a department of France
Guadalajara   Admin capital of Jalisco, a state of Mexico
Guadeloupe   An overseas department of France, its admin capital is Basse-Terre
Guanajuato   A state of Mexico, its admin capital is of the same name
Guanare   Admin capital of Portuguesa, a state of Venezuela
Guangdong (Canton)   A province of China, its admin capital is Guangzhou
Guangxi Zhuang   A province of China, its admin capital is Nanning
Guangzhou   Admin capital of Guangdong (Canton), a province of China
Guantánamo   One of the main cities of Cuba
Guárico   A state of Venezuela, its admin capital is San Juan de Los Morros
Guatemala City   Capital of Guatemala
Guayaquil   One of the main cities of Ecuador
Guéret   Admin capital of Creuse, a region of Limousin, a department of France
Guerrero   A state of Mexico, its admin capital is Chilpancingo
Guiyang   Admin capital of Guizhou, an autonomous region of China
Guizhou   An autonomous region of China, its admin capital is Guiyang
Gujarat   A state of India, its admin capital is Gandhinagar
Gusau   Admin capital of Zamfara, a state of Nigeria
Hai Pong   One of the main cities of Vietnam
Haifa   One of the main cities of Israel
Haikou   Admin capital of Hainan, an autonomous region of China
Hainan   An autonomous region of China, its admin capital is Haikou
Hainault   A province of Belgium, its admin capital is Mons
Hakha   Admin capital of Chin, a state of Myanmar (Burma)
Halab   One of the main cities of Syria
Halifax   Admin capital of Nova Scotia, a province of Canada
Hamah   One of the main cities of Syria
Hamburg   A Land of Germany, its admin capital is Hamburg
Hamilton   One of the main cities of Canada
Hangzhou   Admin capital of Zhejiang, an autonomous region of China
Hannover   Admin capital of Lower Saxony, a Land of Germany
Hanoi   Capital of Vietnam
Harare   Capital of Zimbabwe
Harbin   Admin capital of Heilongjiang, an autonomous region of China
Hargeysa   One of the main cities of Somalia
Harnarfjordur   One of the main cities of Iceland
Harper   One of the main cities of Liberia

Hasselt   Admin capital of Limburg, a province of Belgium

Haute-Corse   A department of Corse, a region of France, its admin capital is Bastia

Haute-Garonne   A department of Midi-Pyrénées, a region of France, its admin capital is Toulouse

Haute-Loire   A department of Auvergne, a region of France, its admin capital is Le Puy

Haute-Marne   A department of Champagne-Ardennes, a region of France, its admin capital is Chaumont

Haute-Normandie (Upper Normandy)   A region of France, its admin capital is Rouen

Haute-Pyrénées   A department of Midi-Pyrénées, a region of France, its admin capital is Tarbes

Hautes-Alpes   A department of Provence-Alpes-Côte d'Azur, a region of France, its admin capital is Gap

Haute-Saône   A department of Franche-Comté, a region of France, its admin capital is Vesoul

Haute-Savoie   A department of Rhône-Alpes, a region of France, its admin capital is Annecy

Haute-Vienne   A department of Limousin, a region of France, its admin capital is Limoges

Haut-Rhin   A department of Alsace, a region of France, its admin capital is Colmar

Hauts-de-Seine   A department of Île-de-France, a region of France, its admin capital is Nanterre

Havana   Capital of Cuba

Hayana   A state of India, its admin capital is Chandigarh

Heard Island and McDonald Islands   A territory of Australia

Heart   One of the main cities of Afghanistan

Hebei   An autonomous region of China, its admin capital is Shijazhuang

Hebron   One of the main cities of Israel   West Bank and Gaza Strip

Hefei   Admin capital of Anhui, a province of China

Heilongjiang   An autonomous region of China, its admin capital is Harbin

Helsinki (Helsingfors)   Capital of Finland

Henan   An autonomous region of China, its admin capital is Zhengzhou

Hérault   A department of Languedoc-Roussillon, a region of France, its admin capital is Montpellier

Herisau   Admin capital of Appenzell-Ausserrhoden, a canton of Switzerland

Hermosillo   Admin capital of Sonora, a state of Mexico

Hesse   A Land of Germany, its admin capital is Wiesbaden

Hidalgo   A state of Mexico, its admin capital is Pachuca de Soto

Himachal Pradesh   A state of India, its admin capital is Shimla

Hims   One of the main cities of Syria
Hlatikulu   One of the main cities of Swaziland
Ho Chi Minh City   One of the main cities of Vietnam
Hobart   Admin capital of Tasmania, a territory of Australia
Hohhot   Admin capital of Nei Mongol, an administrative region of China
Holetown   One of the main cities of Barbados
Holguín   One of the main cities of Cuba
Homyel'   One of the main cities of Belarus
Hong Kong Special   An autonomous region of China, its admin capital is of the same name
Honiara   Capital of Solomon Islands
Hrodna   One of the main cities of Belarus
Hubei   An administrative region of China, its admin capital is Wuhan
Hunan   An administrative region of China, its admin capital is Changsha
Hyderabad   Admin capital of Andhra Pradesh, a state of India
Iasi   One of the main cities of Romania
Ibadan   Admin capital of Oyo, a state of Nigeria
Ikeja   Admin capital of Lagos, a state of Nigeria
Île-de-France   A region of France, its admin capital is Paris
Ille-et-Vilaine   A department of Bretagne, a region of France, its admin capital is Rennes
Ilorin   Admin capital of Kwara, a state of Nigeria
Imo   A state of Nigeria, its admin capital is Owerri
Imphal   Admin capital of Manipur, a state of India
Inchon   One of the main cities of Korea, Rep of (South)
Indre   A department of Centre-Val de Loire, a region of France, its admin capital is Châteauroux
Indre-et-Loire   A department of Centre-Val de Loire, a region of France, its admin capital is Tours
Ingushetia   A republic of Russia, its admin capital is Nazran
Innsbruck   Admin capital of Tirol, a province of Austria
Ipoh   Admin capital of Perak, a state of Malaysia
Iqaluit   Admin capital of Nunavut, a province of Canada
Irbid   One of the main cities of Jordan
Irbil   An autonomous region of Iraq
Irian Jaya   A province of Indonesia, its admin capital is Jayapura
Irkutsk   A region (oblast) of Russia
Isafjordur   One of the main cities of Iceland
Isère   A department of Rhône-Alpes, a region of France, its admin capital is Grenoble
Islamabad   Capital of Pakistan
Ismailia   One of the main cities of Egypt
Istanbul   One of the main cities of Turkey
Itanagar   Admin capital of Arunachal Pradesh, a state of India

Ivanovo   A region (oblast) of Russia
Izhevsk   Admin capital of Udmurtia, a republic of Russia
Izmir   One of the main cities of Turkey
Jaffna   One of the main cities of Sri Lanka
Jaipur   Admin capital of Rajasthan, a state of India
Jakarta   Admin capital of Jakarta Raya, a province of Indonesia
Jakarta   Capital of Indonesia
Jakarta Raya   A province of Indonesia, its admin capital is Jakarta
Jalalabad   One of the main cities of Afghanistan
Jalapa Enríquez   Admin capital of Veracruz, a state of Mexico
Jalingo   Admin capital of Taraba, a state of Nigeria
Jalisco   A state of Mexico, its admin capital is Guadalajara
Jambi   A province of Indonesia, its admin capital is of the same name
Jammu and Kashmir   A state of India, its admin capital is Srinagar/ Jammu
Jawa Barat   A province of Indonesia, its admin capital is Bandung
Jawa Tengah   A province of Indonesia, its admin capital is Semerang
Jawa Timur   A province of Indonesia, its admin capital is Surabaya
Jayapura   Admin capital of Irian Jaya, a province of Indonesia
Jelgava   One of the main cities of Latvia
Jericho   One of the main cities of Israel   West Bank and Gaza Strip
Jiangsu   An administrative region of China, its admin capital is Nanjing
Jiangxi   An administrative region of China, its admin capital is Nanchang
Jiddah   One of the main cities of Saudi Arabia
Jigawa   A state of Nigeria, its admin capital is Dutse
Jilin   An administrative region of China, its admin capital is Changchun
Jinan   Admin capital of Shandong, an autonomous region of China
Jinja   One of the main cities of Uganda
João Pessoa   Admin capital of Paraiba, a state of Brazil
Johannesburg   Admin capital of Gauteng, a province of South Africa
Johore   A state of Malaysia, its admin capital is Johore Bahru
Johore Bahru   Admin capital of Johore, a state of Malaysia
Jos   Admin capital of Plateau, a state of Nigeria
Jujuy   A province of Argentina; its admin capital is San Salavador de Jujuy
Jura   1. A canton of Switzerland, its admin capital is Delémont; 2. A department of Franche-Comté, a region of France, its admin capital is Lons-le-Saunier
Jurmala   One of the main cities of Latvia
Kabardino-Balkaria   A republic of Russia, its admin capital is Nalchik
Kabul   Capital of Afghanistan
Kabwe   One of the main cities of Zambia
Kachin   A state of Myanmar (Burma), its admin capital is Myitkyina

Kaduna   A state of Nigeria, its admin capital is of the same name

Kalimantan Barat   A province of Indonesia, its admin capital is Pontianak

Kalimantan Seletan   A province of Indonesia, its admin capital is Bankarmasin

Kalimantan Tengah   A province of Indonesia, its admin capital is Palangkaraya

Kalimantan Timur   A province of Indonesia, its admin capital is Samarinda

Kaliningrad   A region (oblast) of Russia

Kalmykia (Lhalmg-Tangch)   A republic of Russia, its admin capital is Elista

Kaluga   A region (oblast) of Russia

Kamchatka   A region (oblast) of Russia

Kampala   Capital of Uganda

Kananga   1. One of the main cities of Congo; 2. One of the main cities of Congo-Brazzaville

Kandy   One of the main cities of Sri Lanka

Kangar   Admin capital of Perlis, a state of Malaysia

Kankan   One of the main cities of Guinea

Kano   A state of Nigeria, its admin capital is of the same name

Kaohsiung   One of the main cities of Taiwan

Karachay-Cherkessia   A republic of Russia, its admin capital is Cherkessk

Karachi   Admin capital of Sind, a province of Pakistan

Karaganda   One of the main cities of Kazakhstan

Karelia   A republic of Russia, its admin capital is Petrozavodsk

Karen   A state of Myanmar (Burma), its admin capital is Pa-an

Karnataka   A state of India, its admin capital is Bangalore

Karyai   Admin capital of Mount Athos (Ayion Oros), an autonomous monk's republic of Greece

Kathmandu   Capital of Nepal

Katowice   One of the main cities of Poland

Katsina   A state of Nigeria, its admin capital is of the same name

Kavaratti   Admin capital of Delhi, a union territory of India

Kayah   A state of Myanmar (Burma), its admin capital is Loi-kaw

Kayes   One of the main cities of Mali

Kazan   Admin capital of Tatarstan, a republic of Russia

Kebbi   A state of Nigeria, its admin capital is Birnin-Kebbi

Kedah   A state of Malaysia, its admin capital is Alor Setar

Kelantan   A state of Malaysia, its admin capital is Kota Bahru

Kemerovo   A region (oblast) of Russia

Kendari   Admin capital of Sulawesi Tenggara, a province of Indonesia

Kerala   A state of India, its admin capital is Trivandrum

Kerry   A county of the Republic of Ireland, its admin capital is Tralee

Khabarovsk   An autonomous territory (krai) of Russia

Khakassia   A republic of Russia, its admin capital is Abakan

Khan Yunis   One of the main cities of Israel   West Bank and Gaza Strip

Khanty-Mansi   An autonomous area of Russia

Khartoum   Capital of Sudan

Kiel   Admin capital of Schleswig-Holstein, a Land of Germany

Kiev   Capital of Ukraine

Kigali   Capital of Rwanda

Kildare   A county of the Republic of Ireland, its admin capital is Naas

Kilkenny   A county of the Republic of Ireland, its admin capital is of the same name

Kimberley   Admin capital of Northern Cape, a province of South Africa

Kindia   One of the main cities of Guinea

Kingston   Capital of Jamaica

Kingstown   Capital of St Vincent and the Grenadines

Kinshasa   Capital of Congo

Kinshasa   Capital of Zaire

Kirov   A region (oblast) of Russia

Kisangani   1. One of the main cities of Congo; 2. One of the main cities of Congo-Brazzaville

Kisimaayo   One of the main cities of Somalia

Kisumu   One of the main cities of Kenya

Kitega   One of the main cities of Burundi

Kitwe   One of the main cities of Zambia

Klagenfurt   Admin capital of Carinthia, a province of Austria

Klaipeda   One of the main cities of Lithuania

Kobe   One of the main cities of Japan

Kofoidua   One of the main cities of Ghana

Kogi   A state of Nigeria, its admin capital is Lokoja

Kohima   Admin capital of Nagaland, a state of India

Kohtla-Järve   One of the main cities of Estonia

Komi   A republic of Russia, its admin capital is Syktyvkar

Komi-Permyak   An autonomous area of Russia

Komrat   Admin capital of Gagauzia, an autonomous republic of Moldova

Konya   One of the main cities of Turkey

Kopavogur   One of the main cities of Iceland

Koror   Capital of Palau (USA)

Koryak   An autonomous area of Russia

Kosice   One of the main cities of Slovak Republic

Kostroma   A region (oblast) of Russia

Kota Bahru   Admin capital of Kelantan, a state of Malaysia

Kota Kinabalu   Admin capital of Sabah, a state of Malaysia

Koudougou   One of the main cities of Burkina Faso

Krakow   One of the main cities of Poland

Krasnodar   An autonomous territory (krai) of Russia

Krasnoyarsk   An autonomous territory (krai) of Russia

Kuala Lumpur   Capital of Malaysia

Kuala Terengganu   Admin capital of Terengganu, a state of Malaysia

Kuanas   One of the main cities of Lithuania

Kuantan   Admin capital of Pahang, a state of Malaysia

Kuching   Admin capital of Sarawak, a state of Malaysia

Kumanovo   One of the main cities of Macedonia

Kumasi   One of the main cities of Ghana

Kunming   Admin capital of Yunnan, an autonomous region of China

Kupang   Admin capital of Nusa Tenggara Timur, a province of Indonesia

Kurgan   A region (oblast) of Russia

Kursk   A region (oblast) of Russia

Kuwait (city)   Capital of Kuwait

Kwara   A state of Nigeria, its admin capital is Ilorin

KwaZulu/Natal   A province of South Africa, its admin capital is Ulundi

Kyoto   One of the main cities of Japan

Kyzyl-Orda   Admin capital of Tyva (formerly Tuva), a republic of Russia

L'Aquila   Admin capital of Abruzzi, a region of Italy

La Asunción   Admin capital of Nueva Esparta, a state of Venezuela

La Ceiba   One of the main cities of Honduras

La Pampa   A province of Argentina; its admin capital is Santa Rosa

La Paz   1. Capital of Bolivia; 2. Admin capital of Baja California Sur, a state of Mexico

La Plata   Admin capital of Buenos Aires, a province of Argentina

La Rioja   1. An Argetinian province whose admin capital bears the same name; 2. A Spanish autonomous community (region), its admin capital is Logroño

La Rochelle   Admin capital of Charente-Maritime, a region of Poitou-Charente, a department of France

La Roche-sur-Yon   Admin capital of Vendée, a region of Pays de la Loire, a department of France

La Vega   One of the main cities of Dominican Republic

Laayoune   Capital of Morocco   Western Sahara

Labé   One of the main cities of Guinea

Lacs   A region of Côte d'Ivoire

Lae   One of the main cities of Papua New Guinea

Lafia   Admin capital of Nassarawa, a state of Nigeria

Lagos   A state of Nigeria, its admin capital is Ikeja

Lagunes   A region of Côte d'Ivoire

Lahore   Admin capital of Punjab, a province of Pakistan

Lakshadweep   A union territory of India

Lalitpur   One of the main cities of Nepal

Lampung   A province of Indonesia, its admin capital is Tanjungkarang

Landes   A department of Aquitaine, a region of France, its admin capital is Mont-de-Marsan

Languedoc-Roussillon   A region of France, its admin capital is Montpellier

Lanzhou   Admin capital of Gansu, a province of China

Laoighs   A county of the Republic of Ireland, its admin capital is Portlaoise

Laon   Admin capital of Aisnes, a region of Picardie, a department of France

Lara   A state of Venezuela, its admin capital is Barquisimeto

Larnaca   One of the main cities of Cyprus

Lausanne   Admin capital of Vaud, a canton of Switzerland

Lautem   One of the main cities of East Timor

Laval   Admin capital of Mayenne, a region of Pays de la Loire, a department of France

Lazio   A region of Italy, its admin capital is Rome

Le Mans   Admin capital of Sarthe, a region of Pays de la Loire, a department of France

Le Puy   Admin capital of Haute-Loire, a region of Auvergne, a department of France

Leinster   A province of the Republic of Ireland

Leitrim   A county of the Republic of Ireland, its admin capital is Carrick-on-Shannon

Leningrad   A region (oblast) of Russia

León   One of the main cities of Nicaragua

Leuven   Admin capital of Flemish Brabant, a province of Belgium

Leyte   One of the Philippine islands

Lhasa   Admin capital of Xizang (Tibet), an municipal province of China

Liaoning   An administrative region of China, its admin capital is Shenyang

Libreville   Capital of Gabon

Liège   A province of Belgium, its admin capital is of the same name

Liepaja   One of the main cities of Latvia

Lieptsk   A region (oblast) of Russia

Liestal   Admin capital of Basel-Landschaft, a canton of Switzerland

Lifford   Admin capital of Donegal, a county of the Republic of Ireland

Liguria   A region of Italy, its admin capital is Genoa

Likasi   1. One of the main cities of Congo; 2. One of the main cities of Congo-Brazzaville

Lille   Admin capital of Nord, a region of Nord-Pas-de-Calais, a department of France

Lilongwe   Capital of Malawi

Lima   Capital of Peru

Limassol   One of the main cities of Cyprus

Limburg   A province of Belgium, its admin capital is Hasselt

Limerick   A county of the Republic of Ireland, its admin capital is of the same name

Limoges   Admin capital of Haute-Vienne, a region of Limousin, a department of France

Limousin   A region of France, its admin capital is Limoges

Linden   One of the main cities of Guyana

Linz   Admin capital of Upper Austria, a province of Austria

Lisbon   Capital of Portugal

Ljubljana   Capital of Slovenia

Lódz   One of the main cities of Poland

Logroño   Admin capital of La Rioja, a Spanish autonomous community (region)

Loi-kaw   Admin capital of Kayah, a state of Myanmar (Burma)

Loire   A department of Rhône-Alpes, a region of France, its admin capital is Saint-Éttiene

Loire-Atlantique   A department of Pays de la Loire, a region of France, its admin capital is Nantes

Loiret   A department of Centre-Val de Loire, a region of France, its admin capital is Orléans

Loir-et-Cher   A department of Centre-Val de Loire, a region of France, its admin capital is Blois

Lokoja   Admin capital of Kogi, a state of Nigeria

Lombardy   A region of Italy, its admin capital is Milan

Lomé   Capital of Togo

Longford   A county of the Republic of Ireland, its admin capital is of the same name

Lons-le-Saunier   Admin capital of Jura, a region of Franche-Comté, a department of France

Lorraine   A region of France, its admin capital is Nancy

Los teques   Admin capital of Miranda, a state of Venezuela

Lot   A department of Midi-Pyrénées, a region of France, its admin capital is Cahors

Lot-et-Garonne   A department of Aquitaine, a region of France, its admin capital is Agen

Louth   A county of the Republic of Ireland, its admin capital is Dundalk

Lower Austria   A province of Austria, its admin capital is St Pölten

Lower Saxony   A Land of Germany, its admin capital is Hannover

Lozère   A department of Languedoc-Roussillon, a region of France, its admin capital is Mende

Luanda   Capital of Angola
Luanshya   One of the main cities of Zambia
Lubumbashi   One of the main cities of Congo
Lubumbashi   One of the main cities of Congo-Brazzaville
Lucerne   A canton of Switzerland, its admin capital is of the same name
Lucknow   Admin capital of Uttar Pradesh, a state of India
Luganville   One of the main cities of Vanuatu
Lusaka   Capital of Zambia
Luxembourg   1. Capital of Luxembourg; 2. A province of Belgium, its admin capital is Arlon
Luzon   One of the Philippine islands
Lyon   Admin capital of Rhône, a region of Rhône-Alpes, a department of France
Macao   Capital of Macao (Portugal)
Macapá   Admin capital of Amapá, a state of Brazil
Maceió   Admin capital of Alagoas, a state of Brazil
Madang   One of the main cities of Papua New Guinea
Madeira   An autonomous region of Portugal, its admin capital is Funchal
Madhya Pradesh   A state of India, its admin capital is Bhopal
Madras   Admin capital of Tamil Nadu, a state of India
Madrid   A Spanish autonomous community (region), its admin capital is of the same name
Madrid   Capital of Spain
Mafikeng   Admin capital of North-West, a province of South Africa
Magadan   A region (oblast) of Russia
Magdeburg   Admin capital of Saxony-Anhalt, a Land of Germany
Mahajanga   One of the main cities of Madagascar
Maharashtra   A state of India, its admin capital is Bombay
Mahilyow   One of the main cities of Belarus
Maiduguri   Admin capital of Borno, a state of Nigeria
Maine-et-Loire   A department of Pays de la Loire, a region of France, its admin capital is Angers
Mainz   Admin capital of Rhineland-Palatinate, a Land of Germany
Majuro   Capital of Marshall Islands
Makhachkala   Admin capital of Daghestan, a republic of Russia
Makurdi   Admin capital of Benue, a state of Nigeria
Malabo   Capital of Equatorial Guinea
Malé   Capital of Maldives
Malmo   One of the main cities of Sweden
Maluku   A province of Indonesia, its admin capital is Amboina
Mamou   One of the main cities of Guinea
Mamoudzou   Admin capital of Mayotte, a territorial collective of France
Managua   Capital of Nicaragua

Manama Capital of Bahrain

Manaus Admin capital of Amazonas, a state of Brazil

Manche A department of Basse-Normandi, a region of France, its admin capital is Saint Lô

Mandeville One of the main cities of Jamaica

Manicaland A province of Zimbabwe

Manila Capital of Philippines

Manipur A state of India, its admin capital is Imphal

Manitoba A province of Canada, its admin capital is Winnipeg

Manzini One of the main cities of Swaziland

Maputo Capital of Mozambique

Mar del Plata One of the main cities of Argentina

Maracaibo Admin capital of Zulia, a state of Venezuela

Maracay Admin capital of Aragua, a state of Venezuela

Marahoue A region of Côte d'Ivoire

Maranhão A state of Brazil, its admin capital is São Luís

Marche A region of Italy, its admin capital is Ancona

Maribor One of the main cities of Slovenia

Mariehamn (Maarianhamina) Admin capital of Åland (Ahvenanmaa), an autonomous province of Finland

Mari-El A republic of Russia, its admin capital is Yoshkar-Ola

Marne A department of Champagne-Ardennes, a region of France, its admin capital is Chalôns-sur-Marne

Marrakesh One of the main cities of Morocco

Marseille Admin capital of Bouches-de-Rhône, a region of Provence-Alpes-Côte d'Azur, a department of France

Martinique An overseas department of France, its admin capital is Fort-de-France

Masaka One of the main cities of Uganda

Masbate One of the Philippine islands

Maseru Capital of Lesotho

Mashad One of the main cities of Iran

Mashonaland Central A province of Zimbabwe

Mashonaland East A province of Zimbabwe

Mashonaland West A province of Zimbabwe

Massawa One of the main cities of Eritrea

Massaya One of the main cities of Nicaragua

Masvingo A province of Zimbabwe

Matabeleland North A province of Zimbabwe

Matabeleland South A province of Zimbabwe

Matadi 1. One of the main cities of Congo; 2. One of the main cities of Congo-Brazzaville

Mataram Admin capital of Nusa Tenggara Barat, a province of Indonesia

Mata-Utu   Admin capital of Wallis and Futuna Islands, an overseas territory of France

Mato Grosso   A state of Brazil, its admin capital is Cuiabá

Mato Grosso do Sul   A state of Brazil, its admin capital is Campo Grande

Matola   One of the main cities of Mozambique

Maturin   Admin capital of Monagas, a state of Venezuela

May Pen   One of the main cities of Jamaica

Mayenne   A department of Pays de la Loire, a region of France, its admin capital is Laval

Maykop   Admin capital of Adygeia, a republic of Russia

Mayo   A county of the Republic of Ireland, its admin capital is Castlebar

Mayotte   A territorial collective of France, its admin capital is Mamoudzou

Mazar-e-Sharif   One of the main cities of Afghanistan

Mazatenango   One of the main cities of Guatemala

Mbabane   Capital of Swaziland

Mbale   One of the main cities of Uganda

Mbandaka   1. One of the main cities of Congo; 2. One of the main cities of Congo-Brazzaville

Mbeya   One of the main cities of Tanzania

Meath   A county of the Republic of Ireland, its admin capital is Trim

Mecklenburg-Western Pomerania (M-Vorpommern)   A Land of Germany, its admin capital is Schwerin

Medan   Admin capital of Sumatera Utara, a province of Indonesia

Medllin   One of the main cities of Colombia

Meghalaya   A state of India, its admin capital is Shillong

Meknes   One of the main cities of Morocco

Melaka   A state of Malaysia, its admin capital bears the same name

Melbourne   Admin capital of Victoria, a territory of Australia

Melilla   A Spanish autonomous community (region), its admin capital is of the same name

Melo   One of the main cities of Uruguay

Melun   Admin capital of Seine-et-Marne, a region of Île-de-France, a department of France

Menado   Admin capital of Sulawesi Utara, a province of Indonesia

Mende   Admin capital of Lozère, a region of Languedoc-Roussillon, a department of France

Mendoza   One of the main cities of Argentina; admin centre of the Province of the same name

Mercedes   One of the main cities of Uruguay

Mérida   1. Admin capital of Yucatán, a state of Mexico; 2. Admin capital of Extremadura, a Spanish autonomous community (region); 3. A state of Venezuela, its admin capital is of the same name

Metz   Admin capital of Moselle, a region of Lorraine, a department of France

Meuse   A department of Lorraine, a region of France, its admin capital is Bar-le-Duc

Meutre-et-Moselle   A department of Lorraine, a region of France, its admin capital is Nancy

Mexicali   Admin capital of Baja California, a state of Mexico

México   A state of Mexico, its admin capital is Toluca de Lerdo

Mexico City   Admin capital of Federal District, a state of Mexico, and the capital of Mexico

Mhlume   One of the main cities of Swaziland

Michoacán   A state of Mexico, its admin capital is Morelia

Midi-Pyrénées   A region of France, its admin capital is Toulouse

Midlands   A province of Zimbabwe

Milan   Admin capital of Lombardy, a region of Italy

Millingar   Admin capital of Westmeath, a county of the Republic of Ireland

Minas   One of the main cities of Uruguay

Minas Gerais   A state of Brazil, its admin capital is Belo Horizonte

Mindanao   One of the Philippine islands

Mindoro   One of the Philippine islands

Minna   Admin capital of Niger, a state of Nigeria

Minsk   Capital of Belarus

Miranda   A state of Venezuela, its admin capital is Los teques

Misiones   A province of Argentina; its admin capital is Posadas

Miskolc   One of the main cities of Hungary

Misratah   One of the main cities of Libya

Mizoram   A state of India, its admin capital is Aizawl

Mogadishu   Capital of Somalia

Molepolole   One of the main cities of Botswana

Molise   A region of Italy, its admin capital is Campobasso

Mombasa   One of the main cities of Kenya

Mon   A state of Myanmar (Burma), its admin capital is Moulmein

Monaco-Ville   Capital of Monaco

Monagas   A state of Venezuela, its admin capital is Maturin

Monaghan   A county of the Republic of Ireland, its admin capital is of the same name

Monrovia   Capital of Liberia

Mons   Admin capital of Hainault, a province of Belgium

Montauban   Admin capital of Tarn-et-Garonne, a region of Midi-Pyrénées, a department of France

Mont-de-Marsan   Admin capital of Landes, a region of Aquitaine, a department of France

Montego Bay   One of the main cities of Jamaica

Montenegro   A republic, its admin capital is Podgorica

Monterrey   Admin capital of Nuevo León, a state of Mexico

Montevideo   Capital of Uruguay

Montpellier   Admin capital of Hérault, a region of Languedoc-Roussillon, a department of France

Montreal   One of the main cities of Canada

Mopti   One of the main cities of Mali

Morbihan   A department of Bretagne, a region of France, its admin capital is Vannes

Mordvinia   A republic of Russia, its admin capital is Saransk

Morelia   Admin capital of Michoacán, a state of Mexico

Morelos   A state of Mexico, its admin capital is Cuernavaca

Moroni   Capital of Comoros

Moscow   The capital of Russia, as well as a region (oblast) of Russia

Moselle   A department of Lorraine, a region of France, its admin capital is Metz

Mostaganem   One of the main cities of Algeria

Mostar   One of the main cities of Bosnia-Hercegovina

Moulins   Admin capital of Allier, a region of Auvergne, a department of France

Moulmein   Admin capital of Mon, a state of Myanmar (Burma)

Mount Athos (Ayion Oros)   An autonomous monk's republic of Greece, its admin capital is Karyai

Mount Hagen   One of the main cities of Papua New Guinea

Moyen-Cavally   A region of Côte d'Ivoire

Moyen-Comoe   A region of Côte d'Ivoire

Mpumalanga   A province of South Africa, its admin capital is Nelspruit

Mufulira   One of the main cities of Zambia

Mumbai   (formerly Bombay) admin capital of Maharashtra, a state of India

Munich (München)   Admin capital of Bavaria, a Land of Germany

Munster   A province of the Republic of Ireland

Murcia   A Spanish autonomous community (region), its admin capital is of the same name

Murmansk   A region (oblast) of Russia

Muscat   Capital of Oman

Muslim Mindanao   A Filipino autonomous region, its admin capital is Cotabato City

Mussay'id   One of the main cities of Qatar

Mutrah   One of the main cities of Oman

Mwanza   One of the main cities of Tanzania
Myitkyina   Admin capital of Kachin, a state of Myanmar (Burma)
Mzuzu   One of the main cities of Malawi
N'Zérékoré   One of the main cities of Guinea
Naas   Admin capital of Kildare, a county of the Republic of Ireland
Nablus   One of the main cities of Israel   West Bank and Gaza Strip
Nagaland   A state of India, its admin capital is Kohima
Nagoya   One of the main cities of Japan
Nairobi   Capital of Kenya
Nakhon Ratchasima   One of the main cities of Thailand
Nakuru   One of the main cities of Kenya
Nalchik   Admin capital of Kabardino-Balkaria, a republic of Russia
Nampula   One of the main cities of Mozambique
Namur   A province of Belgium, its admin capital is of the same name
Nanchang   Admin capital of Jiangxi, an administrative region of China
Nancy   Admin capital of Meutre-et-Moselle, a region of Lorraine, a
   department of France
Nanjing   Admin capital of Jiangsu, an administrative region of China
Nanning   Admin capital of Guangxi Zhuang, a province of China
Nanterre   Admin capital of Hauts-de-Seine, a region of Île-de-France, a
   department of France
Nantes   Admin capital of Loire-Atlantique, a region of Pays de la Loire, a
   department of France
Nanthanburi   One of the main cities of Thailand
Naples   Admin capital of Campania, a region of Italy
Narva   One of the main cities of Estonia
Nassarawa   A state of Nigeria, its admin capital is Lafia
Nassau   Capital of Bahamas
Natal   Admin capital of Rio Grande do Norte, a state of Brazil
Nauru   Capital of Nauru
Navarre   A Spanish autonomous community (region), its admin capital
   is Pamplona
Naxçivan   Autonomous Republic of Azerbaijan, its admin capital is of
   the same name
Nayarit   A state of Mexico, its admin capital is Tepic
Nazran   Admin capital of Ingushetia, a republic of Russia
Ndjaména   Capital of Chad
Ndola   One of the main cities of Zambia
Negri Sembilan   A state of Malaysia, its admin capital is Sereban
Negros   One of the Philippine islands
Nei Mongol   An administrative region of China, its admin capital is
   Hohhot
Nelspruit   Admin capital of Mpumalanga, a province of South Africa
Nenets   An autonomous area of Russia

Nequén   An Argetinian province whose admin capital bears the same name

Netherlands Antilles   An overseas territory of the Netherlands, its admin capital is Willemstad

Neuchatel   A canton of Switzerland, its admin capital is of the same name

Nevers   Admin capital of Nièvre, a region of Bourgogne, a department of France

New Amsterdam   One of the main cities of Guyana

New Brunswick   A province of Canada, its admin capital is Fredericton

New Caledonia   An overseas territory of France, its admin capital is Nouméa

New South Wales   A territory of Australia, its admin capital is Sydney

Newfoundland and Labrador   A province of Canada, its admin capital is St John's

Nhangano   One of the main cities of Swaziland

Niamey   Capital of Niger

Nice   Admin capital of Alpes-Maritimes, a region of Provence-Alpes-Côte d'Azur, a department of France

Nicosia   Capital of Cyprus

Nidwalden   A canton of Switzerland, its admin capital is Stans

Nièvre   A department of Bourgogne, a region of France, its admin capital is Nevers

Niger   A state of Nigeria, its admin capital is Minna

Nîmes   Admin capital of Gard, a region of Languedoc-Roussillon, a department of France

Ningxia Hui   An autonomous region of China, its admin capital is Yinchuan

Niort   Admin capital of Deux-Sèvres, a region of Poitou-Charente, a department of France

Nizhny Novgorod   A region (oblast) of Russia

Nord   A department of Nord-Pas-de-Calais, a region of France, its admin capital is Lillee

Nord-Pas-de-Calais   A region of France, its admin capital is Lille

Norfolk Island   A territory of Australia, its admin capital is Kingston

North Island   One of the islands of New Zealand

North Ossetia (Alania)   A republic of Russia, its admin capital is Vladikavkaz

North Rhine-Westphalia (Nordrhein-Westfalen)   A Land of Germany, its admin capital is Düsseldorf

Northern   A province of South Africa, its admin capital is Pietersburg

Northern Cape   A province of South Africa, its admin capital is Kimberley

Northern Territory   A territory of Australia, its admin capital is Darwin

North-West   A province of South Africa, its admin capital is Mafikeng
North-West Frontier Province   A province of Pakistan, its admin capital is Peshawar
Northwest Territories   A province of Canada, its admin capital is Yellowknife
Nouméa   Capital of New Caledonia, an overseas territory of France
Nousakschott   Capital of Mauritania
Nova Scotia   A province of Canada, its admin capital is Halifax
Novgorod   A region (oblast) of Russia
Novosibirsk   A region (oblast) of Russia
Nueva Esparta   A state of Venezuela, its admin capital is La Asunción
Nuevo León   A state of Mexico, its admin capital is Monterrey
Nuku'alofa   Capital of Tonga
Nunavut [born of Northwest Territories 1999]   A province of Canada, its admin capital is Iqaluit
Nusa Tenggara Barat   A province of Indonesia, its admin capital is Mataram
Nusa Tenggara Timur   A province of Indonesia, its admin capital is Kupang
Nyala   One of the main cities of Sudan
N'zi-Comoe   A region of Côte d'Ivoire
Oaxaca   A state of Mexico, its admin capital is Oaxaca de Juárez
Oaxaca de Juárez   Admin capital of Oaxaca, a state of Mexico
Obwalden   A canton of Switzerland, its admin capital is Sarnen
Ocho Rios   One of the main cities of Jamaica
Odense   One of the main cities of Denmark
Offaly   A county of the Republic of Ireland, its admin capital is Tullamore
Ogun   A state of Nigeria, its admin capital is Abeokuta
Oise   A department of Picardie, a region of France, its admin capital is Beauvais
Oistins   One of the main cities of Barbados
Ondangwa   One of the main cities of Namibia
Ondo   A state of Nigeria, its admin capital is Akure
Ontario   A province of Canada, its admin capital is Toronto
Oradea   One of the main cities of Romania
Oran   One of the main cities of Algeria
Orange Walk   One of the main cities of Belize
Oranjestad   Admin capital of Aruba, an overseas territory of the Netherlands
Orel   A region (oblast) of Russia
Orenburg   A region (oblast) of Russia
Orissa   A state of India, its admin capital is Bhubaneswar

Orléans   Admin capital of Loiret, a region of Centre-Val de Loire, a department of France

Orne   A department of Basse-Normandi, a region of France, its admin capital is Alençon

Oruro   One of the main cities of Bolivia

Osaka   One of the main cities of Japan

Oshakati   One of the main cities of Namibia

Oshogbo   Admin capital of Osun, a state of Nigeria

Osijek   One of the main cities of Croatia

Oslo   Capital of Norway

Ostrava   One of the main cities of Czech Republic

Osun   A state of Nigeria, its admin capital is Oshogbo

Ottawa   Capital of Canada

Ouagadougou   Capital of Burkina Faso

Oujda   One of the main cities of Morocco

Oviedo   Admin capital of Asturias, a Spanish autonomous community (region)

Owerri   Admin capital of Imo, a state of Nigeria

Oyo   A state of Nigeria, its admin capital is Ibadan

Pa-an   Admin capital of Karen, a state of Myanmar (Burma)

Pachuca de Soto   Admin capital of Hidalgo, a state of Mexico

Padang   Admin capital of Sumatera Barat, a province of Indonesia

Pago Pago   Capital of Samoa, America (USA)

Pahang   A state of Malaysia, its admin capital is Kuantan

Pakanbaru   Admin capital of Riau, a province of Indonesia

Palangkaraya   Admin capital of Kalimantan Tengah, a province of Indonesia

Palawan   One of the Philippine islands

Pale   Admin capital of Republika Srpska, a state of Bosnia-Hercegovina

Palembang   Admin capital of Sumatera Seletan, a province of Indonesia

Palermo   Admin capital of Sicily, a region of Italy

Palikir   Capital of Micronesia, Fed. States of

Palma de Mallorca   Admin capital of Balaerics, a Spanish autonomous community (region)

Palmas   Admin capital of Tocantins, a state of Brazil

Palu   Admin capital of Sulawesi Tengah, a province of Indonesia

Pamplona   Admin capital of Navarre, a Spanish autonomous community (region)

Panaji   Admin capital of Goa, a state of India

Panama City   Capital of Panama

Panay   One of the Philippine islands

Papeete   Admin capital of French Polynesia, an overseas territory of France

Paphos   One of the main cities of Cyprus

Pará   A state of Brazil, its admin capital is Belém

Paraiba   A state of Brazil, its admin capital is João Pessoa

Paramaribo   Capital of Suriname

Paraná   1. Admin capital of Entre Rios, a province of Argentina; 2. A state of Brazil, its admin capital is Curitiba

Paris   A department of Île-de-France, a region of France, its admin capital   and that of the country   is Paris

Pärnu   One of the main cities of Estonia

Pas-de-Calais   A department of Nord-Pas-de-Calais, a region of France, its admin capital is Arras

Patna   Admin capital of Bihar, a state of India

Pau   Admin capital of Pyrénées, a region of Aquitaine, a department of France

Pavlodar   One of the main cities of Kazakhstan

Pays de la Loire   A region of France, its admin capital is Nantes

Paysandú   One of the main cities of Uruguay

Pécs   One of the main cities of Hungary

Penang   A state of Malaysia, its admin capital is Georgetown

Penza   A region (oblast) of Russia

Perak   A state of Malaysia, its admin capital is Ipoh

Périgeux   Admin capital of Dordogne, a region of Aquitaine, a department of France

Peripignan   Admin capital of Pyrénées-Orientales, a region of Languedoc-Roussillon, a department of France

Perlis   A state of Malaysia, its admin capital is Kangar

Perm   A region (oblast) of Russia

Pernambuco   A state of Brazil, its admin capital is Recife

Perth   Admin capital of Western Australia, a territory of Australia

Perugia   Admin capital of Umbria, a region of Italy

Peshawar   Admin capital of North-West Frontier Province, a province of Pakistan

Peter the First Island   An Antarctic territory of Norway

Petrozavodsk   Admin capital of Karelia, a republic of Russia

Phnom Penh   Capital of Cambodia

Piauí   A state of Brazil, its admin capital is Teresina

Picardie (Picardy)   A region of France, its admin capital is Amiens

Piemonte   A region of Italy, its admin capital is Turin

Pietersburg   Admin capital of Northern, a province of South Africa

Pigg's peak   One of the main cities of Swaziland

Plateau   A state of Nigeria, its admin capital is Jos

Ploiesti   One of the main cities of Romania

Plovdiv   One of the main cities of Bulgaria

Plzen   One of the main cities of Czech Republic

Podgorica   Admin capital of Montenegro

Pointe Noire   One of the main cities of Congo-Brazzaville

Poitiers   Admin capital of Vienne, a region of Poitou-Charente, a department of France

Poitou-Charentes   A region of France, its admin capital is Poitiers

Pondicherry   A union territory of India

Ponta Delgada   Admin capital of Azores, a region of Portugal

Pontianak   Admin capital of Kalimantan Barat, a province of Indonesia

Pontoise   Admin capital of Val d'Oise, a region of Île-de-France, a department of France

Port Blair   Admin capital of Andaman and Nicobar Islands, a union territory of India

Port Louis   Capital of Mauritius

Port Moresby   Capital of Papua New Guinea

Port of Spain   Capital of Trinidad and Tobago

Port Said   One of the main cities of Egypt

Port Sudan   One of the main cities of Sudan

Port Vila   Capital of Vanuatu

Port-au-Prince   Capital of Haïti

Port-Harcourt   Admin capital of Rivers, a state of Nigeria

Portlaoise   Admin capital of Laoighs, a county of the Republic of Ireland

Pôrto Alegre   Admin capital of Rio Grande do Sul, a state of Brazil

Porto Novo   Capital of Benin

Pôrto Velho   Admin capital of Rondônia, a state of Brazil

Portuguesa   A state of Venezuela, its admin capital is Guanare

Posadas   Admin capital of Misiones, a province of Argentina

Potenza   Admin capital of Basilicata, a region of Italy

Potosi   One of the main cities of Bolivia

Potsdam   Admin capital of Brandenburg, a Land of Germany

Poznan   One of the main cities of Poland

Prague   Capital of Czech Republic

Praia   Capital of Cape Verde Islands

Pretoria and Cape Town   Capital of South Africa

Prilep   One of the main cities of Macedonia

Primorye   An autonomous territory (krai) of Russia

Prince Edward Island   A province of Canada, its admin capital is Charlottetown

Princess Ragnhild Land   An Antarctic territory of Norway

Privas   Admin capital of Ardèche, a region of Rhône-Alpes, a department of France

Provence-Alpes-Côte d'Azur   A region of France, its admin capital is Marseille

Pskov   A region (oblast) of Russia

Puebla   A state of Mexico, its admin capital is Puebla de Zaragoza
Puebla de Zaragoza   Admin capital of Puebla, a state of Mexico
Puente Alto   One of the main cities of Chile
Puerto Ayacucho   Admin capital of Amazonas, a state of Venezuela
Puerto Barquerizo Moreno   Capital of Ecuador – Galápagos Islands
Puerto Barrios   One of the main cities of Guatemala
Puerto Cortés   One of the main cities of Honduras
Puerto Plata   One of the main cities of Dominican Republic
Puglia   A region of Italy, its admin capital is Bari
Punjab   1. A province of Pakistan, its admin capital is Lahore; 2. A state of India, its admin capital is Chandigarh
Punta Arenas   One of the main cities of Chile
Punta del Este   One of the main cities of Uruguay
Pusan   One of the main cities of Korea, Rep of (South)
Puy-de-Dôme   A department of Auvergne, a region of France, its admin capital is Clermont-Ferrand
Pyongyang   Capital of Korea, DPR (North)
Pyrénées-Atlantiques   A department of Aquitaine, a region of France, its admin capital is Pau
Pyrénées-Orientales   A department of Languedoc-Roussillon, a region of France, its admin capital is Perpignan
Qandahar   One of the main cities of Afghanistan
Qingdo   One of the main cities of China
Qinghai   An autonomous region of China, its admin capital is Xining
Qom   One of the main cities of Iran
Quatre Bornes   One of the main cities of Mauritius
Québec   A province of Canada, its admin capital is Québec
Québec   One of the main cities of Canada
Queen Maud Land   An Antarctic territory of Norway
Queensland   A territory of Australia, its admin capital is Brisbane
Querétao   A state of Mexico, its admin capital is of the same name
Quetta   Admin capital of Baluchistan, a province of Pakistan
Quetzaltenango   One of the main cities of Guatemala
Quimper   Admin capital of Finistère, a region of Bretagne, a department of France
Quintana Roo   A state of Mexico, its admin capital is Chetumal
Quito   Capital of Ecuador
Rabat   Capital of Morocco
Rabaul   One of the main cities of Papua New Guinea
Rafah   One of the main cities of Israel   West Bank and Gaza Strip
Rajasthan   A state of India, its admin capital is Jaipur
Rakhine   A state of Myanmar (Burma), its admin capital is Sittwe
Ramallah   One of the main cities of Israel – West Bank and Gaza Strip

Ras al-Khaimah An emirate of United Arab Emirates, its admin capital is of the same name

Rawson Admin capital of Chubut, a province of Argentina

Recife Admin capital of Pernambuco, a state of Brazil

Recife One of the main cities of Brazil

Regina Admin capital of Saskatchewan, a province of Canada

Rehoboth One of the main cities of Namibia

Rennes Admin capital of Ille-et-Vilaine, a region of Bretagne, a department of France

Republika Srpska A state of Bosnia-Hercegovina, its admin capital is Pale

Resistencia Admin capital of Chaco, a province of Argentina

Réunion An overseas department of France, its admin capital is St-Denis

Reykjanesbær One of the main cities of Iceland

Reykjavik Capital of Iceland

Rhineland-Palatinate (R-Pfalz) A Land of Germany, its admin capital is Mainz

Rhône A department of Rhône-Alpes, a region of France, its admin capital is Lyon

Rhône-Alpes A region of France, its admin capital is Lyon

Riau A province of Indonesia, its admin capital is Pakanbaru

Riga Capital of Latvia

Rijeka One of the main cities of Croatia

Rio Branco Admin capital of Acre, a state of Brazil

Rio de Janeiro A state of Brazil, its admin capital is of the same name

Rio Gallegos Admin capital of Santa Cruz, a province of Argentina

Rio Grande do Norte A state of Brazil, its admin capital is Natal

Rio Grande do Sul A state of Brazil, its admin capital is Pôrto Alegre

Rio Negro A province of Argentina; its admin capital is Viedma

Rishon Le'Zion One of the main cities of Israel

Rivera One of the main cities of Uruguay

Rivers A state of Nigeria, its admin capital is Port-Harcourt

Riyadh Capital of Saudi Arabia

Rodez Admin capital of Aveyron, a region of Midi-Pyrénées, a department of France

Rome Admin capital of Lazio, a region of Italy

Rome Capital of Italy

Rondônia A state of Brazil, its admin capital is Pôrto Velho

Roraima A state of Brazil, its admin capital is Boa Vista

Rosatio One of the main cities of Argentina

Roscommon A county of the Republic of Ireland, its admin capital is of the same name

Roseau Capital of Dominica

Rotstov   A region (oblast) of Russia

Rouen   Admin capital of Seine-Maritime, a region of Haute-Normandie, a department of France

Rufisque   One of the main cities of Senegal

Ruwi   One of the main cities of Oman

Ryazan   A region (oblast) of Russia

Saarbrücken   Admin capital of Saarland, a Land of Germany

Saarland   A Land of Germany, its admin capital is Saarbrücken

Sabah   A state of Malaysia, its admin capital is Kota Kinabalu

Saint Lô   Admin capital of Manche, a region of Basse-Normandi, a department of France

Saint-Brieuc   Admin capital of Côtes-d'Armor, a region of Bretagne, a department of France

Saint-Étienne   Admin capital of Loire, a region of Rhône-Alpes, a department of France

Saipan   Capital of Northern Mariana Islands (USA)

Sakha (formerly Yakutia)   A republic of Russia, its admin capital is Yakutsk

Sakhalin   A region (oblast) of Russia

Salalah   One of the main cities of Oman

Salta   An Argetinian province whose admin capital bears the same name

Saltillo   Admin capital of Coahuila, a state of Mexico

Salto   One of the main cities of Uruguay

Salvador   Admin capital of Bahia, a state of Brazil

Salvador   One of the main cities of Brazil

Salzburg   A province of Austria, its admin capital is of the same name

Salzburg   One of the main cities of Austria

Samar   One of the Philippine islands

Samara   A region (oblast) of Russia

Samarinda   Admin capital of Kalimantan Timur, a province of Indonesia

Samarkand   One of the main cities of Uzbekistan

San Carlos   Admin capital of Cojedes, a state of Venezuela

San Cristóbal   1. One of the main cities of Dominican Republic; 2. Admin capital of Táchira, a state of Venezuela

San Felipe   Admin capital of Yaracuy, a state of Venezuela

San Fernando   One of the main cities of Trinidad and Tobago

San Fernando de Apure   Admin capital of Apure, a state of Venezuela

San Fernando del Valle de Catamarca   Admin capital of Catamarca, a province of Argentina

San Ignacio   One of the main cities of Belize

San José   Capital of Costa Rica

San Juan   1. An Argetinian province whose admin capital bears the same name; 2. One of the main cities of Dominican Republic

San Juan de Los Morros   Admin capital of Guárico, a state of Venezuela

San Lorenzo   One of the main cities of Paraguay

San Luis   An Argetinian province whose admin capital bears the same name

San Luis Potosí   A state of Mexico, its admin capital is San Luis Potosi

San Marino   Capital of San Marino

San Miguel   One of the main cities of El Salvador

San Miguel de Tucumán   Admin capital of San Miguel de Tucumán, a province of Argentina

San Pedro Sula   One of the main cities of Honduras

San Salvador de Jujuy   Admin capital of Juyjuy, a province of Argentina

San Salvador   Capital of El Salvador

Sana'a'   Capital of Yemen

Santa Ana   One of the main cities of El Salvador

Santa Catarina   A state of Brazil, its admin capital is Florianópolis

Santa Clara   One of the main cities of Cuba

Santa Crus de Tenerife and Las Palmas   Admin capital of Canaries, a Spanish autonomous community (region)

Santa Cruz   1. A province of Argentina; its admin capital is Rio Gallegos; 2. One of the main cities of Bolivia

Santa Fé   An Argetinian province whose admin capital bears the same name

Santa Rosa   Admin capital of La Pampa, a province of Argentina

Santander   Admin capital of Cantabria, a Spanish autonomous community (region)

Santiago   1. Capital of Chile; 2. One of the main cities of Cuba

Santiago de Compostela   Admin capital of Galicia, a Spanish autonomous community (region)

Santiago de los Caballeros   One of the main cities of Dominican Republic

Santiago del Estero   An Argetinian province whose admin capital bears the same name

Santo Domingo   Capital of Dominican Republic

São Luís   Admin capital of Maranhão, a state of Brazil

São Paulo   A state of Brazil, its admin capital is of the same name

São Tomé   Capital of São Tomé and Príncipe

Saôane-et-Loire   A department of Bourgogne, a region of France, its admin capital is Tours

Sapporo   One of the main cities of Japan

Sarajevo   Capital of Federation of Bosnia-Herzegovnia, a state of Bosnia-Hercegovina

Saransk   Admin capital of Mordovinia, a republic of Russia

Saratov   A region (oblast) of Russia

Sarawak   A state of Malaysia, its admin capital is Kuching

Sardinia   A region of Italy, its admin capital is Cagkiari

Sarnen   Admin capital of Obwalden, a canton of Switzerland

Sarthe   A department of Pays de la Loire, a region of France, its admin capital is Le Mans

Saskatchewan   A province of Canada, its admin capital is Regina

Savanes   A region of Côte d'Ivoire

Savoie   A department of Rhône-Alpes, a region of France, its admin capital is Chambéry

Saxony (Sachsen)   A Land of Germany, its admin capital is Dresden

Saxony-Anhalt (Sachsen-A)   A Land of Germany, its admin capital is Magdeburg

Sayda   One of the main cities of Lebanon

Scarborough   One of the main cities of Trinidad and Tobago

Schaffhausen   A canton of Switzerland, its admin capital is of the same name

Schleswig-Holstein   A Land of Germany, its admin capital is Kiel

Schwerin   Admin capital of Mecklenburg-Western Pomerania, a Land of Germany

Schwyz   A canton of Switzerland, its admin capital is of the same name

Segou   One of the main cities of Mali

Seine-et-Marne   A department of Île-de-France, a region of France, its admin capital is Melun

Seine-Maritime   A department of Haute-Normandie, a region of France, its admin capital is Rouen

Seine-Saint-Denis   A department of Île-de-France, a region of France, its admin capital is Bobigny

Selebi-Phikwe   One of the main cities of Botswana

Selngor   A state of Malaysia, its admin capital is Shah Alam

Semarang   Admin capital of Jawa Tengah, a province of Indonesia

Seoul   Capital of Korea, Rep of (South)

Seremban   Admin capital of Negri Sembilan, a state of Malaysia

Sergipe   A state of Brazil, its admin capital is Aracajú

Setif   One of the main cities of Algeria

Seville   Admin capital of Andalucia, a Spanish autonomous community (region)

Sfax   One of the main cities of Tunisia

Shaanxi   An autonomous region of China, its admin capital is Xian

Shah Alam   Admin capital of Selngor, a state of Malaysia

Shan   A state of Myanmar (Burma), its admin capital is Taunggyi

Shandong   An autonomous region of China, its admin capital is Jinan

Shanghai   Admin capital of Shanghai, an autonomous region of China

Shanxi   A municipal province of China, its admin capital is Taiyuan

Sharjah   An emirate of United Arab Emirates, its admin capital is of the same name

Shenyang   Admin capital of Liaoning, an administrative region of China

Shenyang   One of the main cities of China

Shijazhuang   Admin capital of Hebei, an autonomous region of China

Shillong   Admin capital of Meghalaya, a state of India

Shimla   Admin capital of Himachal Pradesh, a state of India

Shiraz   One of the main cities of Iran

Shymkent   One of the main cities of Kazakhstan

Sichuan   A Municipal province of China, its admin capital is Chengdu

Sicily   A region of Italy, its admin capital is Palermo

Sidi-Bel-Abbes   One of the main cities of Algeria

Siglufjordur   One of the main cities of Iceland

Siguiri   One of the main cities of Guinea

Sikasso   One of the main cities of Mali

Sikkin   A state of India, its admin capital is Gangtok

Silvassa   Admin capital of Chandigarh, a union territory of India

Simferopol   Admin capital of Crimea, an autonomous republic of Ukraine

Sinaloa   A state of Mexico, its admin capital is Culiacán Rosales

Sind   A province of Pakistan, its admin capital is Karachi

Sion   Admin capital of Valais, a canton of Switzerland

Sirte   One of the main cities of Libya

Siteki   One of the main cities of Swaziland

Sittwe   Admin capital of Rakhine, a state of Myanmar (Burma)

Skikda   One of the main cities of Algeria

Skopje   Capital of Macedonia

Sligo   A county of the Republic of Ireland, its admin capital is of the same name

Smolensk   A region (oblast) of Russia

Snares Islands   One of the islands of New Zealand

Sofia   Capital of Bulgaria

Sokoto   A state of Nigeria, its admin capital is of the same name

Solander   One of the islands of New Zealand

Solothurn   A canton of Switzerland, its admin capital is of the same name

Somme   A department of Picardie, a region of France, its admin capital is Amiens

Songkhla   One of the main cities of Thailand

Sonora   A state of Mexico, its admin capital is Hermosillo

Sousse   One of the main cities of Tunisia

South Australia   A territory of Australia, its admin capital is Adelaide

South Island   One of the islands of New Zealand

Spanish Town   One of the main cities of Jamaica

Speightstown   One of the main cities of Barbados
Split   One of the main cities of Croatia
Srinagar/Jammu   Admin capital of Jammu and Kashmir, a state of India
St Denis   Capital of Réunion (French)
St Gallen   A canton of Switzerland, its admin capital is of the same name
St George's   Capital of Grenada
St John's   1. Admin capital of Newfoundland and Labrador, a province of Canada; 2. Capital of Antigua and Barbuda
St Pierre and Miquelon   A territorial collective of France, its admin capital is St-Pierre
St Pölten   Admin capital of Lower Austria, a province of Austria
Stans   Admin capital of Nidwalden, a canton of Switzerland
St-Denis   Admin capital of Réunion, an overseas department of France
Stewart Island   One of the islands of New Zealand
Stockholm   Capital of Sweden
St-Pierre   Admin capital of St Pierre and Miquelon, a territorial collective of France
Strasbourg   Admin capital of Bas-Rhin, a region of Alsace, a department of France
Stravropol   An autonomous territory (krai) of Russia
Stuttgart   Admin capital of Baden-Württemberg, a Land of Germany
Styria   A province of Austria, its admin capital is Graz
Sucre   1. One of the main cities of Bolivia; 2. A state of Venezuela, its admin capital is Cumaná
Sud-Bandama   A region of Côte d'Ivoire
Sud-Comoe   A region of Côte d'Ivoire
Suez   One of the main cities of Egypt
Suhar   One of the main cities of Oman
Sukhumi   Admin capital of Akhazia, an autonomous republic of Georgia
Sulawesi Seletan   A province of Indonesia, its admin capital is Ujung Padang
Sulawesi Tengah   A province of Indonesia, its admin capital is Palu
Sulawesi Tenggara   A province of Indonesia, its admin capital is Kendari
Sulawesi Utara   A province of Indonesia, its admin capital is Menado
Sumatera Barat   A province of Indonesia, its admin capital is Padang
Sumatera Seletan   A province of Indonesia, its admin capital is Palembang
Sumatera Utara   A province of Indonesia, its admin capital is Medan
Sumqayit   One of the main cities of Azerbaijan
Sur   1. One of the main cities of Lebanon; 2. One of the main cities of Oman
Surabaya   Admin capital of Jawa Timur, a province of Indonesia

Suva Capital of Fiji
Svalbard and Jan Mayen Island A territory of Norway
Sverdlovsk A region (oblast) of Russia
Swakopmund One of the main cities of Namibia
Sydney Admin capital of New South Wales, a territory of Australia
Syktyvkar Admin capital of Komi, a republic of Russia
Szczecin (Steltin) One of the main cities of Poland
Szeged One of the main cities of Hungary
Ta'izz One of the main cities of Yemen
Tabasco A state of Mexico, its admin capital is Villahermosa
Tabriz One of the main cities of Iran
Tabuk One of the main cities of Saudi Arabia
Táchira A state of Venezuela, its admin capital is San Cristóbal
Taegu One of the main cities of Korea, Rep of (South)
Taichung One of the main cities of Taiwan
Taimyr An autonomous area of Russia
Tainan One of the main cities of Taiwan
Taipei Capital of Taiwan
Taiyuan Admin capital of Shanxi, a municipal province of China
Takoradi One of the main cities of Ghana
Talinn Capital of Estonia
Tamale One of the main cities of Ghana
Tamaulipas A state of Mexico, its admin capital is Cuidad Victoria
Tambov A region (oblast) of Russia
Tamil Nadu A state of India, its admin capital is Madras
Tanga One of the main cities of Tanzania
Tanjungkarang Admin capital of Lampung, a province of Indonesia
Taraba A state of Nigeria, its admin capital is Jalingo
Tarabulus One of the main cities of Lebanon
Tarawa Capital of Kiribati
Tarbes Admin capital of Haute-Pyrénées, a region of Midi-Pyrénées, a
    department of France
Tarn A department of Midi-Pyrénées, a region of France, its admin
    capital is Albi
Tarn-et-Garonne A department of Midi-Pyrénées, a region of France,
    its admin capital is Montauban
Tartu One of the main cities of Estonia
Tashauz One of the main cities of Turkmenistan
Tashkent Capital of Uzbekistan
Tasmania A territory of Australia, its admin capital is Hobart
Tatarstan A republic of Russia, its admin capital is Kazan
Taunggyi Admin capital of Shan, a state of Myanmar (Burma)
Tbilisi Capital of Georgia
Tegucigalpa Capital of Honduras

Tehran   Capital of Iran
Tel Aviv   Capital of Israel
Tela   One of the main cities of Honduras
Tepic   Admin capital of Nayarit, a state of Mexico
Terengganu   A state of Malaysia, its admin capital is Kuala Terengganu
Teresina   Admin capital of Piauí, a state of Brazil
Territoire de Belfort   A department of Franche-Comté, a region of France, its admin capital is Belfort
The Basque country   A Spanish autonomous community (region), its admin capital is Vitoria
The Kermadec Group   One of the islands of New Zealand
The Three Kings   One of the islands of New Zealand
The Valley   Capital of Anguilla
Thies   One of the main cities of Senegal
Thimphu   Capital of Bhutan
Thurgau   A canton of Switzerland, its admin capital is Frauenfeld
Thuringia (Thüringen)   A Land of Germany, its admin capital is Erfurt
Tianjin   One of the main cities of China
Tianjin (Tientsin)   A municipal province of China, its admin capital is of the same name
Ticino   A canton of Switzerland, its admin capital is Bellinzona
Tierra del Fuego   A province of Argentina; its admin capital is Ushuaia
Tighina   Admin capital of Trannsdniestria, an autonomous republic of Moldova
Timbuktu   One of the main cities of Mali
Timisoara   One of the main cities of Romania
Tipperary   A county of the Republic of Ireland, its admin capital is Clonmel
Tirana   Capital of Albania
Tirol   A province of Austria, its admin capital is Innsbruck
Tizi Ouzou   One of the main cities of Algeria
Tlaxcala   A state of Mexico, its admin capital is of the same name
Tlemcen   One of the main cities of Algeria
Toamasina   One of the main cities of Madagascar
Tocantins   A state of Brazil, its admin capital is Palmas
Tokyo   Capital of Japan
Toledo   Admin capital of Castilla-La Mancha, a Spanish autonomous community (region)
Toluca de Lerdo   Admin capital of México, a state of Mexico
Tomsk   A region (oblast) of Russia
Toronto   Admin capital of Ontario, a province of Canada
Tórshavn   Capital of Denmark   Færøe Islands

Toulon   Admin capital of Var, a region of Provence-Alpes-Côte d'Azur, a department of France

Toulouse   Admin capital of Haute-Garonne, a region of Midi-Pyrénées, a department of France

Tours   Admin capital of Indre-et-Loire, a region of Centre-Val de Loire, a department of France

Tours   Admin capital of Saôane-et-Loire, a region of Bourgogne, a department of France

Tralee   Admin capital of Kerry, a county of the Republic of Ireland

Trannsdniestria   An autonomous republic of Moldova, its admin capital is Tighina

Trentino-Alto Adige   A region of Italy, its admin capital is Bolanzon-Bozen and Trento

Trieste   Admin capital of Friuli-Venzia Guilia, a region of Italy

Trim   Admin capital of Meath, a county of the Republic of Ireland

Trincomalee   One of the main cities of Sri Lanka

Tripoli   Capital of Libya

Tripura   A state of India, its admin capital is Agartala

Trivandrum   Admin capital of Kerala, a state of India

Troyes   Admin capital of Aube, a region of Champagne-Ardennes, a department of France

Trujillo   1. One of the main cities of Peru; 2. A state of Venezuela, its admin capital is Trujillo

Tucumán   A province of Argentina; its admin capital is San Miguel de Tucumán

Tucupita   Admin capital of Delta Amacuro, a state of Venezuela

Tula   A region (oblast) of Russia

Tullamore   Admin capital of Offaly, a county of the Republic of Ireland

Tulle   Admin capital of Corrèze, a region of Limousin, a department of France

Tunis   Capital of Tunisia

Turin   Admin capital of Piemonte, a region of Italy

Tuscany   A region of Italy, its admin capital is Florence

Tuxtla Gutiérrez   Admin capital of Chiapas, a state of Mexico

Tuzla   One of the main cities of Bosnia-Hercegovina

Tver   A region (oblast) of Russia

Tyumen   A region (oblast) of Russia

Tyva (formerly Tuva)   A republic of Russia, its admin capital is Kyzyl-Orda

Udmurtia   A republic of Russia, its admin capital is Izhevsk

Ufa   Admin capital of Bashkortostan, a republic of Russia

Ujung Padang   Admin capital of Sulawesi Seletan, a province of Indonesia

Ulan Bator   Capital of Mongolia

Ulan-Ude   Admin capital of Buryatia, a republic of Russia
Ulster   A province of the Republic of Ireland
Ulundi   Admin capital of KwaZulu/Natal, a province of South Africa
Ulyanovsk   A region (oblast) of Russia
Umbria   A region of Italy, its admin capital is Perugia
Umm al-Qaiwan   An emirate of United Arab Emirates, its admin capital is of the same name
Umuahia   Admin capital of Abia, a state of Nigeria
Upper Austria   A province of Austria, its admin capital is Linz
Uppsala   One of the main cities of Sweden
Uri   A canton of Switzerland, its admin capital is Altdorf
Ürümqi   Admin capital of Xinjiang Uygur (Sinkiang), an autonomous region of China
Ushuaia   Admin capital of Tierra del Fuego, a province of Argentina
Ust-Orda-Buryat   An autonomous area of Russia
Uttar Pradesh   A state of India, its admin capital is Lucknow
Uyo   Admin capital of Akwa Ibom, a state of Nigeria
Vacoas-Phoenix   One of the main cities of Mauritius
Vaduz   Capital of Liechtenstein
Val d'Oise   A department of Île-de-France, a region of France, its admin capital is Pontoise
Valais   A canton of Switzerland, its admin capital is Sion
Val-de-Marne   A department of Île-de-France, a region of France, its admin capital is Créteil
Valence   Admin capital of Drôme, a region of Rhône-Alpes, a department of France
Valencia   1. A Spanish autonomous community (region), its admin capital is of the same name; 2. Admin capital of Carabobo, a state of Venezuela
Valladolid   Admin capital of Castill-Leon, a Spanish autonomous community (region)
Valle d'Aosta   A region of Italy, its admin capital is Aosta
Vallee du Bandama   A region of Côte d'Ivoire
Valletta   Capital of Malta
Valparaíso   One of the main cities of Chile
Vancouver   One of the main cities of Canada
Vannes   Admin capital of Morbihan, a region of Bretagne, a department of France
Var   A department of Provence-Alpes-Côte d'Azur, a region of France, its admin capital is Toulon
Varna   One of the main cities of Bulgaria
Vatican City   Capital of Vatican City State
Vaucluse   A department of Provence-Alpes-Côte d'Azur, a region of France, its admin capital is Avignon

Vaud   A canton of Switzerland, its admin capital is Lausanna

Vendée   A department of Pays de la Loire, a region of France, its admin capital is La Roche-sur-Yon

Venetia   A region of Italy, its admin capital is Venice

Venice   Admin capital of Venetia, a region of Italy

Ventspils   One of the main cities of Latvia

Veracruz   A state of Mexico, its admin capital is Jalapa Enríquez

Versailles   Admin capital of Yvelines, a region of Île-de-France, a department of France

Vesoul   Admin capital of Haute-Saône, a region of Franche-Comté, a department of France

Victoria   1. A territory of Australia, its admin capital is Melbourne; 2. Admin capital of British Columbia, a province of Canada; 3. Capital of Seychelles

Victoria de Durango   Admin capital of Durango, a state of Mexico

Viedma   Admin capital of Rio Negro, a province of Argentina

Vienna   A province of Austria, its admin capital – and the capital of the country – is of the same name

Vienne   A department of Poitou-Charentes, a region of France, its admin capital is Poitiers

Vientiane   Capital of Laos

Villahermosa   Admin capital of Tabasco, a state of Mexico

Vilnius   Capital of Lithuania

Vitória   Admin capital of Espirito Santo, a state of Brazil

Vitoria   Admin capital of The Basque Country, a Spanish autonomous community (region)

Vitsyebsk   One of the main cities of Belarus

Vladikavkaz   Admin capital of North Ossetia (Alania), a republic of Russia

Vladimir   A region (oblast) of Russia

Volgograd   A region (oblast) of Russia

Vologda   A region (oblast) of Russia

Vorarlberg   A province of Austria, its admin capital is Bregenz

Voronezh   A region (oblast) of Russia

Vosges   A department of Lorraine, a region of France, its admin capital is Épinal

Wallis and Futuna Islands   An overseas territory of France, its admin capital is Mata-Utu

Wallonia   A region of Belgium

Walloon Brabant   A province of Belgium, its admin capital is Wavre

Walvis Bay   One of the main cities of Namibia

Warsaw   Capital of Poland

Waterford   A county of the Republic of Ireland, its admin capital is of the same name

Wavre   Admin capital of East Flanders, a province of Belgium
Wellington   Capital of New Zealand
West Bengal   A state of India, its admin capital is Calcutta
West Flanders   A province of Belgium, its admin capital is Bruges
Western Australia   A territory of Australia, its admin capital is Perth
Western Cape   A province of South Africa, its admin capital is Cape Town
Westmeath   A county of the Republic of Ireland, its admin capital is Millingar
Wewak   One of the main cities of Papua New Guinea
Wexford   A county of the Republic of Ireland, its admin capital is of the same name
Whitehorse   Admin capital of Yukon Territory, a province of Canada
Wicklow   A county of the Republic of Ireland, its admin capital is of the same name
Wiesbaden   Admin capital of Hesse, a Land of Germany
Willemstad   Admin capital of Aruba, an overseas territory of the Netherlands
Windhoek   Capital of Namibia
Winnipeg   Admin capital of Manitoba, a province of Canada
Worodougou   A region of Côte d'Ivoire
Wroclaw (Breslau)   One of the main cities of Poland
Wuhan   Admin capital of Hubei, an autonomous region of China
Wuhan   One of the main cities of China
Wuxi   One of the main cities of China
Xian   Admin capital of Shaanxi, an autonomous region of China
Xining   Admin capital of Qinghai, an autonomous region of China
Xinjiang Uygur (Sinkiang)   An autonomous region of China, its admin capital is Ürümqi
Xizang (Tibet)   A municipal province of China, its admin capital is Lhasa
Yakutsk   Admin capital of Sakha (formerly Yakutia), a republic of Russia
Yamal-Nenets   An autonomous area of Russia
Yamoussoukro   Capital of Côte d'Ivoire
Yangon (Rangoon)   Capital of Myanmar (Burma)
Yantai   One of the main cities of China
Yaoundé   Capital of Cameroon
Yaracuy   A state of Venezuela, its admin capital is San Felipe
Yaroslavl   A region (oblast) of Russia
Yellowknife   Admin capital of Northwest Territories, a province of Canada
Yenagoa   Admin capital of Bayelsa, a state of Nigeria
Yinchuan   Admin capital of Ningxia Hui, an autonomous region of China

Yobe   A state of Nigeria, its admin capital is Damaturu

Yogyakarta   A province of Indonesia, its admin capital is of the same name

Yokohama   One of the main cities of Japan

Yola   Admin capital of Adamawa, a state of Nigeria

Yonne   A department of Bourgogne, a region of France, its admin capital is Auxerre

Yoshkar-Ola   Admin capital of Mari-El, a republic of Russia

Yucatán   A state of Mexico, its admin capital is Mérida

Yukon Territory   A province of Canada, its admin capital is Whitehorse

Yunnan   An autonomous region of China, its admin capital is Kunming

Yvelines   A department of Île-de-France, a region of France, its admin capital is Versailles

Zacatecas   A state of Mexico, its admin capital is of the same name

Zagreb   Capital of Croatia

Zamfara   A state of Nigeria, its admin capital is Gusau

Zanzan   A region of Côte d'Ivoire

Zaozhuang   One of the main cities of China

Zaragoza   Admin capital of Aragon, a Spanish autonomous community (region)

Zenica   One of the main cities of Bosnia-Hercegovina

Zhejiang   An autonomous region of China, its admin capital is Hangzhou

Zhengzhou   Admin capital of Henan, an autonomous region of China

Ziguinchor   One of the main cities of Senegal

Zomba   One of the main cities of Malawi

Zug   A canton of Switzerland, its admin capital is of the same name

Zulia   A state of Venezuela, its admin capital is Maracaibo

Zürich   A canton of Switzerland, its admin capital is of the same name

Largest islands

Name	Area (sq mi / km)		Location	Status
Greenland	840,000	2,176,166	Arctic Ocean	Internally self-governed part of kingdom of Denmark
New Guinea	306,000	792,746	western Pacific	Indonesia and Papua New Guinea
Borneo	280,100	725,545	Indian Ocean	Indonesia, Malaysia and Brunei
Madagascar	226,658	587,196	Indian Ocean	republic
Baffin Island	195,928	507,585	Arctic Ocean	Nunavut Territory, Canada
Sumatra (Sumatera)	165,000	427,461	Indian Ocean	Indonesia
Honshu	87,805	227,474	NW Pacific	Japan
Great Britain	84,186	218,098	N Atlantic	UK
Victoria Island	83,897	217,349	Arctic Ocean	Northwest Territories, Canada
Ellesmere Island	75,767	196,287	Arctic Ocean	Northwest Territories, Canada
Celebes (Sulawesi)	69,000	178,756	Indian Ocean	Indonesia
South Island, NZ	58,305	151,049	SW Pacific	NZ
Java (Jawa)	48,900	126,683	Indian Ocean	Indonesia
Cuba	44,218	114,554	Caribbean Sea	Republic
North Island, NZ	44,035	114,080	SW Pacific	NZ
Newfoundland	42,030	108,886	NW Atlantic	Canada
Luzon	40,880	105,906	western Pacific	Philippines
Iceland	39,770	103,031	N Atlantic	Republic
Mindanao	36,775	95,272	western Pacific	Philippines
Ireland	31,839	82,484	N Atlantic	Rep Ireland and Northern Ireland
Hokkaido	30,077	77,920	NW Pacific	Japan
Hispaniola	29,418	76,212	Caribbean Sea	Dominican Rep and Haiti
Sakhalin	28,597	74,085	NW Pacific	Russia
Sri Lanka	25,332	65,627	Indian Ocean	Republic
Tasmania	24,868	64,424	SW Pacific	Australia

Peninsulas

A narrow strip of land projecting into a sea or lake from the mainland.

Name	Area miles²	Area km²
Arabia	1,250,000	3,250,000
Southern India	800,000	2,072,000
Alaska	580,000	1,500,000
Labrador	500,000	1,300,000
Scandinavia	309,000	800,300
Iberian Peninsula	225,500	584,000

Deserts

	Name	Territories	Area (miles²)	(km²)
1	Sahara	Algeria, Chad, Libya, Mali, Mauritania, Niger, Sudan, Tunisia, Egypt, Morocco – embraces the Libyan and Nubian Deserts	3,250,000	8,400,000
2	Australian	Australia – embraces the Great Sandy, Great Victoria, Simpson, Gibson and Sturt Deserts	600,000	1,550,000
3	Arabian	Southern Arabia, Saudi Arabia, Yemen. Includes the Ar Rab'al Khali or Empty Quarter and An Nafud Deserts	500,000	1,300,000
4	Gobi	Mongolia and China (Inner Mongolia)	400,000	1,040,000
5	Kalahari	Botswana	200,000	520,000
6	Takla Makan	Sinkiang, China	125,000	320,000
7	Sonoran	Arizona and California, USA and Mexico	120,000	310,000
8	Namib	In south west Africa (Namibia)	120,000	310,000
9	Kara Kum	Turkmenistan, USSR	105,000	270,000
10	Thar	North-western India and Pakistan	100,000	260,000
11	Somali	Somalia	100,000	260,000
12	Atacama	Northern Chile	70,000	180,000
13	Kyzyl Kum	Uzbekistan–Kazakhstan, USSR	70,000	180,000
14	Dasht-e-Lut	Eastern Iran (sometimes called Iranian Desert)	20,000	52,000
15	Mojave	Southern California, USA	13,500	35,000
16	Desierto de Sechura	North-west Peru	10,000	26,000

Countries with the shortest coastlines

Country	miles	km
Monaco	3.5	5.6
Nauru	12	19
Bosnia	13	20
Jordan	16	25
Slovenia	19	30

Canada, including its islands has the longest coastline at 244,800km, 152,100 miles.

Mountains

A landmass is considered to be a mountain when it is approaches 1,000ft (300 meters) high. Most of the earth's mountains form part of ranges or at the very least loosely connected chains, which might be considered to be ranges. Individual mountains which are not part of a range are nearly always related to a volcano.

Types of mountain
There are four basic types of mountain, depending on the method of formation:

(a) Fold   Formed when two of the earth's plates crashed into each other, forcing the sea bed between them up into folds. The mountains are usually old and high, and are distinguished by jagged peaks, often cone-shaped. Examples: Alps in Europe; Andes in South America; Himalayas in Asia.

(b) Fault-block   Formed at fault-lines in the earth's crust when two plates of earth shifted, the wedge of rock between them was forced up between the faults. The resulting mountains are wedge-shaped. (If the wedge of rock between the fault lines was forced downwards, it would have created a steep-sided valley.) Examples: Massif Central, France; Sierra Nevada, USA; mountains in East Africa.

(c) Dome   Formed when magma (molten rock) deep in the earth rose to the surface but was unable to break through the earth's crust or find a crack to seep through. The resulting pressure under the earth's surface forced the rock upwards into a huge bulging shape. These mountains are rounded, humped, dome-shaped hills with gentle slopes. Examples: Black Hills, USA; Lake District, England.

(d) Volcano Formed when red-hot magma erupted through a crack in the earth's surface. The magma solidified in the air into lava; lava rock builds up in layers over time to form a mountain. Characterised by cone shapes with very steep but sloping sides. Examples: Aconcagua, Argentina; Etna, Italy; Mauna Loa, Hawaii.

Highest mountain

Everest is the highest mountain in the world. It was named after Sir George Everest (*pron* Eve-Rest; 1790–1866), who first measured its height. Up to then it was called Peak XV, although its local names are Chumolungma (Tibetan = Mother Goddess of the World) and Sagarmatha (Nepali = Goddess of the Sky). Everest is still growing, by about 13 mm a year, as the earth's plates continue to move underneath it, pushing the mountain folds even higher. Mountaineers aiming to climb Everest today have to climb about 65 centimeters higher than Tensing Norgay and Edmund Hillary, who first reached the peak on 29 May, 1953.

The seven summits – the highest mountains of each continent

Mountain	Continent	Location	Height		First ascent
			ft	metres	
1 Everest	Asia	Nepal/Tibet	29,035	8,850	1953
2 Aconcagua	South America	Argentina	22,841	6,962	1897
3 Mount McKinley	North America	Alaska Range	20,320	6,194	1913
4 Kilima-Njaro	Africa	Tanzania	19,563	5,963	1889
5 El'brus	Europe	Russia	18,481	5,633	1874
6 Puncak Jaya (Carstensz Pyramid)	Australia/ Oceania	Irian Jaya	16,502	5,030	1862
7 Vinson Massif	Antarctica	Sentinel Range, Ellsworth Mts	16,066	4,897	1966

Longest mountain ranges

The Andes

The longest mountain range in the world at more than 4,500 miles (7,250 km), running the length of South America through Venezuela, Colombia, Ecuador, Peru, Chile, Bolivia and Argentina. The range is primarily a 138–165 million years old fold, formed when the Pacific Ocean plate dived under South America. Like many large mountain ranges, it is so high that it affects climate: the Andes blocks winds and rain so the west side is dusty desert. The words Sierra and Cordillera, both meaning mountain range, are often applied to parts of the Andes, which also contains a chain of extinct volcanoes.

The Rocky Mountains
At 3,000 miles (4,800 km), the Rockies form the second longest range. They contain over 100 individual ranges; like the Andes, they are fold mountains, formed some 80 million years ago.

The Himalayas
Includes the Himalaya, Karakorum and Hindu Kush ranges, creating the third longest range, and also the world's highest range, with all 10 of the world's top 10 peaks. Again created by a fold in the earth, the Himalayas are 30–50 million years old, running through Tibet (China), Nepal, India, Bhutan, Pakistan and Afghanistan. The range is so high that it prevents the summer monsoon crossing north to Tibet, so north of the Himalayas is a dry desert. However, millions of years ago the mountains were under ocean, and seashells can still be found there.

The Alps
At 750 miles (1,200 km) the Alps are not particularly long, nor are they very old. Fold mountains, they were formed only about 15 million years ago, running through France, Italy, Switzerland, Austria and Germany. They contain a 26-mile (42 km) long glacier, the Aletsch Glacier, in Switzerland.

Main mountain ranges, with subsidiary ranges

Africa

Aberdare Range	Kenya
Atlas Mountains	Algeria, Morocco
Cherangany Hills	Kenya
Drakensberg	Lesotho, South Africa
Central Range	
Marloti Mountains	
Ethiopian Highlands	Ethiopia
Ahmar Mountains	
Mitumba Mountains	Democratic Republic of the Congo
Ruwenzori Range	Uganda
('Mountains of the	
Moon')	
Tibesti Mountains	Chad
Virunga Mountains	Democratic Republic of the Congo, Rwanda, Uganda

North America

Alaska Range	Alaska
Aleutian Range	Alaska
Appalachian Mountains	
White Mountains	New Hampshire
Green Mountains	
Vermont	
Adirondack Mountains	New York
Catskills	New York
Allegheny Mountains	Pennsylvania
Blue Ridge Mountains	North Carolina and Virginia
Basin Ranges	
Schell Creek Range	Nevada
Snake Range	Nevada
Toiyabe Range	Nevada
White Mountains	California
Black Hills	South Dakota
Boston Mountains	Arkansas
Brooks Range	Alaska
Cascade Range/	British Columbia, Canada, south to
Cascade Mountains	California
Okanogan Range	Washington
Coast Mountains	
Wrangell Mountains	Alaska
St Elias Mountains	Alaska/British Columbia
Coast Mountains	British Columbia
Diablo Range	California
San Gabriel Mountains	California to Riverside County, California
Santa Monica Mountains	California
Santa Susana Mountains	California
Ouachita Mountains	Oklahoma/Arkansas
Laurentides	Quebec
Long Range Mountains	Newfoundland, Canada
Ozark Mountains	Arkansas/Missouri/Oklahoma/ Kansas
Pacific Chain	
Sierra Nevada	California
Rocky Mountains	western United States and Canada (over 100 individual ranges)

Absaroka Range	Montana, Wyoming
Bear River Range	Utah, Wyoming
Beaverhead Mountains	Montana, Idaho
Bighorn Mountains	Wyoming
Bitteroot Range	Montana and Idaho
Cariboo Mountains	British Columbia
Columbia Mountains	British Columbia
Crazy Mountains	Montana
Elkhorn Mountains	Montana
Granite Mountains	Wyoming
Green Mountains	Wyoming
Flathead Range	Montana
Franklin Mountains	Texas
Front Range of the Rockies	Colorado
Kettle River Range	Washington
Laramie Mountains	Wyoming
Lemhi Range	Idaho
Lewis Range	Montana
Livingston Range	Montana
John Long Mountains	Montana
MacDonald Range	British Columbia
Madison Range	Montana
Manzana Mountains	New Mexico
Monashee Mountains	British Columbia
Organ Mountains	New Mexico
Ortiz Mountains	New Mexico
Owl Creek Mountains	Wyoming
Pryor Mountains	Montana
Percell Mountains	Montana
Pioneer Mountains	Montana
Purcell Mountains	British Columbia
Salmon River Mountains	Idaho
Sacramento Mountains	New Mexico
Salish Mountains	Montana
Salmon River Mountains	Idaho
Sangre de Christo Mountains	Colorado
San Juan Mountains	Colorado
Sawatch Range	Colorado

Selkirk Mountains	British Columbia
Shoshone Range	Idaho
Swan Range	Montana
Teton Range	Wyoming
Tobacco Root Mountains	Montana
Uinta Mountains	Utah
Wasatch Range	Utah
Wind River Range	Wyoming
Whitefish Range	Montana
Wolf Mountains	Montana

Sierra Madre	Mexico
Sierra Madre Occidental	
Sierra Madre Oriental	
White Mountains	Arizona

Central America
Guatemala/Honduras
  Mountains

South America
Andes

Cordillera de Merida	Venezuela
Cordillera Occidental	Colombia
Cordillera Oriental	Colombia
Cordillera Central	Peru
Cordillera Occidental	Peru
Cordillera Oriental	Peru
Cordillera Real	Bolivia
Guiana Highlands	Venezuela, Guyana, Brazil
Pakaraima Mountains	
Serra da Manitqueira	Brazil
Serra do Mar	Brazil

Antarctica
Ellsworth Mountains
  Sentinel Range
Queen Elizabeth Range
Pensicola Mountains
Prince Charles Mountains
Shackleton Range
Transantarctic Mountains

Queen Maud Mountains
Queen Alexandra Range

Asia

Altai Mountains	Mongolia, Russia, China
Altun Shan	China
Anti-Lebanon	Lebanon, Syria
Arabian Mountains	Saudi Arabia, Yemen
Arakan Yoma	Myanmar (Burma)
Chin Hills	
Caucasus	Russia, Georgia, Azerbaijan, Armenia
Eastern Ghats	India
Elburz Mountains	Iran
Hangayn Mountains	Mongolia
Himalayas	Tibet (China), Nepal, India, Bhutan, Pakistan and Afghanistan
Great Himalaya	
Hindu Kush	
Karakoram	
Pamir	
Japanese Alps	
Akashi Mountains	
Hida Mountains	
Kiso Mountains	
Khingan Mountains	China, Mongolia
Kunlun Shan	China
Sayan Mountains	Russia
Sierra Madre	Philippines
Stanovoi Range	Russia
Tangula Shan	China
Toros (Taurus) Mountains	Turkey
Tien Shan	China, Kazakhstan, Kyrgyzstan
Ural Mountains	Russia
Western Ghats	India
Zagros Mountains	Iran

Australasia

Barisan Range	Sumatra
Crocker Range	Borneo
Flinders Ranges	South Australia

Great Dividing Range	Queensland/New South Wales/ Victoria, Australia
Blue Mountains	New South Wales
Snowy Mountains	New South Wales
Victorian Alps	Victoria
Kairanawa Mountains	New Zealand
King Leopold Ranges	Western Australia
MacDonnell Ranges	central Australia
New Guinea Highlands	Papua New Guinea
Bismarck Range	
Pegunungan Maoke	Irian Jaya, Papua New Guinea
Owen Stanley Range	Papua New Guinea
Southern Alps	New Zealand
Hammersley Range	Western Australia

Europe

Alps	Austria, Germany, Italy, Switzerland, France, Slovenia
Bavarian Alps	
Cottian Alps	
Dolomites	
Hohe Tauern	
Julian Alps	
Jura Mountains	
Lepontine Alps	
Maritime Alps	
Pennine Alps	
Rhaetian Alps	
Apennines	Italy
Balkan Mountains	Bulgaria
Cambrian Mountains	Wales, UK
Cantabrian Mountains	Spain
Carpathian Mountains	Slovakia, Poland, Romania
Tatra Mountains	
Beskidy Mountains	
Transylvanian Alps	
Dinaric Alps	Croatia, Bosnia-Herzegovina
Grampians	Scotland, UK
Luberon	France
Alpilles	

Northwest Highlands	Scotland, UK
Ore Mountains (Erzgebirge)	Germany, Czech Republic
Pennines	England, UK
Pindus Mountains	Greece
Pyrenees	France, Spain
Rhodope Mountains	Bulgaria, Greece
Scandinavian Mountains	Norway, Sweden
Sierra Nevada	Spain
Sistema Central	Spain
Sudeten Mountains	Germany, Poland, Czech Republic
Karkonosze	Poland
Urals	Russia
Vosges	France
Wicklow Mountains	Ireland

	Mountain	ft	m	Range	First ascent
1	Chumolungma (Everest)	29,028	8,848	Himalaya	29 May 1953
2	Qogir K 2 (Godwin-Austen)	28,250	8,610	Karakoram	31 July 1954
3	Kangchenjunga I	28,208	8,597	Himalaya	25 May 1955
4	Lhotse I	27,923	8,511	Himalaya	18 May 1956
5	Makalu I	27,824	8,481	Himalaya	15 May 1955
6	Dhaulagiri I	26,795	8,167	Himalaya	13 May 1960
7	Manaslu I (Kutang I)	26,760	8,156	Himalaya	9 May 1956
8	Cho Uyo	26,750	8,153	Himalaya	19 October 1954
9	Nanga Parbat (Diamir)	26,660	8,125	Himalaya	3 July 1953
10	Annapurna I	26,546	8,091	Himalaya	3 June 1950
11	Gasherbrum I (Hidden Peak)	26,470	8,068	Karakoram	5 July 1958
12	Broad Peak I	26,400	8,047	Karakoram	9 June 1957
13	Gasherbrum II	26,360	8,034	Karakoram	7 July 1956
14	Shisha Pangma (Gosainthan)	26,291	8,013	Himalaya	2 May 1964
15	Gasherbrum III	26,090	7,952	Karakoram	11 August 1975
16	Annapurna II	26,041	7,937	Himalaya	17 May 1960
17	Gasherbrum IV	26,000	7,924	Karakoram	6 August 1958
18	Gyachung Kang	25,990	7,921	Himalaya	10 April 1964
19	Kangbachen	25,925	7,902	Himalaya	26 May 1974
20	Disteghil Sar I	25,868	7,884	Karakoram	9 June 1960
21	Himal Chuli	25,801	7,864	Himalaya	24 May 1960
22	Khinyang Chhish	25,762	7,852	Karakoram	26 August 1971
23	Nuptse	25,762	7,841	Himalaya	16 May 1961

24	Peak 29 (Manaslu II)	25,705	7,835	Himalaya	October 1970
25	Masherbrum East	25,660	7,821	Karakoram	6 July 1960
26	Nanda Devi	25,645	7,816	Himalaya	29 August 1936
27	Chomo Lönzo	25,640	7,815	Himalaya	30 October 1954
28	Ngojumba Ri (Cho Uyo II)	25,610	7,805	Himalaya	5 May 1965
29	Rakaposhi	25,550	7,788	Karakoram	25 June 1958
30	Batura Muztagh I (Hunza Kunji I)	25,542	7,785	Karakoram	Unclimbed
31	Zemu Peak	25,526	7,780	Himalaya	Unclimbed
32	Kanjut Sar	25,460	7,760	Karakoram	19 July 1959
33	Kamet	25,447	7,756	Himalaya	21 June 1931
34	Namcha Barwa	25,445	7,755	Himalaya	Unclimbed
35	Dhaulagiri II	25,429	7,751	Himalaya	18 May 1971
36	Saltori Kangri I	25,400	7,741	Karakoram	24 July 1962
37	Batura Muztagh II (Hunza Kunji II)	25,361	7,730	Karakoram	Unclimbed
38	Gurla Manhata	25,355	7,728	Himalaya	Unclimbed
39	Ulugh Muztagh	25,340	7,725	Kunlun Shan	Unclimbed
40	Qungar II	25,326	7,719	Pamir	Unclimbed
41	Dhaulagiri III	25,318	7,715	Himalaya	23 October 1973
42	Jannu	25,294	7,709	Himalaya	27 April 1962
43	Tirich Mir	25,282	7,706	Hindu Kush	21 July 1950
44	Saltoro Kangri II	25,280	7,705	Karakoram	Unclimbed
45	Disteghil Sar E	25,262	7,710		Unclimbed
46	Saser Kangri I	25,170	7,672	Karakoram	Unclimbed
47	Chogolisa II	25,164	7,669	Karakoram	Unclimbed
48	Phola Gangchhen	25,135	7,661	Himalaya	Unclimbed
49	Dhaulagiri IV	25,134	7,661	Himalaya	9 May 1975
50	Shahkang Sham	25,131	7,660		Unclimbed
51	Makalu II (Kangshungste)	25,120	7,656	Himalaya	22 October 1954
52	Chogolisa I ('Bride Peak')	25,110	7,654	Karakoram	4 August 1958
53	Trivor	25,098	7,650	Karakoram	17 August 1960
54	Ngojumba Ri II	25,085	7,646		Unclimbed
55	Khinyang Chhish S	25,000	7,620		Unclimbed
56	Shispare	21,997	7,619	Karakoram	21 July 1974
57	Dhaulagiri V	24,993	7,618	Hi	1 May 1975
58	Qungar I	24,918	7,595	Pamir	16 August 1956
59	Peak 38 (Lhotse II)	24,898	7,589	Himalaya	Unclimbed
60	Minya Konka	24,891	7,587	Sikiang, China	28 October 1932
61	Annapurna III	24,787	7,555	Himalaya	6 May 1961
62	Khula Kangri II	24,784	7,554	Himalaya	Unclimbed
63	Changtse (North Peak)	24,780	7,552	Himalaya	Unclimbed
64	Huztagh Ata	24,757	7,546		Unclimbed
65	Skyang Kangri	24,751	7,544	Karakoram	Unclimbed
66	Khula Kangri II	24,740	7,541	Himalaya	Unclimbed

67	Khula Kangri III	24,710	7,532	Himalaya	Unclimbed
68	Yalung Peak	24,710	7,532		Unclimbed
69	Yushkin Gardas Sar	24,705	7,530		Unclimbed
70	Manmstong Kangri	24,692	7,526	Karakoram	Unclimbed
71	Annapurna IV	24,688	7,525	Himalaya	30 May 1955
72	Khula Kangri IV	24,659	7,516	Himalaya	Unclimbed
73	Saser Kangri	24,649	7,513	Karakoram	Unclimbed

	South America	ft	m	Country
S01	Cerro Aconcagua	22,834	6,960	Argentina
S02	Ojos del Salado	22,598	6,888	Argentina-Chile
S03	Nevado de Pissis	22,241	6,779	Argentina-Chile
S04	Huascarán, South Peak	22,205	6,768	Peru
S05	Llullaillaco volcén	22,057	6,723	Argentina-Chile
S06	Mercedario	21,884	6,670	Argentina-Chile
S07	Huascarán N	21,834	6,655	Peru
S08	Yerupaja	21,758	6,632	Peru
S09	Nevados des Tres Crucés C	21,720	6,620	Argentina-Chile
S10	Coropuna	21,705	6,616	Peru
S11	Nevado incahuasi	21,657	6,601	Argentina-Chile
S12	Tupungato	21,490	6,550	Argentina-Chile
S13	Sajama	21,427	6,531	Bolivia
S14	Nevado González	21,326	6,500	Argentina
S15	Cerro del Nacimiento	21,302	6,493	Argentina
S16	Illimani	21,260	6,480	Bolivia
S17	Anto Falla	21,162	6,450	Argentina
S18	Ancohuma (Sorata N)	21,086	6,427	Bolivia
S19	Nevado Bonete	21,031	6,410	Argentina
S20	Cerro de Ramada	21,031	6,410	Argentina

	North America	ft	m	Country
N01	McKinley, South Peak	20,320	6,193	Alaska
N02	Logan	19,850	6,050	Canada
N03	Citlaltépetl or Orizaba	18,700	5,700	Mexico
N04	St Elias	18,008	5,489	Alaska-Canada
N05	Popocatépetl	17,887	5,451	Mexico
N06	Foraker	17,400	5,304	Alaska
N07	Lucania	17,150	5,227	Alaska
N08	King Peak	17,130	5,221	Alaska
N09	Iztaccihuatl	17,000	5,128	Mexico
N10	Steele	16,625	5,073	Alaska
N11	Bona	16,500	5,029	Alaska
N12	Blackburn	16,390	4,996	Alaska
N13	Sanford	16,237	4,949	Alaska

	Africa	ft	m	Location
B01	Kilima-Njaro	19,340	5,894	Tanganyika
B02	Mount Kenya	17,058	5,199	Kenya
B03	Mount Stanley	16,763	5,109	Congo-Uganda
B04	Duwoni or Mt Speke (Victorio Emanuele Peak)	16,042	4,889	Uganda
B05	Mount Baker (Edward Peak)	15,889	4,842	Uganda
B06	Mount Emin	15,797	4,814	Congo (Kinshasa)
B07	Mount Gessi (Iolanda Peak)	15,470	4,715	Uganda
B08	Mount Luigi di Savoia	15,179	4,626	Uganda
B09	Ras Dashan (Dejen)	15,158	4,620	Simien Mts, Ethiopia
B10	Humphreys Peak	15,021	4,578	Uganda

	Europe – Asia = The Caucasus range	ft	m
E01	El'brus, West Peak	18,481	5,633
E02	El'brus, East Peak	18,356	5,594
E03	Shkara	17,060	5,199
E04	Dych Tau	17,054	5,198
E05	Pik Shota Rustaveli	17,028	5,190
E06	Janga, West Peak	16,572	5,051
E07	Dzhangi Tau	16,565	5,049
E08	Kazbek	16,558	5,046
E09	Katuintau (Adish)	16,355	4,985
E10	Mishirgitau, West Peak	16,148	4,921
E11	Kunjum Mishikgi	16,011	4,880
E12	Gestola	15,940	4,858
E13	Tetnuld	15,938	4,857

	Highest European Alps	ft	m	Country	First ascent
L01	Mont Blanc	15,771	4,807.0	France	1786
L02	Monte Rosa	15,203	4,634.0	Switzerland	1855
L03	Dom	14,911	4,545.4	Switzerland	1858
L04	Lyskamm (Liskamm)	14,853	4,527.2	Swiss–Italian border	1861
L05	Weisshorn	14,780	4,505.5	Switzerland	1861
L06	Taschhorn	14,733	4,490.7	Switzerland	1862
L07	Matterhorn	14,683	4,475.5	Swiss–Italian border	1865
L08	La Dent Blanche	14,293	4,356.6	Switzerland	1862
L09	Nadelhorn	14,196	4,327.0	Switzerland	1858
L10	Le Grand Combin de Grafaneire	14,153	4,314.0	Switzerland	1859
L11	Lenzspitze	14,087	4,294.0	Switzerland	1871
L12	Finsteraarhorn	14,021	4,273.8	Switzerland	1829

MOUNTAINS

	Antarctica	ft	m	Location
T01	Vinson Massif	16,863	5,140	Sentinel range, Ellsworth Mts
T02	Mt Tyree	16,289	4,965	Sentinel range, Ellsworth Mts
T03	Mt Shinn	15,750	4,800	Sentinel range, Ellsworth Mts
T04	Mt Gardner	15,354	4,688	Sentinel range, Ellsworth Mts
T05	Mt Kirkpatrick	14,860	4,529	Queen Alexandra Range
T06	Mt Elizabeth	14,698	4,480	Queen Elizabeth Range
T07	Mt Markham	14,250	4,343	Queen Elizabeth Range
T08	Mt MacKellar	14,082	4,292	Queen Alexandra Range
T09	Mt Kaplan	13,960	4,255	Queen Maud Range
T10	Mt Sidley	13,850	4,221	Executive Committee Range
T11	Mt Ostenso	13,711	4,179	Sentinel range, Ellsworth Mts
T12	Mt Minto	13,648	4,160	Queen Elizabeth Range
T13	Mt Long Gables	13,622	4,152	Sentinel range, Ellsworth Mts
T14	Mt Miller	13,600	4,145	Queen Elizabeth Range
T15	Mt Falla	13,500	4,115	Queen Alexandra Range
T16	Mt Fridtjof Nansen	13,350	4,069	Queen Maud Range
T17	Mt Fisher	13,340	4,066	Queen Maud Range
T18	Mt Wade	13,330	4,063	Queen Maud Range
T19	Mt Lister	13,205	4,025	Royal Society Range
T20	Mt Huggins	12,870	3,923	Royal Society Range

	Oceania	ft	m	Location
U01	Ngga Pulu (formerly Mt Sakarno)	16,500	5,029	Irian Jaya (W New Guinea)
U02	Idenburg Peak	15,748	4,800	W Irian
U03	Mt Mohammed Yamin (Wilhelmina Top)	15,525	4,732	Irian Jaya (W New Guinea)
U04	Mt Trikora (Juliana Top)	15,420	4,700	Irian Jaya (W New Guinea)
U05	Mt Wilhem	15,400	4,694	NE New Guinea
U06	Mt Kabur	14,300	4,359	NE New Guinea
U07	Mt Herbert	14,000	4,267	NE New Guinea
U08	Mt Leonard Darwin	13,887	4,233	W Irian
U09	Mauna Kea	13,796	4,205	Hawaii, Hawaiian Is
U10	Mauna Loa	13,680	4,170	Hawaii, Hawaiian Is
U11	Mt Giluwe	13,660	4,164	Papua (SE New Guinea)
U12	Mt Bangeta	13,473	4,107	NE New Guinea
U13	Mt Kinabalu	13,455	4,101	Borneo
U14	Mt Victoria	13,363	4,073	Papua (SE New Guinea)
U15	Sneeuw Gebergte Peak	13,125	4,000	Irian Jaya (W New Guinea)
U16	Mt Albert Edward	13,100	3,993	Papua (SE New Guinea)
U17	Mokuaweoweo	13,018	3,968	Hawaii, Hawaiian Is
U18	Burgess Mt	13,000	3,962	NE New Guinea
U19	Lua Hohonu	12,805	3,903	Hawaii, Hawaiian Is
U20	Mt Auriga	12,728	3,878	NE New Guinea
U21	Mt Sirius	12,631	3,850	NE New Guinea

Mountain ranges

Range	Location	Length (mi / km)		Peak	Height (ft / m)	
Andes	western South America	4,500	7,200	Cerro Aconcagua	22,834	6,960
Rocky Mountains	western North America	3,000	4,800	Mt Elbert	14,436	4,400
Himalaya-Karakorum-Hindu Kush	southern central Asia	2,400	3,861	Mt Everest	29,078	8,863
Great Dividing Range	eastern Australia	2,250	3,620	Mt Kosciusko	7,316	2,230
Trans Antarctic Range	Antarctica	2,200	3,540	Mt Vinson	16,864	5,140
Brazilian Atlantic Coast Range	eastern Brazil	1,900	3,057	Pico de Bandeira	9,482	2,890
West Sumatran–Java Range	west Sumatra and Java	1,800	2,896	Mt Kerintji	12,484	3,805
Aleutian Range	Alaska and NW Pacific	1,600	2,574	Shishaldin	9,386	2,861
Tien Shan	Kyrgyzstan/China	1,400	2,252	Pik Pobedy	24,406	7,439
Central New Guinea Range	Irian Jaya/Papua New Guinea	1,250	2,011	Ngga Pulu	16,503	5,030
Altai Mountains	Russia/Mongolia	1,250	2,011	Gora Belukha	14,783	4,505
Ural Mountains	Russia	1,250	2,011	Gora Narodnaya	6,214	1,894
Kamchatka Mountains	eastern Russia	1,200	1,930	Klyuchevskaya Sopka	15,912	4,850
Atlas Mountains	north-west Africa	1,200	1,930	Jebel Toubkal	13,665	4,165
Verkhoyanskiy Mountains	Russia	1,000	1,609	Gora Mas Khaya	9,708	2,959
Western Ghats	India	1,000	1,609	Anai Madi	8,842	2,694
Sierra Madre Oriental	Mexico	950	1,528	Volcan Citlaltépetl (Pico de Orizaba)	18,406	5,610
Zagros Mountains	Iran	950	1,528	Mt Zard Kuh	14,918	4,547
Scandinavian Range	Norway/Sweden	950	1,528	Mt Galdhöpiggen	8,098	2,469
Semien Mountains	Ethiopia	900	1,448	Ras Dashan	15,157	4,620
Sierra Madre Occidental	Mexico	900	1,448	Nevado de Colima	13,993	4,265
Malagasy Range	Madagascar	850	1,367	Tsaratanana peak	9,436	2,876
Drakensberg	southern Africa	800	1,287	Mt Thabana Ntlenyana	11,425	3,482
Chersky Range	Russia	800	1,287	Gora Pobeda	10,325	3,147

Caucasus	Georgia/Russia/ Azerbaijan	750	1,206	Mt Elbrus	18,510	5,642
Alaska Range	Alaska, USA	700	1,126	Mt McKinley	20,320	6,194
Assam Burma Range	Assam (India)– W Burma	700	1,126	Hkakado Razi	19,296	5,881
lparCascade Range	NW USA/Canada	700	1,126	Mt Rainer	14,409	4,392
Central Borneo Range	Borneo (Indonesia)/ Malaysia	700	1,126	Mt Klnabalu	13,455	4,101
Apennines	Italy	700	1,126	Corno Grande	9,616	2,931
Appalchians	eastern USA	700	1,126	Mt Mitchell	6,683	2,037
Alps	central Europe	650	1,050	Mont Blanc	15,771	4,807
Elburz Mountains	Iran	560	900	Mt Damavand	18,386	5589
Allegheny Mountains	USA	500	800	Spruce Knob	4,862	1478
Pyrenees	France/Spain	270	434	Mt Aneto (Spain)	11,178	3398
Jura		225	360	Crêt de la Neige (France)	5,636	1713

Active volcanoes of the world

By height

Name	Location	Eruption dates	Height (ft / m)	
Ojos del Salado	Argentinean–Chilean Andes	1981	22,572	6,880
Volcan Llullaillaco	Argentinean–Chilean Andes	1877	22,057	6,723
Volcan Guallitri	Andes, Chile	1960, 1993	19,882	6,069
Lascar	Andes, Chile	1951	19,652	5,990
Cotopaxi	Andes, Ecuador	1940, 1975	19,347	5,897
Volcán Misti	Andes, Peru		19,167	5842
Tupungatito	Andes, Chile	1959, 1986	18,504	5,640
Lascar	Chilean Andes	2000	18,346	5,591
Popocatépetl	Altiplano de Mexico	1932, 1999, 2003	17,930	5,465
Nevado del Ruiz	Colombia	1845, 1985, 1991	17,457	5,321
Sangay	Andes, Ecuador	1946, 1998, 2002	17,159	5,230
Irruputuncu	Chile	1995	16,939	5,163
Cotacachi	Andes, Ecuador	1955	16,192	4,935
Klyuchevskaya sopta	Sredinnyy Khrebet (Kamchatka Peninsula), USSR	1962	15,913	4,850
Klyuchevskaya Sopka	Kamchatka Peninsula, Russia	2000–3	15,863	4,835
Guagua Pichincha	Andes, Ecuador	2001	15,696	4,784
Puracé	Andes, Colombia	1950, 1977	15,604	4,756
Shasta	California USA	1786	14,163	4,316

Wrangell	Alaska, USA	1907	14,163	4,316
Galeras	Colombia	2000	14,028	4,275
Tajumulco	Guatemala	Rumbles	13,812	4,210
Mauna Loa	Hawaii	1950, 1984, 1987, 2003	13,680	4,170
Cameroon Mt	Cameroon	1959, 2000	13,435	4,095
Tacama	Sierra Madre, Guatemala		13,333	4,064
Fuego	Sierra Madre, Guatemala	1973	12,582	3,835
Erebus	Ross Island, Antarctica	1998, 2001	12,448	3,784
Fuji	Honshu, Japan	1708	12,388	3,775
Santa Maria	Guatemala	2000	12,375	3,772
Rindjani	Lombok, Indonesia	1964	12,224	3,726
Pico de Tiede	Teneriffe		12,198	3,718
Tolbachik	USSR	1941	12,080	3,682
Semeru	Java, Indonesia	1963, 2003	12,060	3,676
Nyiragongo	Democratic Republic of Congo	1972, 2003–3	11,400	3,474
Koryakskaya	Kamchatka Peninsula, USSR	1957	11,339	3,456
Irasu	Cordillera Central, Costa Rica	1963	11,268	3,432
Chiriqui	Cadelia de Talamanca, Panama		11,253	3,430
Slamat	Java, Indonesia	1953	11,247	3,428
Mt Spurr	Alaska Range, USA	1953	11,070	3,374
Etna, Mount	Sicily	1169, 1669, 1993, 1996–9, 2000–3	11,053	3,368
Raung	Java	2000, 2002	10,932	3,322
Sheveluch	Kamchatka Peninsula, Russia	1997, 1999, 2000–1, 2003	10,771	3,283
Mt Etna	Sicily, Italy	1974	10,705	3,363
Llaima	Chile	1998, 2003	10,253	3,125
Tambora	Sumbawa, Indonesia		9,351	2,850
St Helens, Mount	Washington State, USA	1980, 1986, 1991, 1998	8,363	2,549
Beerenberg	Jan Mayen Island	1985	7,470	2,277
The Peak	Tristan de Cahuna, S Atlantic	1961	6,760	2,060
Mt Lamington	Papua New Guinea	1951	5,535	1,687
Pinatubo	Luzon, Philippines	1991, 1995, 2002	5,249	1,598
Hekla	Iceland	1981, 1991, 2000	4,892	1,491
La Soufrière	Basselerre Island, Guadaloupe		4,813	1,467
Mt Pelée	Martinique	1902	4,800	1,463
Hekla	Iceland	1948	4,747	1,447
Unzen, Mount	Kyushu, Japan	1792, 1991, 1996, 2000	4,462	1,360
Vesuvius	Bay of Naples, Italy	79[†], 1631, 1944, 1944	4,198	1,280

Kilauea	Hawaii, USA	1973, 1997, 2000–3	4,077	1,240
Soufrière	St Vincent	1902, 1979, 1997	3,865	1,178
Stromboli	Lipari Islands, Italy	1971, 1996, 1998, 2000, 2002–3	3,038	926
Soufrière Hills	Montserrat	1997–2003	3,001	914
Krakatau	Straits of Sunda, Indonesia	1883[†], 1995, 1999, 2001	2,667	813
Santorini (Thera)	Aegean Sea, Greece	1628 BCE[†], 1950	1,850	564
Tristan da Cunha	South Atlantic	1961	800	243
Surtsey	Off SE Iceland	1963–7	568	173
Anak Krakatau	Island, Indonesia	1960	510	155

[†] Famous eruptions

Deepest depressions

Name	Location	Maximum depth below sea level	
		ft	m
Dead Sea	Jordan/Israel	1,338	408
Lake Assal	Djibouti	511	156
Turfan Depression	Sinkiang, China	505	153
Qattara Depression	Egypt	436	132
Mangyshlak peninsula	Kazakhstan	433	131
Danakil Depression	Ethiopia	383	116
Death Valley	California, USA	282	86
Salton Sink	California, USA	235	71
W. of Ustyurt plateau	Kazakhstan,	230	70
Prikaspiyskaya Nizmennost'	Russia/Kazakhstan	220	67
Lake Sarykamysh	Uzbekistan/Turkmenistan	148	45
El Faiyûm	Egypt	147	44
Península Valdés	Chubut, Argentina	131	40
Lake Eyre	South Australia	52	16

Deep caves of the world

Continent	Country	Deepest caves	Depth ft	m
Europe	France	Reseau du Foillis, Haute Savoie	4,773	1,455
Europe	France / Spain	Gouffre de la Pierre Saint-Martin, Pyrenees	4,363	1,330
Europe	France	Reseau de la Pierre St Martin, Haute Savoie	4,334	1,321
Asia	USSR	Snezhnaya, Caucasus	4,200	1,280
Europe	France	Gouffre Jean Bernard, Savoie Alps	4,133	1,260
North America	Mexico	Sistema Huautla	4,002	1,220
Europe	France	Gouffre Berger	3,930	1,198
Europe	Spain	Sima de Ukendi	3,887	1,185
Europe	Spain	Avenc B15, Pyrenees	3,772	1,150
Europe	France	Gouffre Berger, Sornin Plateau, Vercors	3,743	1,143
Europe	Austria	Schneeloch, Salzburg	3,645	1,111
Europe	Spain	Sima G E S Malaga	3,602	1,098
Europe	Austria	Lamprechtsofen	3,359	1,024
Europe	France	Reseau Felix Trombe	3,339	1,018
Europe	France	Chourun des Aguilles, Dauphine Alps	3,214	980
Europe	France	Gouffre André Touya, Western Pyrénées	3,116	950
Europe	Italy	Grotta di Monte Cucco, Appenines	3,024	922
Europe	Italy	Grotta di Monte Cucco, Perugia	3,024	922
Europe	Italy	Abisso Michele Gortani, Julian Alps	3,018	920
Europe	France	Gouffre de Cambou de Liard, Central Pyrénées	2,979	908
Europe	France	Réseau Félix Trombe, Eastern Pyrénées	2,952	900
Europe	Italy	Spluga Della Preta, Dolomites	2,870	875
Europe	Austria	Grüberhornhöle Dachstein	2,802	854
Europe	Spain	Sumidero de Cellagua, Cantabria	2,798	853
Europe	Ukraine	Holloch, Muotathal, Schwyz	2,651	808
Europe	Poland	Jaskini Snieznej Tatras	2,467	752
Asia	Iran	Ghar Parua, Zagros Mountains	2,463	751
Africa	Morocco	Kef Toghobeit	2,221	674
Europe	Slovenia	Poloska Jama	2,211	671
Asia	Lebanon	Gouffre de Faour Dara	2,040	621
North America	Mexico	Sótano de San Augustin , El (has the longest vertical pitch of 410m, 1345ft)	2,009	611
Europe	Norway	Ragge favreraige	1,885	574

North America	Mt Robso, Brit Columbia, Canada	Arctomys Pot	1,720	524
Africa	Algeria	Anou Boussouil, Djurdjura	1,690	515
Oceania	Papua New Guinea	Bibina Cave, Kundiawa	1,620	493
Europe	Greece	Epos Cavern	1,454	443
Asia	Japan	Oumi Senri	1,350	411
South America	Peru	Clima de Milpo, La	1,336	407
Asia	Crimea	Schachta Oktjabviskaya,	1,312	400
North America	Utah, USA	Neffs Canyon Cave	1,184	361
Oceania	New Zealand	Harwood Hole	1,171	356
Europe	Romania	Izvorul Tausoarelor, Rodna	1,115	340
Oceania	Australia	Khazad-Dum, Tasmania	1,053	321
Europe	Wales	Ogof Fynnon Ddu	1,011	307
Europe	England	Oxlow Cavern, Giant's Hole, Derbyshire	642	196
Europe	Ireland, Republic of	Carrowmore, Co. Sligo	460	140

Water

Oceans / seas

Ocean	Area		Percentage of sea area
	sq mile	km	
Pacific	64,190,000	166,240,000	46
Atlantic	33,420,000	86,560,000	23.9
Indian	28,350,000	73,430,000	20.3
Arctic	5,110,000	13,230,000	3.7
Other seas	8,600,000	22,280,000	6.1

Sea	Area		Average depth	
	sq mile	km	ft	m
South China Sea	1,148,500	2,974,600	4,000	1,200
Caribbean Sea	1,063,000	2,753,000	8,000	2,400
Mediterranean Sea	966,750	2,503,000	4,875	1,485
Bering Sea	875,750	2,268,180	4,700	1,400
Gulf of Mexico	595,750	1,542,985	5,000	1,500
Sea of Okhotsk	589,800	1,527,570	2,750	840
East China Sea	482,300	1,249,150	600	180
Hudson Bay	475,800	1,232,300	400	120
Sea of Japan	389,000	1,007,500	4,500	1,370
Andaman Sea	308,000	797,700	2,850	865
North Sea	222,125	575,300	300	90
Black Sea	178,375	461,980	3,600	1,100
Red Sea	169,000	437,700	1,610	490
Baltic Sea	163,000	422,160	190	55
Persian Gulf	92,200	238,790	80	24
Gulf of St Lawrence	91,800	237,760	400	120
Gulf of California	62,530	162,000	2,660	810
English Channel	34,700	89,900	177	54
Irish Sea	34,200	88,550	197	60
Bass Strait	28,950	75,000	230	70

Deepest sea trenches

		Name	Location	Deepest point	Depth	
					ft	m
1400	2250	Mariana Trench	Western Pacific	Challenger Deep	36,160	11,022
1600	2575	Tonga-Kermadec Trench	Southern Pacific	Vityaz 11 (Tonga)	35,702	10,882
1400	2250	Kuril-Kamchatka Trench	Western Pacific		34,587	10,542
825	1325	Philippine Trench	Western Pacific	Galathea Deep	34,439	10,497
		Idzu-Bonin Trench (sometimes included in the Japan Trench)			32,185	9,810
200	320	New Hebrides Trench	Southern Pacific	North Trench	30,069	9,165
400	640	New Britain Trench	Southern Pacific		29,988	9,140

500	800	Puerto Rico Trench	Western Atlantic	Milwaukee Deep		30,249	9,220
350	560	Yap Trench	Western Pacific			27976	8527
1000	1600	Japan Trench	Western Pacific			27599	8412
600	965	South Sandwich Trench	Southern Atlantic	Meteor Deep		27112	8263
2000	3200	Aleutian Trench	North Pacific			26574	8100
2200	3540	Peru-Chile (Atacama) Trench	East Pacific	Bartholomew Deep		26454	8064
		Palau Trench (sometimes included in Yap Trench)				26420	8050
600	965	Romanche Trench	North South Atlantic			25800	7864
1400	2250	Java (Sunda) Trench	Indian Ocean	Planet Deep		25344	7725
600	965	Cayman Trench	Caribbean			24720	535
650	1040	Nansei Shotó (Ryukyu) Trench	West Pacific			24630	7505
150	240	Banda Trench	Banda Sea			24155	7360

Glaciers and glaciation

		Length	
Name	Location	km	miles
Lambert–Fisher Ice Passage	Antarctica (disc 1956–7)	515	320
Novaya Zemlya, North Island	USSR (1160 miles, 3004km)	418	260
Arctic Institute Ice Passage, Victoria Land	E Antarctica	362	225
Nimrod-Lennox-King Ice Passage	E Antarctica	289	180
Denman Glacier	E Antarctica	241	150
Beardmore Glacier	E Antarctica (disc 1908)	225	140
Recovery Glacier	W Antarctica	225	140
Petermanns Gletscher, Knud Rasmussen Land	Greenland	200	124
Unnamed Glacier, SW Ross Ice Shelf	W Antarctica	193	120
Slessor Glacier	W Antarctica	185	115

Other notable glaciers

Name	Location	Length miles	Length km	Area miles²	Area km²
Vatnajökull	Iceland	88	141	3400	8800
Hispar-Biafo Ice Passage	Karakoram	76	122	125,240	323,620
haJostedalsbre	Norway	62	100	415	1075
Fedtschenko	Pamirs	47	75	520	1346
Siachen Glacier	Karakoram	47	75	444	1150
Nabesna Glacier	Alaska	43.5	70	770	1990
Malaspina Glacier	Alaska	26	41	1480	3830
Tasman Glacier	New Zealand	18	29	53	137
Aletschgletscher	Alps	16.5	26.5	44	144
Kangchenjunga	Himalaya	12	19	177	458

Glaciated areas

South Polar regions	Area miles²	Area km²
South Polar regions	5,250,000	13,597,000
North Polar regions	758,500	1,965,000
Alaska–Canada	22,700	58,800
Asia	14,600	37,800
South America	4,600	11,900
Europe	4,128	10,700
New Zealand	380	984
Africa	92	238
Total	6,055,000	15,682,422

The world's largest rivers
See table opposite.

River	Source	Course	Length (miles)	Length (km)	Basin area (miles²)	Basin area (km²)	Outflow (ft³/s)	Outflow (m³/s)	L	B
Nile	Kagera River, Burundi	Tanzania–Uganda–Sudan–Egypt–E Mediterranean	4,145	6,670	1,293,000	3,350,000	110,000	3,120	1	4
Amazon	Apurimac River, Peru	Peru–Columbia–Equatorial Brazil–S Atlantic	4,007	6,447	2,722,000	7,050,000	6,350,000	180,000	2	1
Mississippi–Missouri	Jefferson (Red Rock) River, Montana	S Montana–Louisiana–Gulf of Mexico	3,710	5,970	1,245,000	3,224,000	650,000	18,400	3	5
Yenisey	Selenga River, Mongolia	Mongolia–Kara Sea (N Russia)	3,442	5,540	996,000	2,580,000	670,00	19,000	4	7
Yangtze (Chang-Jiang)	Kunlun Mts, China	W China–Yellow Sea	3,436	5,530	765,000	1,960,000	770,00	21,800	5	9
Yellow River (Huang Ho)	Qinghai, China	Tsing Province–N Pacific	3,395	5,462	378,000	979,000	378,000	*22,650	7	22
Ob´–Irtysh	Altai Mts, Russia	Mongolia–Kara Sea (N Russia)	3,362	5,410	1,150,000	2,978,000	550,000	15,600	6	6
Paraná	Paranaíba and Grande confluence, Brazil	Brazil–S Atlantic	3,032	4,878	1,600,000	4,145,000	970,000	27,500	14	2
Zaïre (Congo)	Chambeshi River, Zambia	Zambia–Zaïre border–S Atlantic	2,920	4,700	1,314,000	3,400,000	1,450,000	41,000	8	3
Amur–Argun	Northern Chinain Khingan Ranges (as Argun')	N China–N Pacific	2,782	4,476	787,000	2,038	438,000	12,400	10	33
Lena	Kirenga River, Siberia	Eastern Russia–ArcticOcean	2,734	4,400	960,000	2,490,000	575,000	16,300	9	8
Mackenzie–Peace	Finlay/Parsnip confluence, BC	British Columbia–Beaufort Sea	2,635	4,240	711,000	1,841,000	400,000	11,300	11	11

Mekong	Lants'ang, Tibet	Central Tibet–S China Sea	2,600	4,180	381,000	987,000	388,000	11,000	12	21
Niger	Loma Mts, Guinea	Guinea–Atlantic	2,590	4,169	730,000	1,890,000	415,000	11,750	13	10
Murray–Darling	Cape Byron, NSW	Queensland–Lake Alexandria, SA	2,330	3,750	408,000	1,059,000	14,000	400	15	19
Zambesi	Kalene Hill, Zambia	Zimbabwe–Indian Ocean	2,200	3,540	514,000	1,330,000	250,000	7,000	17	15
Volga	Valdai Hills, nr Moscow	Russia–N Caspian Sea	2,193	3,530	525,000	1,360,000	287,000	8,200	16	14
Madeira	Mamoré and Beni Rivers, Bolivia	Bolivia–Ilha Tupinamboram, Amazon River	2,082	3,352	—	—	530,000	15,000	—	—
Jurua	Puerto Portillo, Peru		2,040	3,282	—	—	—	—	—	—
Purus	Peru: as the Alto Purus	Peru–Brazil, Amazon	1,995	3,210	—	—	—	—	—	—
St Lawrence	St Louis River, Minnesota	Minnesota–N Atlantic	1,945	3,130	532,000	1,378,000	10,200	10,200	19	13
Rio Grande	Rockies, Colorado	SW Colorado–Atlantic Ocean	1,885	3,033	172,000	445,000	3000	85	20	30
Yukon	Tagish Lake, Yukon–BC	NW British Columbia–Bering Sea	1,875	3,017	330,000	855,000	—	—	18	24
São Francisco	Serra da Canastra, Minais Gerais, Brazil	Brazil–S Atlantic	1,811	2,914	270,000	700,000	—	—	22	26
Indus	Tibet: as Sengge	Tibet–N Arabian Sea	1,790	2,880	450,000	1,166,000	195,000	5,500	23	16
Danube	Black Forest, Germany	SW Germany–Black Sea	1,775	2,816	315,000	815,000	250,000	7,000	24	25
Salween	Tibet in Tanglha range	Tibet–Andaman Sea	1,750	2,810	125,000	325,000	—	—	25	31
Orinoco	Venezuela–Brazil border	SE Venezuela–Atlantic	1,700	2,740	400,000	1,036,000	—	—	26=	20

River	Source	Flow						B	L
Tocantins	Brazil: near Braziliia as Paraná	Brazil–S Atlantic	1,700	2,740	350,000	905,000	360,000	10,000	26=	23
Si Kiang	China: in Yünnan plateau as Nanp'an	Yünnan Plateau–S China Sea	1,650	2,650	232,300	602,000	—	—	29	27
Kolyma	USSR: in Khrebet Suntarkhayata (as Kulu)	Khrebat–Siberian Sea	1,616	2,600	206,000	534,000	134,000	3,800	30	28
Nelson–Saskatchewan	Canada: Bow Lake, British Colombia	E Alberta–Hudson Bay	1,600	2,575	414,000	1,072,000	80,000	2,250	31=	18
Amu–Dar'ya (Oxus)	Wakhan, Afghanistan, on the border with Sinkiang China	Sinkiang China–Aral Sea	1,600	2,575	179,500	465,000	—	—	31=	29
Ural	USSR: South-central Urals	South-Central Urals–Caspian Sea	1,575	2,540	84,900	220,000	—	—	33	32
Ganges–Brahmaputra	Indian Himalayas	SWTibet–Indian Ocean	1,553	2,498	626,000	1,620,000	1,360,000	38,500	21	12
Paraguay	Brazil in the Mato Grosso as Paraguai	Brazil-Paraná	1,500	2410	444,000	—	—	—	34	–
Tigris	South-west Turkey	E Turkey–Persian Gulf	1,180	2,740	430,000	1,115,000	50,000	*2,700	26=	17

* maximum
B – order by basin area
L – order by length

Other rivers of 1000 miles (1600km) or longer

Miles	km	Name and location	Area of basin (miles²)	(km²)
1,450	2,335	Arkansas, USA	Tributary of No.3	—
1,450	2,335	Colorado, USA	228,000	590,000
1,420	2,285	Dnepr (Dnieper), USSR	194,200	503,000
1,400	2,255	Rio Negro, Columbia-Brazil	Tributary of No.2	—
1,360	2,188	Orange (Oranje), South Africa	394,000	1020,000
1,343	2,160	Olenek, USSR	95,000	246,000
1,330	2,140	Syr-Dar'ya, USSR	175,000	453,000
1,306	2,100	Ohio-Allegheny, USA	Tributary of No.3	—
1,250	2,010	Irrawaddy, China-Burma	166,000	430,000
1,224	1,969	Don, USSR	163,000	422,000
1,210	1,950	Columbia Snake, Canada-USA	258,000	688,000
1,180	1,900	Indigirka-Khastakh, USSR	139,000	360,000
1,150	1,850	Sungari (or Sunghua), China	Tributary of No.10	—
1,150	1,850	Tigris, Turkey-Iraq	Included in No.26	—
1,112	1790	Pechora, USSR	126,000	326,000
1,018	1,638	Red River, USA	Tributary of No.3	—
1,000	1,600	Churchill, Canada	15,000	390,000
1,000	1,600	Uruguay, Brazil-Uruguay-Argentina	Included in No.14	—
1,000	1,600	Pilcomayo, Bolivia-Argentina-Paraguay	Tributary of Paraguay and Sub-tributary of Parana	—

Note: Some sources state that the Amazon tributary the Jurua is over 1,133 miles (1,823 km) long and the Lena tributary, the Victim, is 1,200 miles (1,931 km) long.

World's highest waterfalls

1 **Angel Falls** 979m or 3,212ft; highest fall 807m or 2,648ft 807; found on Carrao River, an upper tributary of the Caroni in Venezuela; ; in this area are other very high but unnamed falls; discovered by pilot Jimmy Angel in 1935 (see 8).

2 **Tugela** 947m or 3,110ft; five falls of which the highest is 410m or 1,350 ft; found on the Tugela River, Natal, South Africa.

3   **Utigård** 800m or 2,625ft; highest fall 600m or 1,970ft;
    found on the Jostedal Glacier, Nesdale, Norway

4   **Mongefossen** 774m or 2,540ft; found on the Monge
    River, Mongebekk, Norway.

5   **Yosemite** 739m or 2,425ft; comprises Upper Yosemite
    435m or 1,430ft, Middle Cascades 205m or 675ft, Lower
    Yosemite 97m or 320ft; found on Yosemite Creek, a
    tributary of the Merced River inYosemite Valley, Yosemite
    National Park, CA, USA (see 12 and 21).

6   **Østre Mudøla Foss** 656m or 2,154ft; highest fall 296m or
    974ft; found on Mardals River, Eikisdal, W Norway.

7   **Tyssestrengane** 646m or 2,120ft; highest fall 289m or
    948ft; found on Tysso River, Hardanger, Norway.

8   **Kukenaam (or Cuquenán)** 610m or 2,000ft; found on
    Arabopó, an upper tributary of the Caroni, Venezuela
    (see 1).

9   **Sutherland** 580m or 1,904ft; highest fall 248m or 815ft;
    found on the Arthur River near Milford Sound, Otago, S.
    Island, New Zealand.

10 **Kile (or Kjellfossen)** 561m or 1,841ft; highest fall 149m
    or 490ft; found on the Naerö fjord feeder near
    Gudvangen, Norway.

11. **Takkakaw** 502m or 1,650ft; highest fall 365m or 1,200ft;
    found on a tributary of the Yoho River, Daly Glacier, British
    Columbia, Canada.

12 **Ribbon** 491m or 1,612ft; found on Ribbon Fall Stream 3
    miles west of Yosemite Falls, Yosemite National Park
    (see 5 and 21).

13 **King George VI** 487m or 1,600ft; found on Utshi River, an
    upper tributary of the Muaruni, Guyana (see 14).

14 **Roraima** 457m or 1,500ft; found on an upper tributary of
    the Muaruni River, Guyana (see 13).

15 **Cleve-Garth** 449m or 1,476ft; found in New Zealand.

16 **Kalambo** 426m or 1,400ft; found on the south-east
    feeder of south-east feeder of Lake Tanzania (formerly
    Tanganyika).

17 **Gavarnie** 421m or 1,384ft; found on the Gave de Pau River, Pyrénées Glaciers, France.

18 **Glass** 403m or 1,325ft; found on the Igazú River, Brazil.

19 **Krimmler Fålle** 390m or 1,280ft; 4 falls, of which the upper is 140m or 460ft; found on the Krimml Glacier, Salzburg, Austria.

20 **Lofoi** 383m or 1,259ft; found in Zaire.

21 **Silver Strand (or Widow's Tears)** 356m or 1,170ft; found on the Merced tributary, Yosemite National Park (see 5 and 12).

World's most voluminous waterfalls

1 **The Seven Cataracts of the Boyoma (formerly Stanley) Falls** a maximum height of 60m or 200ft; maximum width 730m or 2,400ft; 17,000ms or some 600,000fts; found on the Zaïre River near Kisangani.

2 **Guaira (or Salto dos Sete Quedas – Seven Falls)** a maximum height of 114m or 374ft; maximum width 4,846m or 15,900ft; 13,000ms or 470fts (although the maximum measured has been 50,000ms or 1,750,000fts); found on the Alto Paraná River, Brazil–Paraguay (see 6).

3 **Khône Falls** a maximum height of 21m or 70ft; maximum width 10,670m or 35,000ft; 11–12,000ms or some 400–420,000fts; found on the Mekong River, Laos.

4 **Niagara Falls** comprising the Horseshoe (Canadian) Falls; a maximum height of 48m or 160ft; maximum width 760m or 2,500ft; and the American Falls; a maximum height of 50m or 167ft; the whole passing 6,000ms or some 212,000fts; found on the Niagara River, Lake Erie to Lake Ontario

5 **Paulo Afonso Falls** a maximum height of 58m or 192ft; passing 2,800ms or some 100,000fts; found on the São Francisco River, Brazil.

6 **Urubu-punga Falls** a maximum height of 12m or 40ft; passing 2,700ms or some 97,000fts; found on the Alto Paraná River, Brazil (see 2).

7   **Cataratas del Iguazú (Quedas do Iguaçu)** a maximum height of 93m or 308ft; some 4,000m or 13,000ft wide; passing 1,700ms or 61,660fts; found on the Iguazú (or Iguaçu) River Brazil–Argentina

8   **Patos–Maribondo Falls** a maximum height of 35m or 115ft; found on the Rio Grande, Brazil.

9   **Mosi-oa-tunya (Victoria) Falls** a maximum height of 108m or 355ft; comprising Leaping Water 33m or 108ft wide, Main Fall 821m or 2,694ft wide and Rainbow Falls 550m or 1,800ft wide; passing 21,100ms or some 38,430fts; found on the Zambezi River, Zambia.

10   **Churchill (formerly Grand) Falls** a maximum height of 75m or 245ft; passing up to 1,100ms or 40,000fts; found on the Churchill (formerly Hamilton) River, Canada.

11   **Kaieteur (Köituök) Falls** a maximum height of 225m or 741ft; maximum width 105m or 350ft; passing up to 660ms or 23,400fts; found on the Potaro River, Guyana.

Lakes of the world

Name	Country	Area (miles²)	Area (km²)	Length (miles)	Length (km)	Maximum depth (ft)	Maximum depth (m)	Average depth (ft)	Average depth (m)	Height of surface above sea level (ft)	Height of surface above sea level (m)
Caspian Sea	Russia, Kazakhstan, Turkmenistan, Azerbaijan, Iran	143,552	371,800	760	1,225	3,215	980	675	205	-92	-28
Superior	Canada and USA	31,795	82,350	350	560	1,333	406	485	147	600.4	183
Victoria (Nyanza)	Uganda, Tanzania, and Kenya	26,834	69,500	225	360	265	80	130	39	3720	1,134
Huron	Canada and USA	23,011	59,600	206	330	750	228	196	59	579	176
Michigan	USA	22,394	58,000	307	494	923	281	275	83	579	176
Aral Sea	Uzbekistan, Kazakhstan	15,444	40,010	280	450	223	68	52	15.8	174	53
Tanganyika	Dominon Rep of Congo, Tanzania, Zambia and Burundi	12,703	32,900	450	725	4,708	1,435	—	—	2,534	772
Great Bear	Northwest Territories (Canada)	12,279	32,800	232	373	270	82	240	73	390	118
Baikal	Russia	11,776	30,500	385	620	6,365	1,940	2,300	700	1,493	455

Lake	Location										
Malawi (formerly Nyasa)	Malawi, Tanzania, and Mozambique	11,429	29,600	360	580	2,226	678	895	272	1,550	472
Great Slave	Northwest Territories (Canada)	11,031	28,500	298	480	535	163	240	73	512	156
Erie	Canada and USA	9,910	25,700	241	387	210	64	60	18.2	572	174
Winnipeg	Manitoba (Canada)	9,417	24,500	266	428	120	36	50	152	713	217
Ontario	Canada and USA	7,550	19,500	193	310	780	237	260	79	246	75
Balkhash	Kazakhstan	7,115	18,433	300	482	85	26	—	—	1,112	339
Chad	Cameroon, Chad, Niger, and Nigeria	6,875	17,764	130	209	13-24	3.9-7.3	5	1.5	787	240
Ladoga	Russia	6,835	17,700	120	193	738	225	170	51	13	3.9
Onega	Russia	3,753	9,600	145	233	361	110	105	32	108	33
Eyre	South Australia	3,600	9,580	115	185	65	19.8	—	—	-39	-11.8
Titicaca	Peru and Bolivia	3,200	8,300	130	209	913	278	328	100	12,506	3,811
Nicaragua	Nicaragua	3,190	8,000	100	160	200	60	—	—	110	33
Athabasca	Canada	3,064	8,100	208	334	407	124	—	—	699	213

Lakes under 3,000 miles (7,770 km) but over 2,000 miles
(5180 km)

Name	Country	Area miles²	Area km²
Turkana (formerly Rudolf)	Kenya and Ethiopia	2,473	6,400
Reindeer	Canada	2,465	6,380
*Issyk Kul'	USSR	2,355	6,100
Torrens	Australia	2,230	5,775
Vanern	Sweden	2,149	5,565
Winnipegosis	Canada	2,105	5,450
Mobutu Sese Seko (formerly Albert)	Uganda and Zaire	2,075	5,375
Kariba (dammed)	Zimbabwe and Zambia	2,050	5,300

* Has a maximum depth of 2,303 feet (700m) and an average depth
of 1,050 ft (320 m). The height of the surface above sea-level is 5,279
ft (1600 m).

Air

Winds around the world

Abroholos Brazil – a frequent coastal squall May through August
between Cabo de Sao Tome and Cabo Frio.

Aejej Morocco – a whirlwind in the Morocco desert.

Aquilo Ancient Rome – a northwesterly wind.

Aquilon North Wind – a Shakespearean epithet.

Auster see Ostria.

Austru Romania – an east or southeast wind, cold in winter; it
may be a local name for a foehn wind.

Bad-I-Sad-O-Bist-Roz Afghanistan – a hot and dry northwesterly
wind June through September.

Baguio a hurricane.

Bali wind East Java – a strong east wind.

Barat Sulawesi (Celebes) – a heavy northwest squall December–
February in Manado Bay on the north coast.

Barber – a strong wind carrying damp snow/sleet/spray that freezes upon contact with objects, especially the beard and hair.

Bayamo Cuba – violent wind blowing from the land on the south coast, especially near the Bight of Bayamo.

Bentu de Soli Sardinia – an east wind on the coast.

Berg South Africa – a hot, dry wind.

Bise, Bize Switzerland – a cold dry northerly wind mainly prevalent in Spring.

Blaast – a frigid wind of the north.

Blizzard – a strong, bitterly cold wind that whips falling snow into a frenzy.

Blue Norther – see Norther.

Bora West coast of the Adriatic – a violent cold North wind that blows (usually in the winter) from the Hungarian basin; see **Fall wind**.

Borasco Mediterranean – a thunderstorm or violent squall.

Boreas, Borras – a Classical name for north winds; may be the origin of Bora.

Brickfielder S Australia – a hot dry wind; similar to the Harmattan.

Brisa, Briza S America – a northeast coastal wind; Puerto Rico – an east wind during the Trade Wind season; Philippines – the north East Monsoon

Brisote Cuba – the strongest northeast trade winds.

Brubu East Indies – a squall.

Bull's Eye Squall S Africa – one forming off the coast in fair weather, so called because of the small isolated cloud marking the top of the invisible vortex of the storm.

Bura, Buran Central Asia – a blizzard blowing from the North, or a summer wind from the North raising dust storms.

Buster SE Australian coast – a sudden violent cold wind.

Cape Doctor, The Doctor South Africa – a strong southeast wind that blows on the coast.

Carabinera Spain – a squall.

Cat's Paw US – a breeze just strong enough to ripple the surface of water.

Caver, Kaver Hebrides – a gentle breeze.

Chi'ing Fung China – a gentle breeze.

Chili Tunisia – the Sirocco.

Chinook, Snow Eater Rocky Mountains – a warm dry wind that descends the eastern slopes and may raise the temperature by up to 40°F in minutes; NW Coast of US – a warm, moist southwest wind; Southern California – the Santa Ana. The Native American Chinook means 'snow eater'; it is a foehn wind.

Chocolatero Mexico Gulf Coast – a hot sandy squall, coloured brown by dust.

Chubasco West coast of Central America – a violent rainy-season squall with thunder and lightning.

Churada Mariana Islands – a severe rain squall during the northeast monsoon, from November through April or May, especially from January through March.

Cierzo – see Mistral.

Contrastes West Mediterranean – Spring and Autumn winds a short distance apart blowing from opposite quadrants.

Cordonazo West coast of Mexico – southerly hurricane winds; the 'Lash of St Francis'. associated with tropical cyclones in the Pacific Ocean. The Cordonazo may occur from May through November, with particular fury about the Feast of St Francis – 4 October.

Coromell La Paz, Gulf of California – a night land breeze prevailing from November through May.

Crivetz Romania – a cold northeasterly blizzard wind.

Cyclone Indian Ocean and Bay of Bengal – a severe tropical storm (winds >64 knots); see also Hurricane and Typhoon. Closed circulations in the midlatitudes and small-scale circulations such as tornadoes may also be termed Cyclones.

Diablo Northern California – Chinook or Santa Ana winds blowing below canyons in Diablo range (East Bay) hills; it may exceed 60 mph. The Diabolo develops when the pressure over Nevada is higher than that over the central California coast.

Doctor Tropics – a cooling sea breeze; South Africa – the Cape Doctor; West Australia – the Fremantle Doctor; the Harmattan.

Doinionn – an Irish wind.

Elephanta Malabar Coast, India – a strong southerly or southeasterly wind blowing during September and October; it marks the end of the southwest monsoon.

Etesian Eastern Mediterranean; Aegean Sea – NW winds of the summer months.

Euros, Eurus in Greek mythology, the rainy, stormy SE wind.

Euroclydon – see Gregale.

Fall wind – a large-scale katabatic wind (air currents descending the lee side of a mountain) that remains cold as it flows. Examples are the Adriatic Bora, the S French Mistral and the extremely cold winds along the coasts of Antarctica.

Foehn, Föhn Alpine valleys – a warm dry katabatic wind whose temperature increases by adiabatic compression as it descends the lee side of a mountain range. Other Foehns include the Chinook and the Santa Ana.

Fremantle Doctor West Australia – a cooling sea breeze, often noted during hot summer-time cricket matches; see Doctor.

Ghibli Libya – the Scirocco (*qv*).

Gregale Central and West Mediterranean – a strong, cold northeast winter wind; may be identified with the Euroclydon wind that sank St. Paul's ship.

Haboob Northern and Central Sudan, especially around Khartum – a strong wind and sand- or dust-storm, followed by rain, occurring some 24 times each year (Arabic *habb* = wind).

Harmattan West African Coast – a dry dusty wind blowing from the Sahara Desert across the Gulf of Guinea and the Cape Verde Islands; sometimes called the Doctor.

Hayate Japan – a gale.

Hurricane Atlantic, Caribbean, Gulf of Mexico and Eastern Pacific – a severe tropical storm; the Caribbean Indian storm god is named Huracan.

Kadja Bali – a steady breeze off the sea.

Kaver – see Caver.

Kamseen, Kamsin, Khamseen, Khamsin Egypt – the Sirocco (*qv*).

Knik Palmer, Alaska – a strong southeast winter wind.

Kohilo Hawaii – a gentle breeze.

Kolawaik Argentina – the southerly wind of the Gran Chaco.

Kona Storm Hawaii – a storm over the islands, characterized by strong southerly or southwesterly winds and heavy rains.

Koshava – a wind that brings Russian snows to the plains of the former Yugoslavia.

Kubang Java – a Chinook or Foehn (*qv*).

Landlash Scotland – a gale.

Leste Madeira and Canary Islands – a hot, dry, easterly wind.

Levanter West Mediterranean and the Straits of Gibraltar – a strong easterly attended by cloudy, foggy, and sometimes rainy weather, especially in winter.

Levantera Adriatic – a persistent east wind usually accompanied by cloudy weather.

Levanto Canary Islands – a hot southeasterly wind.

Leveche Spain – a Foehn or hot southerly wind; a Sirocco.

Libecchio, Libeccio West coast of Corsica – a strong westerly (or southwesterly) wind off the sea.

Maestro Coasts of Corsica and Sardinia, and the Adriatic – a northwesterly wind with fine weather, especially in summer.

Mamatele Malta – a hot northwesterly wind.

Maria – a fictional wind appearing in the book *Storm* by George R Stewart, and taken up in *Paint Your Wagon* (Lerner and Lowe, 1951) and by the Kingston Trio (1959).

Matanuska Wind Palmer, Alaska – a strong, gusty, northeast winter wind.

Mato Wamniyomi Dakota – Native American for whirlwind, dust devil or tornado.

Mistral Mediterranean; Gulf of Lions – a strong cold dry northeast wind that blows from the Rhone valley; a Fall Wind also called Cierzo.

Moncao Portugal – a northeasterly trade wind (*qv*).

Myatel – a North Russian wind.

Nashi, N'aschi Iranian coast of the Persian Gulf and the Makran coast – a northeast winter wind similar to but less severe than the Bora; it may be associated with an outflow from the central Asiatic anticyclone that extends over the high land of Iran..

Nor'easter, Northeaster New England coast – a strong northeast wind presaging a gale or storm.

Norte Mexico and the Gulf of Mexico – a strong cold northeasterly wind resulting from an outbreak of cold air from the north; the Mexican extension of a Norther (*qv*).

Norther, Blue Norther Southern United States, particularly Texas – a cold winter wind that blows from the north resulting in a drastic drop in air temperatures; a fall of 50°F in a few hours has been noted

Nor'wester the province of Canterbury, New Zealand, especially in the city of Christchurch – it is a very warm wind which may blow for days on end; it comes in from the Tasman Sea, dries as it rises over the Southern Alps, and heats as it decends.

Notus – a Classical south wind.

Ostria Bulgarian coast – a warm southerly wind, considered a precursor of bad weather.

Pali Pali Pass, Honolulu – local name for the strong winds that blow through it.

Pampero Southern Argentina – a strong cold wind from the south or southwest that blows across the Pampas.

Papagayo Pacific coast of Nicaragua and Guatemala – a violent northeasterly fall wind (*qv*); the cold air mass of a Norte (*qv*) which has overridden the mountains of Central America; see Tehuantepecer.

Papagayos Costa Rica – a cool wind from the north.

Pittarak Greenland – a wind from the north west.

Puna Andes – probably the harshest cold wind.

Purgas – a Siberian wind.

Quexalcoatl Aztec – a wind from the west.

Samiel Arabian and North African deserts; Turkey – a hot, dry sand-laden wind, also known as Simoom or Simoon (*qv*).

Santa Ana Santa Ana Pass, California – a Chinook (*qv*) from the Californian desert.

Shaitan Middle East – a dust storm.

Shamal Iraq and the Persian Gulf – a summer northwesterly wind often stronger during the day than the night.

Sharki Persian Gulf – an occasional southeasterly wind.

Shawondasee Hudson Bay – the Algonquin lazy wind that blows from the south in the late summer.

Scirocco, Sirocco North Africa and the North Mediterranean coastline – a hot, dry, dusty wind, either a foehn or a hot southerly wind in advance of a low pressure area moving from the Sahara or Arabian deserts; in Spain, Leveche.

Solano Andalusia, Northern Spain – a hot, dry, often sand-laden south-easterly wind that brings suffocating weather.

Souther – a south gale

Squamish the fjords of British Columbia – a strong and often violent wind; Squamishes occur in those fjords oriented such that cold polar air can be funneled westward. They are notable in Jervis, Toba, and Bute inlets and in Dean Channel and Portland Canal. They lose their strength when free of the confining fjords, and are not noticeable 15 to 20 miles offshore.

Steppenwind – a wind of the Russian Steppes.

Suestada Uruguay and Argentina – a strong, rainy gale.

Suestado the coasts of Argentina, southern Brazil and Uruguay – a winter storm with southeast gales, caused by intense cyclonic activity.

Sukhovey Mongolia – a warm, easterly dust storm wind in the Gobi Desert.

Sumatra Straits of Malacca – a brief but violent nocturnal squall that emanates from Sumatra especially during the southwest monsoon.

Sundowner Southern California coast in the vicinity of Santa Barbara – warm downslope winds; the name refers to their typical occurrence in the late afternoon or early evening, though they may occur at any time of the day. Wind speeds may exceed gale force, with temperatures in excess of 100°F.

Taku Wind Juneau, Alaska – a strong, gusty, east-northeast wind, blowing between October and March; at the mouth of the Taku River, after which the wind is named, it sometimes attains hurricane force.

Tehuantepecer in the Gulf of Tehuantepec (south of southern Mexico) – a violent squally winter wind from the north or north-northeast, originating in the Gulf of Mexico as a Norther that crosses the isthmus and blows through the gap between the Mexican and Guatamalan mountains. It may be felt up to 100 miles out to sea; see also Papagayos.

Tokalau Fiji – a wind from the northeast.

Trade Winds Equator ±30° – blowing generally from the north east in the Northern hemisphere, and from the south east in the Southern hemisphere, they are noted for their constancy of direction and speed, and therefore helpful to sailing ships plying their trade.

Tramontana Italy – a cold northeasterly or north wind of the fine weather mistral type off the west coast.

Twister – a tornado.

Typhon – a whirlwind.

Typhoon Western Pacific – a severe tropical storm; perhaps from the Chinese *ty fung*.

Vardar, Vardarac the Vardar Valley, Greece to the Gulf of Salonica – a cold fall wind blowing from the northwest that often occurs in winter when atmospheric pressure over eastern Europe is higher than that over the Aegean Sea.

Vind Gnyr Ancient Ireland – a blustery thunderstorm downdraft, described in the Norse Sagas.

Vind-Blaer Icelandic Sagas – a breeze.

Virugas – a Siberian wind.

Warm Braw the Schouten Islands north of New Guinea – a foehn wind.

White Squall – in the tropics, a sudden and unexpected strong gust of wind, signed by whitecaps or white, broken water; in clear weather, usually seen as a whirlwind.

Whittle England – a gust of wind gust so named when Captain Whittle's coffin was upset.

Williwaw, Williwau, Willy Waw Straits of Magellan or the Aleutian Islands and coast of Alaska – a strong gust of cold wind blowing seawards from a mountainous coast.

Willy-willy Australia (especially SW) – a tropical cyclone (> 33 knots); a dust-devil.

Xlokk Malta – a hot, dry wind.

Yamo Uganda – a whirlwind.

Zephyr Italy – a mild breeze bringing pleasant weather.

Zephyros Ancient Greek – the West wind.

Zonda Argentina – a hot, humid air that blows from the north across the plains; an Andes Chinook.

Space

Rockets and spaceships

Humanity's first entrance into space came about as a result of war. Immense power is needed to project an object out of the earth's atmosphere – the required speed is 28,200 kilometres per hour and to achieve orbit around the earth the object must reach a height of at least 160 kilometres above ground. This power can only be achieved (at our present state of scientific knowledge) by rockets, which achieve their initial lift-off and subsequent forward motion through the vacuum of space by pushing a jet of hot gas out behind them. The gases are produced by burning liquid fuel and an oxidant. Rocket science itself is very much a by-product of war, and it was the pressure from the military for better, longer-distance weapons during the Second World War which led to great advances in the field.

Because rocket engines are huge and heavy, several separate ones might be used for each space launch, and as each uses up its fuel, it is jettisoned. Apollo 11, for example, used three rocket stages to reach orbit around the moon, becoming smaller and smaller as each rocket stage fired and was jettisoned. Similarly, the moon lander module was in two parts, with the lander part abandoned after being used as a launching pad for the upper part when the astronauts left the moon. When the lunar module returned to the command module Apollo 11, it in turn was discarded and, just before re-entry into the earth's atmosphere, the command module also jettisoned the service module which contained the main engine. Only the small conical pod of the command module returned to earth.

Space shuttles are largely re-usable, although they do jettison their fuel tanks when emptied. They are launched by booster rockets, which separate from the shuttle and are later recovered for re-use, and when the shuttle returns to earth it finishes its journey by gliding to a runway to land like a conventional plane.

Important space missions

No	Mission	Launch date	Country	Achievement
1	Sputnik 1	4 October 1957	USSR	First successful space launch (unmanned). First artificial satellite
2	Sputnik 2	3 November 1957	USSR	Launched the dog Laika into space. (She died on re-entry)
3	Explorer 1	1 February 1958	USA (NASA)	First successful NASA space launch (unmanned)
4	Luna 2	12 September 1959	USSR	Probe crashed on the moon
5	Luna 3	4 October 1959	USSR	First photo of dark side of the moon
6	Vostok 1	12 April 1961	USSR	Yuri Gagarin first man in space
7	Mercury MR3	5 May 1961	USA	Alan Shephard first American in space
8	Mariner 2	26 August 1962	USA	Passed Venus
9	Vostok 6	16 June 1963	USSR	Valentina V. Tereschkova first woman in space
10	Mariner 4	28 November 1964	USA	Photos from Mars flyby
11	Voshkod 2	18 March 1965	USSR	First space-walk, by Alexei Leonov
12	A-1 Asterix	26 November 1965	France	First western European satellite
13	Gemini 7/7A	4/15December 1965	USA	First rendezvous between 2 craft in space

14	Apollo 1	27 January 1967	USA	Crew of 3 killed at launch
15	Luna 9	31 January 1966	USSR	First soft landing on the moon
16	Soyuz 1	23 April 1967	USSR	Vladimir M. Komarov killed on re-entry
17	WRESAT	29 November 1967	Australia	First Australian satellite
18	Apollo 8	21 December 1968	USA	First manned lunar orbit
19	Soyuz 4/5	14/15 January 1969	USSR	First transfer of crew in space
20	Apollo 11	16 July 1969	USA	First men on the moon
21	Oshumi	11 February 1970	Japan	First Japanese satellite
22	Apollo 13	11 April 1970	USA	Emergency return to earth after on-board explosion
23	Long March	24 April 1970	China	First Chinese satellite
24	Venera 7	17 August 1970	USSR	First soft landing on Venus
25	Luna 17	10 November 1970	USSR	Unmanned moon rover
26	Salyut 1	19 April 1971	USSR	First space station
27	Mars 2	19 May 1971	USSR	First orbit of Mars
28	Mars 3	28 May 1971	USSR	First soft landing on Mars
29	Soyuz 11	6 June 1971	USSR	Crew of 3 killed on re-entry
30	Prospero	28 October 1971	Britain	First British satellite
31	Pioneer 10	3 March 1972	USA	First probe past the asteroid belt. Flew past Jupiter, escaped solar system
32	Skylab 1	14 May 1973	USA	Space station
33	Apollo/Soyuz	15 July 1975	USA/USSR	First international link-up in space
34	Voyager 2	20 August 1977	USA	Flyby of Jupiter, Saturn, Uranus, Neptune
35	Ariane/CAT	24 December 1979	European Space Agency (ESA)	First co-operative European launch
36	Rohini	18 July 1980	India	First Indian satellite
37	STS 1	12 April 1981	USA	First space shuttle
38	Soyuz T9	27 June 1983	USSR	First construction in space
39	Giotto	2 July 1985	ESA	Close-up of Halley's Comet
40	Mir 1	19 February 1986	USSR	Space station
41	Hubble Space Telescope	24 April 1990	USA/ESA	Huge space telescope
42	Mars Pathfinder	4 December 1996	USA	Explored surface of Mars
43	Zarya	20 November 1998	Canada/ESA/ Japan/Russia/ USA	To begin assembly of International Space Station
44	Expedition 1	31 October 2000	Canada/ESA/ Japan/Russia/ USA	First occupants of International Space Station
45	Beagle 2	2 June 2003	ESA	Mars probe (lost)
46	Spirit/ Opportunity	10 June/7 July 2003	USA	Mars exploration rovers

Moon landings

Space mission	Launched	Landed on moon	Moon walkers (mission commander, moon lander pilot)	Command module pilot	Where landed	Name of command module	Name of moon lander module	Returned to Earth
Apollo 11	16 July 1969	20 July 1969	Neil Armstrong Edwin 'Buzz' Aldrin	Michael Collins	Sea of Tranquillity	Columbia	Eagle	24 July 1969
Apollo 12	14 November 1969	19 Nov 1969	Charles Conrad Alan Bean	Richard Gordon	Ocean of Storms	Yankee Clipper	Intrepid	24 Nov 1969
Apollo 14	31 January 1971	5 Feb 1971	Alan Shephard Edgar Mitchell	Stuart Roosa	Fra Mauro area	Kitty Hawk	Antares	9 February 1971
Apollo 15	26 July 1971	30 July 1971	David Scott James Irwin	Alfred Worden	Hadley Rille	Endeavour	Falcon	7 August 1971
Apollo 16	16 April 1972	20 April 1972	John Young Charles Duke	Thomas Mattingly	Descartes region	Casper	Orion	27 April 1972
Apollo 17	7 December 1972	11 December 1972	Eugene Cernan Harrison Schmitt	Ronald Evans	Taurus-Littrow region	America	Challenger	19 December 1972

Space Shuttles	First launch
Discovery	24 January 1985
Challenger	29 April 1985 (exploded 28 January 1986)
Atlantis	3 October 1985
Columbia	12 January 1986 (exploded 1 February 2003)
Endeavor	7 May 1992

Some space spin-offs

Discoveries and Inventions arising from or improved by the Space Programme

Artificial limbs	Miniaturised cameras
Bar code scanning in shops	Reflective emergency blankets
Dried foods	Shock-absorbing foam
Insulin pump	Ski goggles
Kidney dialysis machines	Strengthened glass
Laser-operated equipment	Thermal clothes
Medical photography	

Lunar features

Like the Earth and the Sun, the Earth's moon does not have a separate name. It is often referred to by the Latin word for moon – Luna. Although it has been a source of mystery, wonder and speculation throughout human history, it was only when decent quality telescopes were developed in the early C17 that it became possible to examine the moon's surface closely and give it three dimensions.

The first astronomers who mapped the moon assumed it would be a world very much like their familiar earth. So, when they saw that the moon's darker areas are smooth, whereas the lighter areas are rough, they thought the dark parts were liquid seas and the light parts were continents and lands. Although we now know that the darker, smoother areas are simply younger, less battered, areas of rock, traditional labels such as 'sea', 'ocean', 'bay' etc are still used to name them.

In 1651 the priest-astronomer Giovanni Battista Riccioli of Bologna published an astronomy textbook *Almagestum Novum* containing his new moon map. The types of names he used have now become standard. He named craters after famous people — mainly astronomers and scientists such as Tycho and Copernicus. Since early telescopes were not as powerful as later ones, the largest and most visible features were named first.

We now know that there are many more craters than renowned astronomers, so later names derive from mythology or earthly features. Riccioli gave the seas symbolic names reflecting phenomena and states of mind. Most of those on the west side of the Moon relate to wet weather: Sea of Rains, Ocean of Storms, Bay of Dew. But those on the east side are more cheerful, such as the Sea of Serenity and the Sea of Tranquility (where *Apollo 11* landed). Today the International Astronomical Union oversees the naming of all astronomical features, and rules that features cannot be named after living people, for political figures after 1800, or after religious figures from the major world religions (Christianity, Judaism, Islam, Hinduism, Buddhism or Confucianism). Astronomers, of course, usually use the Latin names for planetary features.

Definition of major features of the surface of the moon

Albedo	Feature area made distinct by large amount of reflected light
Crater	Circular depression formed when meteoroids struck the moon's surface at high speeds. There are hundreds of thousands of recognised craters, ranging in size from hundreds of kilometers to one meter
Lacus (Lake)	Small, dark, relatively smooth area; a lava plain, formed when a crater was filled by lava
Mare (Sea)	Large, dark area (Lava plain)
Mons (Mountain)	Mountain, plural Monte; a large, rounded bump on the surface
Oceanus (Ocean)	Very large dark area (Lava plain)
Palus (Swamp)	Small dark area (Lava plain)
Promontorium (Cape)	Headland. Lighter area sticking out into a lava plain
Sinus (Bay)	Small plain (Lava area)
Vallis (Valley)	Valley; shallow depression

Name	Lattitude	Longitude	Diameter (km)	Meaning of name / named after
Albedo feature				
Reiner Gamma	7.5N	59.0W	70.0	nearby crater
Lakes				
Lacus Aestatis	15.0S	69.0W	90.0	Lake of Summer
Lacus Autumni	9.9S	83.9W	183.0	Lake of Autumn
Lacus Bonitatis	23.2N	43.7E	92.0	Lake of Goodness
Lacus Doloris	17.1N	9.0E	110.0	Lake of Sorrow
Lacus Excellentiae	35.4S	44.0W	184.0	Lake of Excellence
Lacus Felicitatis	19.0N	5.0E	90.0	Lake of Happiness
Lacus Gaudii	16.2N	12.6E	113.0	Lake of Joy
Lacus Hiemalis	15.0N	14.0E	50.0	Wintry Lake
Lacus Lenitatis	14.0N	12.0E	80.0	Lake of Softness
Lacus Luxuriae	19.0N	176.0E	50.0	Lake of Luxury
Lacus Mortis	45.0N	27.2E	151.0	Lake of Death
Lacus Oblivionis	21.0S	168.0W	50.0	Lake of Forgetfulness
Lacus Odii	19.0N	7.0E	70.0	Lake of Hatred
Lacus Perseverantiae	8.0N	62.0E	70.0	Lake of Perseverance
Lacus Solitudinis	27.8S	104.3E	139.0	Lake of Solitude
Lacus Somniorum	38.0N	29.2E	384.0	Lake of Dreams
Lacus Spei	43.0N	65.0E	80.0	Lake of Hope
Lacus Temporis	45.9N	58.4E	117.0	Lake of Time
Lacus Timoris	38.8S	27.3W	117.0	Lake of Fear
Lacus Veris	16.5S	86.1W	396.0	Lake of Spring
Seas				
Mare Anguis	22.6N	67.7E	150.0	Serpent Sea
Mare Australe	38.9S	93.0E	603.0	Southern Sea
Mare Cognitum	10.0S	23.1W	376.0	Sea that has become known
Mare Crisium	17.0N	59.1E	418.0	Sea of Crises
Mare Fecunditatis	7.8S	51.3E	909.0	Sea of Fecundity
Mare Frigoris	56.0N	1.4E	1596.0	Sea of Cold
Mare Humboldtianum	56.8N	81.5E	273.0	Humboldt, Alexander von; German natural historian (1769–1859)
Mare Humorum	24.4S	38.6W	389.0	Sea of Moisture
Mare Imbrium	32.8N	15.6W	1123.0	Sea of Showers
Mare Ingenii	33.7S	163.5E	318.0	Sea of Cleverness
Mare Insularum	7.5N	30.9W	513.0	Sea of Islands
Mare Marginis	13.3N	86.1E	420.0	Sea of the Edge
Mare Moscoviense	27.3N	147.9E	277.0	Sea of Muscovy
Mare Nectaris	15.2S	35.5E	333.0	Sea of Nectar
Mare Nubium	21.3S	16.6W	715.0	Sea of Clouds
Mare Orientale	19.4S	92.8W	327.0	Eastern sea

Mare Serenitatis	28.0N	17.5E	707.0	Sea of Serenity
Mare Smythii	1.3N	87.5E	373.0	Smyth, William Henry; British astronomer (1788–1865)
Mare Spumans	1.1N	65.1E	139.0	Foaming Sea
Mare Tranquillitatis	8.5N	31.4E	873.0	Sea of Tranquility
Mare Undarum	6.8N	68.4E	243.0	Sea of Waves
Mare Vaporum	13.3N	3.6E	245.0	Sea of Vapors

Mountains

Mons Agnes	18.6N	5.3E	1.0	Greek female name
Mons Ampère	19.0N	4.0W	30.0	André Marie; French physicist (1775–1836)
Mons André	5.2N	120.6E	10.0	French male name
Mons Ardeshir	5.0N	121.0E	8.0	Persian (Iranian) king's name
Mons Argaeus	19.0N	29.0E	50.0	peak in Asia Minor (now Erciyas Dagi)
Mons Bradley	22.0N	1.0E	30.0	James; British astronomer (1692–1762)
Mons Delisle	29.5N	35.8W	30.0	nearby crater
Mons Dieter	5.0N	120.2E	20.0	German male name
Mons Dilip	5.6N	120.8E	2.0	Indian male name
Mons Esam	14.6N	35.7E	8.0	Arabic male name
[Mons Euler]	23.3N	29.2W	27.0	Leonhard; Swiss mathematician (1707–1783); now called Mons Vinogradov
Mons Ganau	4.8N	120.6E	14.0	African male name
Mons Gruithuisen	36.0N	39.5W	20.0	nearby Delta crater
Mons Gruithuisen	36.6N	40.5W	20.0	nearby Gamma Crater
Mons Hadley	26.5N	4.7E	25.0	Hadley, John; British instrument maker (1682–1743)
Mons Hadley Delta	25.8N	3.8E	15.0	nearby crater
Mons Hansteen	12.1S	50.0W	30.0	nearby crater
Mons Herodotus	27.5N	53.0W	5.0	nearby crater
Mons Huygens	20.0N	2.9W	40.0	Christian; Dutch astronomer, mathematician, physicist (1629–1695)
Mons La Hire	27.8N	25.5W	25.0	Philippe De; French mathematician, astronome (1640–1718)
Mons Maraldi	20.3N	35.3E	15.0	nearby crater
Mons Moro	12.0S	19.7W	10.0	Antonio Lazzaro; Italian Earth scientist (1687–1764)
Mons Penck	10.0S	21.6E	30.0	Albrecht; German geographer (1858–1945)
Mons Pico	45.7N	8.9W	25.0	Spanish for peak
Mons Piton	40.6N	1.1W	25.0	Mt. Piton on Tenerife in the Canary Islands

Mons Rümker	40.8N	58.1W	70.0	Karl Ludwig Christian; German astronomer (1788–1862)
Mons Usov	12.0N	63.0E	15.0	Mikhail A.; Soviet geologist (1883–1933)
Mons Vinogradov	22.4N	32.4W	25.0	Aleksandr Pavlovich; Soviet geochemist and cosmochemist (1895–1975); formerly called Mons Euler
Mons Vitruvius	19.4N	30.8E	15.0	nearby crater
Mons Wolff	17.0N	6.8W	35.0	Christian, Baron von; German philosopher (1679–1754)
Mont Blanc	45.0N	1.0E	25.0	Named for terrestrial mountain in Alps
Montes Agricola	29.1N	54.2W	141.0	Georgius; German Earth scientist (1494–1555)
Montes Alpes	46.4N	0.8W	281.0	terrestrial Alps
Montes Apenninus	18.9N	3.7W	401.0	terrestrial Apennines
Montes Archimedes	25.3N	4.6W	163.0	nearby crater
Montes Carpatus	14.5N	24.4W	361.0	terrestrial Carpathians
Montes Caucasus	38.4N	10.0E	445.0	terrestrial Caucasus Mountains
Montes Cordillera	17.5S	81.6W	574.0	Spanish for mountain chain
Montes Haemus	19.9N	9.2E	560.0	Named for range in the Balkans
Montes Harbinger	27.0N	41.0W	90.0	Harbingers of dawn on crater Aristarchus
Montes Jura	47.1N	34.0W	422.0	terrestrial Jura Mountains
Montes Pyrenaeus	15.6S	41.2E	164.0	terrestrial Pyrenees
Montes Recti	48.0N	20.0W	90.0	Latin for straight range
Montes Riphaeus	7.7S	28.1W	189.0	range in Asia (now Ural Mountains)
Montes Rook	20.6S	82.5W	791.0	Lawrence; British astronomer (1622–1666)
Montes Secchi	3.0N	43.0E	50.0	nearby crater
Montes Spitzbergen	35.0N	5.0W	60.0	German for sharp peaks,
Montes Taurus	28.4N	41.1E	172.0	terrestrial Taurus Mts
Montes Teneriffe	47.1N	11.8W	182.0	terrestrial island

Oceans

Oceanus Procellarum	18.4N	57.4W	2568.0	Ocean of Storms

Swamps

Palus Epidemiarum	32.0S	28.2W	286.0	Marsh of Epidemics
Palus Putredinis	26.5N	0.4E	161.0	Marsh of Decay
Palus Somni	14.1N	45.0E	143.0	Marsh of Sleep

Promontories

Promontorium Agarum	14.0N	66.0E	70.0	cape in Sea of Azov

Promontorium Agassiz	42.0N	1.8E	20.0	Jean Louis Rodolphe; Swiss zoologist, geologist (1807–1873)
Promontorium Archerusia	16.7N	22.0E	10.0	cape on the Black Sea
Promontorium Deville	43.2N	1.0E	20.0	Sainte-Claire Charles; French geologist (1814–1876)
Promontorium Fresnel	29.0N	4.7E	20.0	Augustin Jean; French optician (1788–1827)
Promontorium Heraclides	40.3N	33.2W	50.0	Ponticus; Greek astronomer (c. 388–310 B.C.)
Promontorium Kelvin	27.0S	33.0W	50.0	William Thomson, Lord Kelvin; Scottish natural philosopher (1824–1907)
Promontorium Laplace	46.0N	25.8W	50.0	Pierre Simon; French mathematician, astronomer (1749–1827)
Promontorium Taenarium	19.0S	8.0W	70.0	cape in Greece; now Matapan or Tainaron

Bays

Sinus Aestuum	10.9N	8.8W	290.0	Seething Bay
Sinus Amoris	18.1N	39.1E	130.0	Bay of Love
Sinus Asperitatis	3.8S	27.4E	206.0	Bay of Roughness
Sinus Concordiae	10.8N	43.2E	142.0	Bay of Harmony
Sinus Fidei	18.0N	2.0E	70.0	Bay of Trust
Sinus Honoris	11.7N	18.1E	109.0	Bay of Honor
Sinus Iridum	44.1N	31.5W	236.0	Bay of Rainbows
Sinus Lunicus	31.8N	1.4W	126.0	Lunik Bay – landing area of Luna (Lunik) 2
Sinus Medii	2.4N	1.7E	335.0	Bay of the center
Sinus Roris	54.0N	56.6W	202.0	Bay of Dew
Sinus Successus	0.9N	59.0E	132.0	Bay of Success

Valleys

Vallis Alpes	48.5N	3.2E	166.0	Alpine Valley
Vallis Baade	45.9S	76.2W	203.0	nearby crater
Vallis Bohr	12.4N	86.6W	80.0	nearby crater
Vallis Bouvard	38.3S	83.1W	284.0	Alexis; French astronomer, mathematician (1767–1843)
Vallis Capella	7.6S	34.9E	49.0	nearby crater
Vallis Inghirami	43.8S	72.2W	148.0	nearby crater
Vallis Palitzsch	26.4S	64.3E	132.0	nearby crater
Vallis Planck	58.4S	126.1E	451.0	nearby crater
Vallis Rheita	42.5S	51.5E	445.0	nearby crater
Vallis Schrödinger	67.0S	105.0E	310.0	nearby crater
Vallis Schröteri	26.2N	50.8W	168.0	Schröter's Valley
Vallis Snellius	31.1S	56.0E	592.0	nearby crater

Planets of our solar system

	Mercury	Venus	Earth	Mars	Jupiter	Saturn	Uranus	Neptune	Pluto
Sidereal orbital period (year) Earth days/years	87.95d	224.70d	365.26d	686.98d	11.6y	29.46y	84.01y	164.79y	247.7y
Rotation period – days and hours	59d	–243d*	23h56m	24h37m	9h55m	10h24m	17h46m	16h7m	153h18m
Mean distance from Sun:									
km.10^6	57.9	108.2	149.6	228.0	778.4	1427.0	2,869.5	4,497.0	5,900.0
miles.10^6	34.7	64.9	89.8	136.8	467.0	856.2	1,721.7	2,698.0	3,540.0
Orbital velocity:									
km/s	48.0	35.0	30.0	24.0	13.0	10.0	7.0	5.0	5.0
miles/s	29.0	21.0	18.0	14.0	8.0	6.2	4.0	3.1	3.1
Equatorial diameter:									
km	4,880	12,104	12,756.3	6,787	142,200	119,300	51,800	49,500	2,200
miles	2,928	7,262	7663.8	4,072	85,320	71,580	31,080	29,700	1,320
Mass: compared with Earth = 1	0.0553	0.815	1.0	0.1074	317.892	95.168	14.559	17.619	?0.17
Mean density:	5.4	5.2	5.52	3.97	1.33	0.69	1.27	1.64	?
Mean day surface temperature: °C	400	470	20	0	–103	–138	–218	–224	–200
°F	752	878	68	32	–153	–216	–360	–371	–328

Natural satellites

Satellites

The stargazer's 'who' does not always reflect the 'what' of astronomy. Some moons within our planetary system have been identified by numbers rather than names. Others, though they have a dignified-sounding name from Greek mythology, may be reckoned as little more than a rock with aspirations. And all the time new satellites are being found, or at least newly thought to exist. Here, then, is a rough guide to the kinds of imagination that have been exercised, not in the description of the solar system's moons, but in their naming.

Earth

Moon – In Greek mythology the moon goddess Selene; to the Romans she was Luna.

Mars

Both moons of this planet are named after mythological attendants on the god of war.

Phobos – Fear
Deimos – Terror

Jupiter

At the most recent count, this planet had 61 satellites. Four of these are large enough to demand mention here.

Io – daughter of the king of Argos, transformed by the enamoured Zeus into a white cow which was then tormented by a gadfly on the prompting of Zeus' wife Hera.
Europa – a Tyrian princess, kidnapped by Zeus in the form of a white bull, who swam away with her on its back to Crete and who later, restored to his own form, promised that a continent would be named after her.
Ganymede – a sublimely beautiful boy, cup-bearer to Zeus, who made him immortal.
Callisto – as one of Zeus' many mortal conquests, Callisto was changed into a bear by the vengeful Hera, in which form she was hunted down by her mistress Artemis.

Saturn

Of Saturn's 33 moons, the following are among the most significant. The largest is Titan, which is remarkable for being the only satellite in the solar system to have an atmosphere – in this case composed of nitrogen.

Pan – half man, half goat-figure, ruler over the wild natural world; to the Romans his equivalent was known as Faunus.

Atlas – one of the Titans, after whom the Atlantic is named; punished for opposing his nephew Zeus by being fated to hold up the world for the rest of his existence.

Prometheus – in Greek myth 'Forethought', the champion of mankind, who brought the gift of fire from heaven; for this Zeus punished Prometheus by chaining him to a rock for thirty thousand years while an eagle ate his liver.

Pandora – seen by the Greeks as the first woman, who brought to earth a box bearing all the world's woes. Forbidden to open it, she did so anyway, letting out everything but Hope.

Epimetheus – one of the Titans, creator of the animals.

Janus – Roman god of archways and doors; represented with two faces.

Tethys – the Titan mother of the Oceanids, or sea nymphs, of Greek mythology.

Calypso – in the *Odyssey*, the divine nymph, daughter of Atlas, who delays Odysseus on her island for seven years.

Dione – one of the Titans, mother of Aphrodite.

Rhea – the Titan mother of Zeus.

Titan – the twelve Titans were seen by the Greeks as being an early race of gods, from before the coming of Zeus.

Hyperion – one of the names of the sun god.

Iapetus – the Titan father of Prometheus and Atlas.

Phoebe – one of the Titans, grandmother to the sun god Apollo.

Uranus

This planet has 27 moons – most of these names belong to characters from Shakespeare; two – Belinda and Umbriel – come from the work of Alexander Pope. Each one is given here with the play or poem in which she/he appears or is mentioned.

Cordelia	*King Lear*
Ophelia	*Hamlet*
Bianca	*The Taming of the Shrew*
Cressida	*Troilus and Cressida*
Desdemona	*Othello*
Juliet	*Romeo and Juliet*
Portia	*The Merchant of Venice*
Rosalind	*As You Like It*
Belinda	*The Rape of the Lock*
Puck	*A Midsummer Night's Dream*

Miranda	*The Tempest*
Ariel	*The Tempest*
Umbriel	*The Rape of the Lock*
Titania	*A Midsummer Night's Dream*
Oberon	*A Midsummer Night's Dream*
Caliban	*The Tempest*
Stephano	*The Tempest*
Sycorax	*The Tempest*
Prospero	*The Tempest*
Setebos	*The Tempest*

Neptune

This planet is currently thought to have 13 moons; only two are substantial.

Triton – son of the Greeks' sea god Poseidon; human above the waist and fish below.

Nereid – The Nereids were the fifty sea-nymph daughters of Nereus, the Old Man of the Sea.

Pluto

Charon – the infernal ferryman of Greek myth, who transported the souls of the newly dead across the underworld River Styx to be judged.

Stellar constellations

Constellations are the patterns which the stars make in the sky. Over time many different patterns have been identified, and they have been known by many different names. In 1930 the International Astronomical Union (IAU) defined 88 constellations, and standardised their names.

Constellation (Latin name)	English name	TLA	Possessive (Latin genitive) *	Area in square degrees	Rank in order of size	Position in the celestial sphere †	Notes stars; alpha star (the brightest) in bold [5]	Optimum View from Earth during the month of ...
Andromeda	Andromeda / Chained Lady	And	Andromedae	722	19	N	**Alpheratz**, Almaak, Mirach	November
Antlia	Air Pump	Ant	Antliae	239	62	S	–	April
Apus	Bird of Paradise	Aps	Apodis	206	67	S	–	July
Aquarius	Water Bearer	Aqr	Aquarii	980	10	S	**Sadal Melik**, Skat, Sadachbia, Sadal Sund, Al Bali	October
Aquila	Eagle	Aql	Aquilae	652	22	N – S	**Altair**	September
Ara	Altar	Ara	Arae	237	63	S	–	July
Aries	Ram	Ari	Arietis	441	39	N	**Hamal**, Sheratan, Mearthim, Botein	December
Auriga	Charioteer	Aur	Aurigae	657	21	N	**Capella**, Menkalinan, Elnath	February
Boötes	Herdsman	Boo	Bootis	907	13	N	**Arcturus**, Izar	June
Caelum	Chisel	Cae	Caeli	125	81	S	–	January
Camelopardalis	Giraffe	Cam	Camelopardalis	757	18	N	–	February
Cancer	Crab	Cnc	Cancri	506	31	N	**Acubens**, Asellus Borealis, Asellus Australis, Tegmeni	March
Canes Venatici	Hunting Dogs	CVn	Canun Venaticorum	465	38	N	**Cor Caroli**	May
Canis Major	Great Dog	CMa	Canis Majoris	380	43	S	**Sirius**	February
Canis Minor	Little Dog	CMi	Canis Minoris	182	71	N	**Procyon**	March
Capricornus	Goat	Cap	Capricorni	414	40	S	**Algedi**, Scheiddih, Nashira, Altair, Gredi, Dabih	September
Carina	Keel	Car	Carinae	494	34	S	**Canopus**, (brightest star in the southern sky)	March

Cassiopeia	Cassiopeia	Cas	Cassiopeiae	598	25	N	**Schedar**, Ruchbah, Caph	November
Centaurus	Centaur	Cen	Centauri	1060	9	S	**Rigil Kentaurus** (aka Alpha Centauri) Hadar	May
Cepheus	Cepheus	Cep	Cephei	588	27	N	**Alderamin**, Alfirk, Errai, Delta Cephei	October
Cetus	Whale	Cet	Ceti	1231	4	S	**Menkar**, Mira, Deneb Kaitos, Baten Kaitos	December
Chamaeleon	Chameleon	Cha	Chamaleontis	132	78	S	–	April
Circinus	Compasses	Cir	Circini	93	85	S	–	June
Columba	Dove	Col	Columbae	270	55	S	**Phact**	February
Coma Berenices	Berenice's Hair	Com	Comae Berenices	386	42	N	**Diadem**	May
Corona Australis	Southern Crown	CrA	Coronae Australis	128	80	S	–	August
Corona Borealis	Northern Crown	CrB	Coronae Borealis	179	72	N	**Alphecca**	July
Corvus	Crow	Crv	Corvi	184	70	S	**Alchiba**	May
Crater	Cup	Crt	Crateris	282	53	S	**Alkes**	April
Crux	Southern Cross	Cru	Crucis	68	88	S	**Acrux**, Mimosa	May
Cygnus	Swan	Cyg	Cygni	804	16	N	**Deneb**, Sadr, Albireo	September
Delphinus	Dolphin	Del	Delphini	189	69	N	**Sualocin**	September
Dorado	Swordfish	Dor	Doradus	179		S	–	January
Draco	Dragon	Dra	Draconis	1083	8	N	**Thuban**, Eltanin	July
Equuleus	Little Horse	Equ	Equulei	72	87	N	**Kitalpha**	September
Eridanus	River Eridanus	Eri	Eridani	1138	6	S	**Achernar**	December
Fornax	Furnace	For	Fornacis	398	41	S	–	December
Gemini	Twins	Gem	Geminorum	514	30	N	**Castor, Pollux**, Alhena, Mekbuda, Wasat, Tejat Prior, Tejat Poster, Mebsouta	February

Constellation (Latin name)	English name	TLA	Possessive (Latin genitive) *	Area in square degrees	Rank in order of size	Position in the celestial sphere †	Notes stars; alpha star (the brightest) in bold §	Optimum View from Earth during the month of....
Grus	Crane	Gru	Gruis	366	45	S	**Alnair**	October
Hercules	Hercules	Her	Herculis	1225	5	N	**Rasalgethi**	July
Horologium	Clock	Hor	Horologii	249	58	S	–	December
Hydra	Hydra (Sea Serpent)	Hya	Hydrae	1303	1	S	**Alphard**	April
Hydrus	Water Snake	Hyi	Hydri	243	61	S	–	December
Indus	Indian	Ind	Indi	294	49	S	–	September
Lacerta	Lizard	Lac	Lacertae	201	68	N	–	October
Leo	Lion	Leo	Leonis	947	12	N	**Regulus**, Denebola, Algiba, *The Sickle*, Chort, Zozma, Aldhafera, Ras Elased Borealis, Ras Elasted Australis, Regolo	April
Leo Minor	Smaller Lion	LMi	Leonis Minoris	232	64	N	–	April
Lepus	Hare	Lep	Leporis	290	51	S	**Arneb**	February
Libra	Scales	Lib	Librae	538	29	S	**Zuben Elgenubi**, Zuben Elschemali, Zuben Elakrab, Zuben Elkaribi	June
Lupus	Wolf	Lup	Lupi	334	46	S	**Men**	June
Lynx	Lynx	Lyn	Lyncis	545	28	N	–	March
Lyra	Harp	Lyr	Lyrae	286	52	N	**Vega**, Sheliak, Sulafat	August
Mensa	Table	Men	Mensae	153	75	S	–	January
Microscopium	Microscope	Mic	Microscopii	210	66	S	–	September
Monoceros	Unicorn	Mon	Monocerotis	482	35	S	–	February

Musca	Fly	Mus	Muscae	138	77	S	–	May
Norma	Carpenter's Square	Nor	Normae	165	74	S	–	July
Octans	Octant	Oct	Octantis	291	50	S	–	October
Ophiucus	Serpent Bearer	Oph	Ophiuchi	948	11	N – S	Rasalhague	July
Orion	Orion	Ori	Orionis	594	26	N – S	Betelgeuse, Bellatrix, Mintaka, Rigel, Saiph, Alnilam	January
Pavo	Peacock	Pav	Pavonis	378	44	S	Peacock	September
Pegasus	Winged Horse	Peg	Pegasi	1121	7	N	Markab	October
Perseus	Perseus	Per	Persei	615	24	N	Mirfak, Algol, Pleiades	December
Phoenix	Phoenix	Phe	Phoenicis	469	37	S	Ankaa	November
Pictor	Easel	Pic	Pictoris	247	59	S	Canopus	February
Pisces	Fishes	Psc	Piscium	889	14	N	Alrescha	November
Piscis Austrinus	Southern Fish	PsA	Pisces Austrini	245	60	S	Fomalhaut	October
Puppis	Stern (of a ship)	Pup	Puppis	673	20	S	–	March
Pyxis	Compass	Pyx	Pyxidis	221	65	S	–	March
Reticulum	Net	Ret	Reticuli	114	82	S	–	January
Sagitta	Arrow	Sge	Sagittae	80	86	N	–	September
Sagittarius	Archer	Sgr	Sagittarii	867	15	S	Rukbat, Kaus Australis, Nunki, Kaus Medius, Kaus Borealis	August
Scorpius	Scorpion	Sco	Scorpii	497	33	S	Antares, Shauka, Graffias, Shaula, Sargas, Sabik, Al Niyat, Akrab, Deschubba	July
Sculptor	Sculptor	Scl	Sculptoris	475	36	S	–	November
Scutum	Shield	Sct	Scuti	109	84	S	–	August
Serpens	Serpent	Ser	Serpentis	637	23	N – S	Unuck al Hai	July

Constellation (Latin name)	English name	TLA	Possessive (Latin genitive) *	Area in square degrees	Rank in order of size	Position in the celestial sphere †	Notes stars; alpha star (the brightest) in bold §	Optimum View from Earth during the month of...
Sextans	Sextant	Sex	*Sextantis*	314	47	S	–	April
Taurus	Bull	Tau	*Tauri*	797	17	N	**Aldebaran**, Hyades, Nebulosa del Granchio, Ladi, Ain, Pleiadi, Alcyone, Cappella	January
Telescopium	Telescope	Tel	*Telescopii*	252	57	S	–	August
Triangulum	Triangle	Tri	*Trianguli*	132	78	N	Ras al Mothallah	December
Triangulum Australe	Southern Triangle	TrA	*Trianguli Australis*	110	83	S	Atria	July
Tucana	Toucan	Tuc	*Tucanae*	295	48	S	–	November
Ursa Major	Great Bear	UMa	*Ursae Majoris*	1280	3	N	**Dubhe**, Megraz, Alioth, Mizar, Alcor, Alkaid, Phecda, Merak	April
Ursa Minor	Little Bear	UMi	*Ursae Minoris*	256	56	N	Polaris	June
Vela	Sails	Vel	*Velorum*	500	32	S	–	March
Virgo	Virgin	Vir	*Virginis*	1294	2	N – S	**Spica**, Vindemiatrix	May
Volans	Flying Fish	Vol	*Volantis*	141	76	S	–	March
Vulpecula	Fox	Vul	*Vulpeculae*	268	54	N	–	September

* The genitive is needed for describing stars within the constellation
† N = northern celestial hemisphere: declination between 0° and +90°
S = southern celestial hemisphere: declination between 0° and –90°
§ If no Alpha star is given, the constellation either does not have any named stars, or all its stars appear equally bright (or equally dim)

Many constellations can, of course, be seen from both hemispheres at different times of the year. Declination in the sky is the equivalent of latitude on earth. 0 marks the celestial equator, and 90 marks the celestial north, above the north pole. It is measured in degrees. Right ascension is the equivalent of earthly longitude, and is the other co-ordinate which enables a constellation's position to be mapped. It is measured from the point where the sun crosses the celestial equator and moves north. This equates to the spring equinox, when the sun is crossing through Pisces. Right ascension is calculated in hours, minutes and seconds, from 0 to 24.

Astronomers often do not refer to an Alpha star by its common name, but rather as 'Alpha of (name of the constellation)'. In the usual astronomical language of Latin, this means for example, that Sirius, the Dog Star, is often referred to as Alpha *Canis Majoris* or Alpha CMa for short. Alternatively, in a list of stars of a particular constellation, astronomers might place the Greek letter Alpha (?) before the star's name. Other stars are also ranked in order of brightness. The second brightest is designated Beta, and given the Greek letter Beta (?), and so on. In many cases, astronomers now know that the Alpha star of a constellation is not actually its brightest star, but the traditional Alpha designations have been kept.

Serpens is the only constellation which is divided into two parts: *Serpens Caput* (Head of the Snake) is 429 sq.deg. and *Serpens Cauda* (Tail of the Snake) measures 208 sq.deg. The two parts of the snake are separated by *Ophiuchus*. *Hydra*, the largest constellation, covers 3.158% of the sky. The brightest constellation is *Crux*. The constellation with the greatest number of visible stars in it is *Centaurus*, with 101 stars. Many constellations contain smaller star patterns within them, such as the Big Dipper or Plough in *Ursa Major*, the Little Dipper in *Ursa Minor*, Keystone in *Hercules*, and the Pleiades in *Taurus*.

Stars: the brightest, as seen from Earth

A star's brightness is called its *magnitude*, which is measured in two ways. *Apparent magnitude* is how bright the star appears to the human eye. This means that stars that are closer to earth will usually appear brighter than ones of the same real magnitude which are farther away. The actual light output from a star is called its *absolute magnitude*. This is the measurement of brightness at a distance of 10 parsecs (32.6 light years) from the star. The brighter an object, the lower its scale of magnitude; a high magnitude number means that the object is less bright. So, the brightest stars have a high negative number. A few stars visibly vary a great deal – sometimes appearing much dimmer than usual depending on atmospheric conditions or position of the earth. Those are marked (var).

Common name	Scientific name	Constellation	Apparent magnitude	Absolute magnitude	Light years from Earth
Sun	Sol	(Solar system)	−26.72	4.8	– (150 M km)
Sirius	Alpha CMa	Canis Major	−1.46	1.4	8.6
Canopus	Alpha Car	Carina	−0.72	−2.5	74
Rigil Kentaurus	Alpha Cen	Centaurus	−0.27	4.4	4.3
Arcturus	Alpha Boo	Boötes	−0.04	0.2	34
Vega	Alpha Lyr	Lyra	0.03	0.6	25
Capella	Alpha Aur	Auriga	0.08	0.4	41
Rigel	Beta Ori	Orion	0.12	−8.1	900
Procyon	Alpha CMi	Canis Minor	0.38	2.6	11.4
Achernar	Alpha Eri	Eridanus	0.46	−1.3	69
Betelgeuse	Alpha Ori	Orion	0.50 (var)	−7.2	427
Hadar	Beta Cen	Centaurus	0.61 (var)	−4.4	320
Acrux	Alpha Cru	Crux	0.76	−4.6	510
Altair	Alpha Aql	Aquila	0.77	2.3	16
Aldebaran	Alpha Tau	Taurus	0.85 (var)	−0.3	60
Antares	Alpha Sco	Scorpius	0.96 (var)	−5.2	600
Spica	Alpha Vir	Virgo	0.98 (var)	−3.2	220
Pollux	Beta Gem	Gemini	1.14	0.7	40
Fomalhaut	Alpha PsA	Piscis Austrinus	1.16	2.0	22
Becrux	Beta Cru	Crux	1.25 (var)	−4.7	460
Deneb	Alpha Cyg	Cygnus	1.25	−7.2	1500
Regulus	Alpha Leo	Leo	1.35	−0.3	69
Adhara	Epsilon CMa	Canis Major	1.50	−4.8	570
Castor	Alpha Gem	Gemini	1.57	0.5	49
Gacrux	Gamma Cru	Crux	1.63 (var)	−1.2	120
Shaula	Lambda Sco	Scorpius	1.63 (var)	−3.5	330

Stars: the nearest to Earth

As scientists develop more sensitive equipment, it is likely that this list will change in the future when 'new' stars are detected.

A light year is 9,460,000 million km – the distance that a beam of light travels in one year. It is one of the basic astronomical measurements of distance, though professional astronomers prefer the parsec = 3.26 light years.

Common name	Scientific name	Constellation	Dist (light years)	Apparent magnitude	Absolute magnitude
Sun	Sol	(Solar system)	– (150 M km)	–26.72	4.8
Proxima Centauri	V645 Cen	Centaurus	4.2	11.05 (var)	15.5
Rigil Kentaurus	Alpha Cen A	Centaurus	4.3	–0.01	4.4
–	Alpha Cen B	Centaurus	4.3	1.33	5.7
Barnard's Star	–	Ophiuchus	6.0	9.54	13.2
Wolf 359	CN Leo	Leo	7.7	13.53 (var)	16.7
Lalande 21185	BD +36 2147	Ursa Major	8.2	7.50	10.5
Luyten 726-8A	UV Cet A	Cetus	8.4	12.52 (var)	15.5
Luyten 726-8B	UV Cet B	Cetus	8.4	13.02 (var)	16.0
Sirius A	Alpha CMa A	Canis Major	8.6	–1.46	1.4
Sirius B	Alpha CMa B	Canis Major	8.6	8.3	11.2
Ross 154	Ross 154	Sagittarius	9.4	10.45	13.1
Ross 248	Ross 248	Andromeda	10.4	12.29	14.8
–	Epsilon Eri	Eridanus	10.8	3.73	6.1
Ross 128	Ross 128	Virgo	10.9	11.10	13.5
–	61 Cyg A (V1803 Cyg)	Cygnus	11.1	5.2 (var)	7.6
–	61 Cyg B	Cygnus	11.1	6.03	8.4
–	Epsilon Ind	Indus	11.2	4.68	7.0
–	BD +43 44 A	Cygnus	11.2	8.08	10.4
–	BD +43 44 B	Cygnus	11.2	11.06	13.4
Luyten 789-6	Luyten 789-6	Aquarius	11.2	12.18	14.5
Procyon A	Alpha CMi A	Canis Minor	11.4	0.38	2.6
Procyon B	Alpha CMi B	Canis Minor	11.4	10.7	13.0
–	BD +59 1915 A	Draco	11.6	8.90	11.2
–	BD +59 1915 B	Draco	11.6	9.69	11.9
Lacaille 9352	CoD -36 15693	Piscis Austrinis	11.7	7.35	9.6

The human world

UK counties and Metropolitan areas post-1974

England

County or area	AC/UA	Admin HQ	Abbreviation	Royal Mail abbreviation	Postcode	Area (km²)	Highest point (ft)	Highest point (m)	Highest point and location
Bedfordshire			Beds	Beds		1,236	798	243	Dunstable Downs in Chilterns, nr Dunstable
Bedfordshire	AC	Bedford			MK	1,192			
Luton	UA	Luton			LU	43			
Berkshire			Berks	Berks		1,259	974	296	Walbury Hill and Inkpen Beacon
Bracknell Forest	UA	Bracknell			RG	109			
Newbury	UA	Newbury			RG	704			
Reading	UA	Reading			RG	40			
Slough	UA	Slough			SL	27			
Windsor and Maidenhead	UA	Maidenhead			SL	198			
Wokingham	UA	Wokingham			RG	179			
Buckinghamshire			Bucks	Bucks		1,877	857	261	Near Ashton Hill
Buckinghamshire	AC	Aylesbury			HP	1,568			
Milton Keynes	UA	Milton Keynes			MK	309			
Cambridgeshire			Cambs	Cambs		3,067	478	145	300 yards (275m) south of the Hall, Great Chishill
Cambridgeshire	AC	Cambridge			CB	3,067			
Peterborough	UA	Peterborough			PE	333			

County / Area	Type	Admin HQ	Abbr	Code	Area	Pop	Height	Highest point
Cheshire			Ches		2,331	1,834	559	Shining Tor
Cheshire	AC	Chester		CH	2,081			
Halton	UA	Widnes		WA	74			
Warrington	UA	Warrington		WA	176			
Cornwall		Truro	Corn	TR	3,530	1,377	419	Brown Willy
Cumbria (was Cumberland)		Carlisle	Cumb	CA	6,817	3,210	978	Scafell Pike
Derbyshire			Derbys		2,629	2,088	621	Kinder Scout, between Crowden Head and Kinder Low
Derby	UA	Derby		DE	78			
Derbyshire	AC	Matlock		DE	2,551			
Devon (was Devonshire)			Devon		6,698	2,038	621	High Willhays, 4 miles south of Okehampton
Devon	AC	Exeter		EX	6,561			
Plymouth	UA	Plymouth		PL	74			
Torbay	UA	Torquay		TQ	63			
Dorset			Dors		2,653	908	276	Pilsdon Pen
Bournemouth	UA	Bournemouth		BH	46			
Dorset	AC	Dorchester		DT	2,542			
Poole	UA	Poole		BH	65			
Durham			Dur	Co Durham	2,726	2,591	798	Mickle Fen
County Durham	AC	Durham		DH	2,231			
Darlington	UA	Darlington		DL	197			
Hartlepool	UA	Hartlepool		TS	94			
Stockton-on-Tees	UA	Stockton-on-Tees		TS	204			
East Sussex			E Ssx		1,794	813	247	Ditchling Beacon
Brighton and Hove	UA	Brighton		BN	81			
East Sussex	AC	Lewes		BN	1,713			
Ely, Isle of (Now part of Cambridgeshire)						120	36	North Hill, Haddenham

County	Type	Admin centre	Abbr.	Code	Area	Highest point (ft)	Highest point (m) & location
Essex			Exx		3,662	480	146 In High Wood, Langley
Essex	AC	Chelmsford		CM	3,456		
Southend	UA	Southend-on-Sea		SS	42		
Thurrock	UA	Grays		RM	164		
Gloucestershire			Glos		3,260	1,083	330 Cleave Hill, 3 miles north-east of Cheltenham
Bristol	UA	Bristol		BS	110		
Gloucestershire	AC	Gloucester		GL	2,653		
South Gloucestershire	UA	Thornbury		BS	497		
Hampshire			Hants		3,777	937	285 Pilot Hill, near Ashmansworth
Hampshire	AC	Winchester		SO	3,685		
Portsmouth	UA	Portsmouth		PO	42		
Southampton	UA	Southampton		SO	50		
Herefordshire		Hereford		HR	2,182	2,306	702 In Black Mountains
Hertfordshire		Hertford	Herts	SG	1,639	802	244 ¼ from Hastoe Village, nr Tring
Huntingdonshire (Now part of Cambridgeshire)			*Hunts*			256	78 *1 mile north of Covington*
Isle of Wight	UA	Newport		PO	380	2,034	619 Snaefell
Kent			Kent		3,728	824	251 Between Westerham and Biggin Hill (old fort trig. point)
Kent	AC	Maidstone		ME	3,537		
The Medway Towns	UA	Strood		ME	191		
Lancashire			Lancs		3,070	2,057	626 Gragareth
Blackburn and Darwen	UA	Blackburn		BB	137		
Blackpool	UA	Blackpool		FY	35		
Lancashire	AC	Preston		PR	2,898		

Leicestershire			Leics	Leics		2,157	912	277	Bardon Hill, 2¼ miles east-south-west of Coalville
Leicester	UA	Leicester			LE	73			
Leicestershire	AC	Glenfield, Leicester			LE	2,084			
Lincolnshire			Lincs	Lincs		6,899	550	167	Near Normanby-le-Wold
Lincolnshire	AC	Lincoln			LN	5,921			
North Lincolnshire	UA	Scunthorpe			DN	786			
North East Lincolnshire	UA	Grimsby			DN	192			
London, Greater						1,578	809	246	33 yds (30m) south-east of 'Westerham Heights' (a house) on the Kent GLC boundary
Barking and Dagenham		Dagenham			RM	34			
Barnet		Hendon			NW	89			
Bexley		Bexleyheath			DA	61			
Brent		Wembley			HA	44			
Bromley		Bromley			BR	152			
Camden		St Pancras			NW	22			
City of London		City of London			EC	2.7			
Croydon		Croydon			CR	87			
Ealing		Ealing			W	55			
Enfield		Enfield			EN	81			
Greenwich		Woolwich			SE	48			
Hackney		Hackney			E	20			
Hammersmith and Fulham		Hammersmith			SW	16			
Haringey		Wood Green			N	30			
Harrow		Harrow			HA	51			
Havering		Romford			RM	178			
Hillingdon		Uxbridge			UB	110			
Hounslow		Hounslow			TW	58			

Name	Place	Code	Area
Islington	Islington	N	15
Kensington and Chelsea	Kensington	W	12
Kingston upon Thames	Kingston upon Thames	KT	38
Lambeth	Brixton	SW	27
Lewisham	Catford	SE	35
Merton	Morden	SW	38
Newham	East Ham	E	36
Redbridge	Ilford	IG	56
Richmond upon Thames	Twickenham	TW	55
Southwark	Camberwell	SE	29
Sutton	Sutton	SM	43
Tower Hamlets	Bethnal Green	E	20
Waltham Forest	Walthamstow	E	40
Wandsworth	Wandsworth	SW	35
Westminster	Westminster	SW	22
Manchester, Greater		GM	1,289 1,774 540 Feathered Moss
Bolton	Bolton	M BL	140
Bury	Bury	M	99
Manchester	Manchester	M	116
Oldham	Oldham	OL	141
Rochdale	Rochdale	OL	160
Salford	Salford	M	97
Stockport	Stockport	SK	126
Tameside	Ashton-under-Lyne	M	103
Trafford	Stretford	M	106
Wigan	Wigan	WN	199

Name	Status	Administrative HQ	Abbr.	Abbr.	Postcode			Highest point
Merseyside			Mers			655	588	179 Billinge Hill
Knowsley		Kirkby			L	97		
Liverpool		Liverpool			L	113		
St Helens		St Helens			WA	133		
Sefton		Bootle			L	153		
Wirral		Wallasey			L	159		
Middlesex – Defunct, although still used for postal addresses			*Mddx*				504	153 *High Road, Bushey Heath*
Norfolk		Norwich	Nflk		NR	5,385	335	102 Sandy Lane, east of Sheringham
North Yorkshire			N Yorks	N Yorkshire		8,608	2,419	737 Whernside
Middlesbrough	UA	Middlesbrough			TS	54		
North Yorkshire	AC	Northallerton			DL	8,007		
Redcar and Cleveland	UA	Eston			TS	245		
York	UA	York			YO	273		
Northamptonshire		Northampton	Northants	Northants	NN	2,367	734	223 Arbury Hill, nr Daventry
Northumberland		Morpeth	Northd	Northd	NE	5,026	2,676	815 The Cheviot
Nottinghamshire		Nottingham	Notts	Notts	NG	2,160	653	199 Herrod's Hill
Nottingham	UA	Nottingham			NG	75		
Nottinghamshire	AC	West Bridgford, Nottingham				2,085		
Oxfordshire		Oxford	Oxon	Oxon	OX	2,583	856	260 White Horse Hill
Rutland		Oakham			LE	394	625	190 Ranksborough Hill, north of Oakham
Shropshire		Shrewsbury			SY	3,488	1,790	545 Brown Clee Hill
Shropshire	AC	Shrewsbury			SY	3,197		
The Wrekin	UA	Telford			TF	290		

Name		Admin centre	Abbr	County	Postcode	Area	Total	Height	Highest point
Somerset			Som			4,178	1,705	519	Dunkery Beacon
Bath and North East Somerset	UA	Bath			BA	351			
North West Somerset	UA	Weston-super-Mare			BS	375			
Somerset	AC	Taunton			TA	3,452			
South Yorkshire			S Yorks	S Yorkshire		1,559	1,791	545	Margery Hill
Barnsley		Barnsley			S	328			
Doncaster		Doncaster			DN	581			
Rotherham		Rotherham			S	283			
Sheffield		Sheffield			S	367			
Staffordshire			Staffs	Staffs		2,715	1,684	513	Oliver Hill
Staffordshire	AC	Stafford			ST	2,623			
Stoke-on-Trent	UA	Stoke-on-Trent			ST	93			
Suffolk		Ipswich	Sflk		IP	3,798	420	128	Rede
Surrey		Kingston upon Thames	Sry		KT		965	294	Leith Hill, nr Dorking
Tyne and Wear			T&W	Tyne and Wear		537	851	259	Nr Chopwell
Gateshead		Gateshead			NE	143			
Newcastle upon Tyne		Newcastle upon Tyne			NE	112			
North Tyneside		North Shields			NE	84			
South Tyneside		South Shields			NE	63			
Sunderland		Sunderland			SR	135			
Warwickshire		Warwick	Warks	Warks	CV	1,979	854	260	Ilmington Downs

									Where?
West Midlands			W Mids	W Midlands		899	876	267	Turner's Hill
Birmingham		Birmingham			B	265			
Coventry		Coventry			CV	97			
Dudley		Dudley			DY	98			
Sandwell		Oldbury			CV	86			
Solihull		Solihull			B	179			
Walsall		Walsall			WS	106			
Wolverhampton		Wolverhampton			WV	69			
West Sussex		Chichester	W Ssx	W Sussex	PO	1,969	919	280	Blackdown Hill, Fernhurst
West Yorkshire			W Yorks	W Yorkshire		2,034	1,908	581	Black Hill
Bradford		Bradford			BD	366			
Calderdale		Halifax			HX	363			
Kirklees		Huddersfield			HD	410			
Leeds		Leeds			LS	562			
Wakefield		Wakefield			WF	333			
Wiltshire	UA		Wilts	Wilts		3,476	964	293	Milk Hill and Tan Hill, 1¼ miles north of Alton Barnes
Swindon	AC	Swindon			SN	230			
Wiltshire		Trowbridge			BA	3,246			
Worcestershire		Worcester			WR	1,742	1,395	425	Worcestershire Beacon, Malvern Hills

Wales

	Abbreviation	Postcode	Area	Highest point and location (ft)	(m)	
Anglesey (Ynys Mon)	C	Llangefni	LL	719	720	219 Caer y Twr
Blaenau Gwent	CB	Ebbw Vale (Glyn Ebwy)	NP	109		
Bridgend (Penybont ar Ogwr)	CB	Bridgend (Penybont ar Ogwr)	CF	246		
Caerphilly (Caerffili)	CB	Ystrad Mynach	CF	279		
Cardiff, City of (Caerdydd)	CB	Cardiff (Caerdydd)	CF	139		
Carmarthenshire (Sir Caerfyrddin)	C	Carmarthen (Caerfyrddin)	Carm	SA	2,398	2,500 762 Carmarthen Fan Foel
Ceredigion	C	Aberaeron	SA	1,797		
Conwy	CB	Conwy	LL	1,130		
Denbighshire (Sir Dinbych)	C	Ruthin (Rhuthun)	Denb	LL	844	2,713 826 Moel Sych and Cader Berwyn
Flintshire (Sir Fflint)	C	Mold (Yr Wyddgrug)	Fl	CH	437	1,820 554 Moel Fammau (Mother of Hills)
Gwynedd	C	Caernarfon	Gynd	LL	2,548	3,560 1,085 Snowdon (YrWyddfa)

County	Type	Administrative centre		Postcode			
Merthyr Tydil (Merthyr Tudful)	CB	Merthyr Tydfil (Merthyr Tudful)		CF	111		
Monmouthshire (Sir Fynwy)	C	Cwmbran	Monm	NP	851	2,28	677 Chwarel-y-Fan
Neath Port Talbot (Castellnedd Port Talbot)	CB	Port Talbot		SA	442		
Newport (Casnewydd)	CB	Newport (Casnewydd)		NP	191		
Pembrokeshire (Sir Benfro)	C	Haverfordwest (Hwlffordd)	Pembs	SA	1,590	1,760	536 Foel Cwmcerwyn
Powys	C	Llandrindod Wells (Llandrindod)	Pwys	LD	5,204	2,907	885 Pen-y-Fan (Cader Arthur)
Rhondda, Cynon, Taff	CB	Clydach Vale (Glyn Clydach)		SA	424		
Swansea, City of	CB	Swansea (Abertawe)		SA	378		
Torfaen	CB	Pontypool (Pontypwl)		NP	126		
Vale of Glamorgan, The (Cyngor Bro Morgannwg)	CB	Barry (Y Barri)		CF	337		
Wrexham (Wrecsam)	CB	Wrexham (Wrecsam)		LL	499		

Scotland

County		Abbreviation	Postcode	Area	(ft)	(m)	Highest point and location
Aberdeen, City of	Aberdeen		AB	182	4,296	1309	Ben Macdhui (shared with Banffshire)
Aberdeenshire	Aberdeen		AB	6,317			
Angus	Forfar		DD	2,184	3,504	1,068	Glas Maol
Argyll and Bute	Lochgilphead		PA	7,023	3,766	1,147	Bidean nam Bian
Clackmannanshire	Alloa		FK	158	2,364	720	Ben Cleugh (Clach) (Ochils)
Dumfries and Galloway	Dumfries	D & G	DG	6,446	2,770	844	Merrick
Dundee, City of	Dundee		DD	55			
East Ayrshire	Kilmarnock		KA	1,275			
East Dunbartonshire	Kirkintilloch		G	176			
East Lothian	Haddington		EH	666	1,755	534	Meikle Says Law
East Renfrewshire	Giffnock		G	168			
Edinburgh, City of	Edinburgh		EH	260			
Falkirk	Falkirk		FK	293			
Fife	Glenrothes	Fife	KY	1,340	1,713	522	West Lomond
Glasgow, City of	Glasgow		G	175			
Highland	Inverness	Hghld	IV	26,119	4,406	1,342	BEN NEVIS
Inverclyde	Greenock		PA	167			
Midlothian	Dalkeith		EH	350	2,137	651	Blackhope Scar

County	Town		Postcode			Highest point
Moray	Elgin		IV	2,237	2,329	709 Carn A 'Ghille Chearr
North Ayrshire	Irvine		KA	888		
North Lanarkshire	Motherwell		ML	476		
Orkney	Kirkwall	Ork	KW	1,025	1,570	478 Ward Hill, Hoy
Perth and Kinross	Perth		PH	5,395		
Renfrewshire	Paisley		PA	262	1,713	522 Hill of Stake (on Ayrshire border)
Scottish Borders, The	Newton St Boswells		TD	4,727		
Shetland	Lerwick	Shetd	ZE	1,471	1,486	452 Ronas Hill, North Mavine
South Ayrshire	Ayr		KA	1,230		
South Lanarkshire	Hamilton		ML	1,778		
Stirling	Stirling		FK	2,243	3,192	972 Ben Lomond
West Dunbartonshire	Dumbarton		G	176		
Western Isles	Stornoway	W Is	PA	3,070	2,622	799 Clisham, Harris
West Lothian	Livingston		EH	427	1,023	311 The Knock

Northern Ireland

	Abbreviation	Postcode	Area	(ft)	Highest point and location (m)	
Antrim	Antrim	Ant	BT	578	1,817	553 Trostàn
Ards	Newtonards		BT	381		
Armagh	Armagh	Arm	BT	671	1,894	577 Slieve Gullion
Ballymena	Ballymena		BT	632		
Ballymoney	Ballymoney		BT	419		
Banbridge	Banbridge		BT	446		
Belfast, City of	Belfast		BT	115		
Carrickfergus	Carrickfergus		BT	82		
Castlereagh	Cregagh		BT	85		
Coleraine	Coleraine		BT	486		
Cookstown	Cookstown		BT	622		
Craigavon	Portadown		BT	379		
Derry	Londonderry/ Derry	Londy	BT	387	2,240	682 Sawel Mountain

Down	Downpatrick	Down	BT	650	2,796	852	SLIEVE DONARD
Dungannon	Dungannon		BT	783			
Fermanagh	Enniskillen	Ferm	BT	1,877	2,188	666	Cuilcagh
Larne	Larne		BT	336			
Limavady	Limavady		BT	586			
Magherafelt	Magherafelt		BT	572			
Moyle	Ballycastle		BT	494			
Newry and Mourne	Newry		BT	909			
Newtonabbey	Ballyclare		BT	151			
North Down	Bangor		BT	82			
Omagh	Omagh		BT	1,130			
Strabane	Strabane		BT	862			

Old British counties

England

Beds	Bedfordshire	Bedford
Berks	Berkshire	Reading
Bucks	Buckinghamshire	Aylesbury
Cambs	Cambridgeshire and the Isle of Ely	Cambridge
Ches	Cheshire	Chester
Corn	Cornwall	Truro
Cumb	Cumberland	The Courts, Carlisle
Derbys	Derbyshire	Matlock
Devon	Devonshire	The Castle, Exeter
Dor	Dorset	Dorchester
Dur, Co Dur	Durham	Durham
Essex	Essex	Chelmsford
Glos	Gloucestershire	Gloucester
Hants	Hampshire	The Castle, Winchester
Here	Herefordshire	Hereford
Herts	Hertfordshire	Hertford
Hunts	Huntingdonshire	Huntingdon
IoM, I of M	Isle of Man	
IoW, I of W	Isle of Wight	
IoS, Is of Sc	Isles of Scilly	
Kent	Kent	Maidstone
Lancs	Lancashire	Preston
Leics	Leicestershire	Grey Friars, Leicester
Lincs	*Lincolnshire:*	
	Holland	Boston
	Kesteven	Sleaford
	Lindsey	Lincoln
	London, Greater	County Hall, S E
Mddx	Middlesex	
Norf	Norfolk	Martineau Lane, Norwich

Northants	Northamptonshire	Northampton
Northd, Northumb	Northumberland	Newcastle on Tyne
Notts	Nottinghamshire	West Bridgford
Oxon	Oxfordshire	Oxford
	Soke of Peterborough	
Rut	Rutland	Catmose, Oakham
Salop	Shropshire	Shrewsbury
Som	Somerset	Taunton
Staf	Staffordshire	Stafford
Suff	Suffolk:	
	East Suffolk	Ipswich
	West Suffolk	Bury St Edmunds
Sy	Surrey	Kingston upon Thames
Ssx	*Sussex:*	
	East Sussex	Lewes
	West Sussex	Chichester
Warw	Warwickshire	Warwick
Westm	Westmorland	Kendal
Wilts	Wiltshire	Trowbridge
Worcs	Worcestershire	Worcester
Yorks	*Yorkshire:*	
	East Riding	Beverley
	North Riding	Northallerton
	West Riding	Wakefield

Administrative areas created from 1 April 1974 that have since disappeared:

Avon – defunct 1 April 1996, became part of Somerset, Gloucestershire and Bristol.
Cleveland – defunct 1 April 1996, became part of Durham and North Yorkshire.
Hereford and Worcester – split into Hereford and Worcestershire 1 April 1998.
Humberside – defunct from 1 April 1996, became part of Lincolnshire or East Riding of Yorkshire.

Wales

Angle	Anglesey	Llangefni
Breck	Brecknockshire	Brecon
Caern	Ca(e)rnarvonshire	Caernarvon
Card	Cardiganshire	Aberystwyth
Carm	Carmarthenshire	Carmarthen
Denb	Denbighshire	Ruthin
Fl	Flintshire	Mold
Glam	Glamorgan	Cardiff
Meri	Merioneth	Dolgellau
Monm	Monmouthshire	Newport
Mont	Montgomeryshire	Welshpool
Pembs	Pembrokeshire	Haverfordwest
Rad	Radnorshire	Llandrindod Wells

Administrative counties of Scotland (1889–1975)

Aber	Aberdeenshire	Aberdeen
	Angus	Forfar
Arg	Argyll	Lochgilphead
Ayr	Ayrshire	Ayr
Banf	Banffshire	Banff
Berw	Berwickshire	Duns
	Buteshire	
Caith	Caithness	Wick
Clack	Clackmannanshire	Alloa
Dumfrie	Dumfriesshire	Dumfries
Dumbar	Dunbartonshire	Dumbarton
	East Lothian	Haddington
Fife	Fife	Cupar
Inver	Inverness-shire	Inverness
Kincar	Kincardineshire	Stonehaven
Kin	Kinross-shire	Kinross
Kirkcud	Kirkcudbrightshire	Kirkcudbright

Lan	Lanarkshire	Hamilton
	Mid Lothian	Edinburgh
	Morayshire	Elgin
Nairn	Nairnshire	Nairn
	Orkney	Kirkwall
Peeb	Peeblesshire	Peebles
Per	Perthshire	Perth
Renf	Renfrewshire	Paisley
R&C	Ross and Cromarty	Dingwall
Roxb	Roxburghshire	Newtown St Boswells
Selk	Selkirk	Selkirk
	Shetland	Lerwick
Stirl	Stirlingshire	Stirling
Suther	Sutherland	Golspie
	West Lothian	
Wig	Wigtownshire	Stranraer

Irish counties

Ireland was originally a kingdom divided into four provinces: Ulster, Leinster, Munster and Connacht (Connaught). Six of the nine counties in Ulster now comprise Northern Ireland while three remain in the Republic of Ireland.

Ulster: Northern Ireland

Antrim	Ant
Armagh	Arm
Down	Down
Fermanagh	Ferm
Londonderry	Londy
Tyrone	Tyr

Ulster (Republic of Ireland)

Cavan	Cav
Donegal	Dngl
Monaghan	Mongh

Leinster

Carlow	Carl
Dublin	Dub
Kildare	Kild
Kilkenny	Kilk
Laois	Laois
Longford	Long
Louth	Louth
Meath	Meath
Offaly	Ofly
Wexford	Wex
Wicklow	Wklw
Westmeath	Wmth

Munster

Clare	Clare
Cork	Cork
Kerry	Kerry
Limerick	Lim
Tipperary	Tipp
Waterford	Wat

Connacht

Galway	Gal
Leitrim	Leit
Mayo	Mayo
Roscommon	Rosc
Sligo	Sligo

British telephone exchanges before panumeration

Note: The numbers on the telephone dials corresponded at that time to the following letters:

1	—
2	ABC
3	DEF
4	GHI
5	JKL
6	MN
7	PRS
8	TUV
9	WXY
0	OQ

Thus you may compare dial letters with exchange names.

021 – Birmingham

Acocks Green	021-706
Ashfield	021-351
Aston Cross	021-359
Bearwood	021-429
Birchfield	021-356
Blackheath	021-559
Broadwell	021-552
Calthorpe	021-440
Castle Bromwich	021-747
Central	021-236
East	021-327
Edgbaston	021-454
Erdington	021-373
Four Oaks	021-308
GPO	021-262
Great Barr	021-357
Halesowen	021-550
Harborne	021-427
Highbury	021-444
Hillside	021-445
James Bridge	021-526
King's Norton	021-458
Marston Green	021-779
Maypole	021-474
Midland	021-643
Northern	021-554
Priory	021-475
Rubery	021-453
Selly Oak	021-472
Sheldon	021-743
Shirley	021-744
Smethwick	021-558
Solihull	021-705
South	021-449
Springfield	021-777
Setchford	021-783
Stone Cross	021-558
Streetly	021-353
Sutton Coldfield	021-354
Tipton	021-557
Victoria	021-772
Wednesbury	021-556
West Bromwich	021-553
Woodgate	021-422

031 – Edinburgh

Abbeyhill	031-661
Caledonian	031-225
Colinton	031-441
Corstorphine	031-334
Craiglockhart	031-443
Davidson's Mains	031-336
Deans	031-332
Donaldson	031-337
Fairmilehead	031-445
Fountainbridge	031-229
GPO	031-550
Granton	031-552
Leith	031-554
Liberton	031-664
Morningside	031-447
Musselburgh	031-667
Newington	031-667
Pentland	031-449
Portobello	031-669
Waverley	031-556

041 – Glasgow

Baillieston	041-771
Barrhead	041-881
Battlefield	041-649
Bearsden	041-942
Bell	041-552
Bishopsbriggs	041-772
Bridgeton	041-554
Busby	041-644
Cambuslang	041-641
Central	041-221
City	041-248
Clydebank	041-952
Cranhill	041-774

Croftfoot	041-634	Bromborough	051-334
Douglas	041-332	Caldy	051-625
Drumchapel	041-944	Central	051-236
Giffnock	041-638	Childwall	051-722
Govan	041-445	Claughton	051-652
GPO	041-220	Cressington Park	051-422
Halfway	041-882	Eastham	051-327
Ibrox	041-427	Ellesmere Port	051-355
Jordanhill	041-954	Garston	051-427
Kelvin	041-334	Gateacre	051-428
Kirkintiloch	041-776	GPO	051-229
Langside	041-632	Great Crosby	051-924
Maryhill	041-946	Hale	051-425
Merrylee	041-637	Hooton	051-339
Milngavie	041-956	Hunts Cross	051-486
Moss Heights	041-883	Huyton	051-489
Newton Mearns	041-639	Irby	051-648
Paisley	041-889	Kirkby	051-547
Parkhead	041-556	Lark Lane	051-727
Pollok	041-423	Lydiate	051-593
Possil	041-336	Maghull	051-526
Provanmill	041-770	Maritime	051-227
Renfrew	041-886	Mountwood	051-608
Rutherglen	041-647	New Brighton	051-639
Scotstoun	041-959	North	051-207
Shettleston	041-778	Prescot	051-426
South	041-429	Rock Ferry	051-645
Springburn	041-558	Royal	051-709
Stepps	041-779	Sefton Park	051-733
Tannahill	041-887	Simonswood	051-546
Thornly Park	041-884	Stanley	051-226
Western	041-339	Stoneycroft	051-228
		Wallasey	051-638
051 – Liverpool		Waterloo	051-928
Aintree	051-525	Windes	051-424
Allerton	051-724	Willaston	051-345
Anfield	051-263		
Argosy	051-274	**061 – Manchester**	
Arrowebrook	051-677	Altrincham	061-928
Birkenhead	051-647	Ardwick	061-273
Bootle	051-922	Ashton-under-Lyme	061-330

Blackfriars	061-834	Woodley	061-430
Bramhall	061-439	Wythenshawe	061-998
Broughton	061-792		
Bury (*Lancashire*)	061-764	**01 – London**	
Central	061-236	Abbey	01-222
Cheetham Hill	061-740	Acorn	01-992
Chorlton-cum-Hardy	061-881	Addiscombe	01-654
Collyhurst	061-205	Advance	01-980
Deansgate	061-832	Albert Dock	01-476
Denton	061-336	Alperton	01-998
Disbury	061-445	Ambassador	01-262
Droylsden	061-370	Amherst	01-985
East	061-223	Archway	01-272
Eccles	061-789	Arnold	01-904
Failsworth	061-681	Atlas	01-568
Gatley	061-428	Avenue	01-283
GPO	061-863	Balham	01-672
Heaton Moor	061-432	Barnet	01-449
Hulme Hall	061-485	Battersea	01-228
Hyde	061-368	Bayswater	01-229
Longford	061-865	Beckenham	01-650
Main (*Oldham*)	061-624	Belgravia	01-235
Medlock Head	061-633	Bermondsey	01-237
Mercury	061-437	Bexleyheath	01-303
Middleton	061-643	Bishopsgate	01-247
Moss Side	061-226	Bluebell	01-656
Pendleton	061-736	Bowes Park	01-888
Prestwich	061-773	Brixton	01-274
Pyramid	061-962	Brunswick	01-278
Radcliffe	061-723	Buckhurst	01-504
Ringway	061-980	Bushey Heath	01-950
Rusholme	061-224	Byron	01-422
Sale	061-973	Bywood	01-668
Stalybridge	061-338	Canonbury	01-226
Stepping Hill	061-483	Central	01-236
Stockport	061-480	Chancery	01-242
Swinton	061-794	Cherrywood	01-540
Trafford Park	061-872	Chiswick	01-994
Urmston	061-748	City	01-248
Walken	061-790	Clerkenwell	01-253
Whitefield	061-766	Clissold	01-254

Clocktower	01-552	Fountain	01-677
Colindale	01-205	Fox Lane	01-882
Concord	01-864	Fremantle	01-373
Coombe End	01-949	Frobisher	01-370
Coppermill	01-520	Fulham	01-385
Covent Garden	01-240	Galleon	01-330
Crescent	01-550	Georgian	01-579
Croyden	01-688	Gerrard	01-437
Crystal Palace	01-659	Gibbon	01-789
Cunningham	01-286	Gipsy Hill	01-670
Danson Park	01-304	Gladstone	01-452
Derwent	01-337	Goodmayes	01-599
Dickens	01-359	Grangewood	01-472
Diligence	01-903	Greenwich	01-858
Dollis Hill	01-450	Grosvenor	01-499
Dominion	01-592	Gulliver	01-485
Drummond	01-908	Hadley Green	01-440
Dryden	01-204	Hampstead	01-435
Duncan	01-690	Harrow	01-427
Ealing	01-567	Hatch End	01-428
East	01-987	Hayes	01-573
Edgware	01-952	Headquarters	01-432
Edmonton	01-807	Hendon	01-202
Elgar	01-965	Highgate Wood	01-444
Elstree	01-953	Hillside	01-445
Eltham	01-850	Hither Green	01-698
Empress	01-603	Hogarth	01-749
Enfield	01-363	Holborn	01-405
Enterprise	01-368	Hop	01-407
Euston	01-387	Hounslow	01-570
Ewell	01-393	Howard	01-804
Fairlands	01-644	Hudson	01-572
Feltham	01-890	Hunter	01-486
Field End	01-868	Hurstway	01-462
Finchley	01-346	Hyde Park	01-493
Fitzroy	01-348	Ilford	01-478
Flaxman	01-352	Imperial	01-467
Fleet Street	01-353	Isleworth	01-560
Floral	01-878	Ivanhoe	01-505
Foots Cray	01-300	Ivydale	01-394
Forest Hill	01-699	Juniper	01-586

Keats	01-366	Municipal	01-686
Kelvin	01-673	Museum	01-636
Kensington	01-589	National	01-628
Kilburn	01-328	New Cross	01-639
Kingston upon Thames	01-546	Noble	01-602
Kipling	01-857	North	01-607
Knightsbridge	01-584	Nuffield	01-848
Laburnum	01-360	Paddington	01-723
Ladbroke	01-969	Palmers Green	01-886
Lakeside	01-947	Park	01-727
Langham	01-580	Peckham Rye	01-732
Larkswood	01-527	Perivale	01-997
Latimer	01-802	Pinner	01-866
Lee Green	01-852	Plumstead	01-855
Leytonstone	01-539	Pollards	01-764
Liberty	01-542	Popesgrove	01-892
Livingstone	01-653	Primrose	01-722
London Wall	01-588	Prospect	01-876
Lords	01-289	Putney	01-788
Loughton	01-508	Raglan	01-556
Lower Hook	01-397	Ravensbourne	01-460
LPR	01-432	Redpost	01-733
LTR	01-587	Regent	01-734
Ludgate Circus	01-583	Reliance	01-735
Macaulay	01-622	Renown	01-736
Maida Vale	01-624	Richmond (*Surrey*)	01-940
Malden	01-942	Rippleway	01-594
Mansion House	01-626	Riverside	01-748
Maryland	01-534	Rodney	01-703
Mayfair	01-629	Royal	01-709
Meadway	01-458	Scott	01-720
Melville	01-643	Seven Kings	01-590
Metropolitan	01-638	Shepherd's Bush	01-743
Mill Hill	01-959	Shoreditch	01-739
Mincing Lane	01-623	Silverthorn	01-529
Mitcham	01-648	Skyport	01-759
Molesey	01-979	Sloane	01-730
Monarch	01-606	Snaresbrook	01-530
Moorgate	01-600	Southall	01-574
Mountview	01-340	Spartan	01-249
Mulberry	01-889	Speedwell	01-455

Springpark	01-777	Turnham Green	01-995
Stamford Hill	01-800	Twickenham Green	01-894
Stepney Green	01-790	Underhill	01-863
Stonegrove	01-958	Uplands	01-660
Streatham	01-769	Upper Clapton	01-806
Sullivan	01-799	Valentine	01-554
Sunnyhill	01-203	Vandyke	01-874
Swiss Cottage	01-794	Victoria	01-834
Sydenham	01-778	Vigilant	01-642
Tabard	01-822	Viking	01-845
Tate Gallery	01-828	Virginia	01-349
TCY	01-829	Wanstead	01-989
Teddington Lock	01-977	Waring Park	01-302
Temple Bar	01-836	Waterloo	01-928
Terminus	01-837	Waxlow	01-578
Thornton Heath	01-684	Welbeck	01-935
Tideway	01-692	Wembley	01-902
Tottenham	01-808	Western	01-937
Townley	01-693	Whitehall	01-930
Trafalgar	01-839	Widmore	01-464
Trevelyan	01-553	Willesden	01-459
Trojan	01-870	Wimbledon	01-946
TSW	01-879	Woolwich	01-854
Tudor	01-883	Wordsworth	01-907
Tulse Hill	01-674		

The rationale for Wimbledon = 946 and Wordsworth = 907 will be apparent.

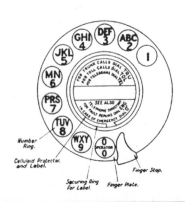

Many compromises had to be made; for example, Hampstead = 426, so Hammersmith became Riverside = 748. As time went on, 'dummy' names such as Acorn, Diligence and Hop had to be introduced.

UK motor vehicle index marks

In the UK, the index marks (registration numbers) of vehicles consist of various combinations of letters and numbers. The letters relate to a vehicle's place of registration, and the numbers to its 'place in the queue'. We give some indication of the antiquity of the marks for the benefit of Vintage and Veteran car buffs. A star* after the letter(s) indicates that they were introduced at the very start of vehicle registration under the Motor Car Act of 1903, which became effective on 1 January 1904.

The dates of later introductions are shown either in the second (present-day area) column or, if the area has changed, after the original area in the third column.

So, for example, AG lately represented Hull, but originally represented Ayrshire from 1925.

	Present area	Original area if different
A*		London
AA*	Bournemouth	Southampton
AB*	Worcester	Worcestershire
AC*	Coventry	Warwickshire
AD*	Gloucester	Gloucestershire
AE*	Bristol	
AF*	Truro	
AG	Hull	Ayr 1925
AH*	Norwich	Norfolk
AI*		Meath County
AJ*	Middlesbrough	Yorkshire: North Riding
AK*	Sheffield	Bradford
AL*	Nottingham	Nottinghamshire
AM*	Swindon	Wiltshire
AN*	Reading	West Ham
AO*	Carlisle	Cumberland
AP*	Brighton	East Sussex
AR*	Chelmsford	Hertfordshire
AS*	Inverness	Nairn
AT*	Hull	
AU*	Nottingham	

AV	Peterborough	Aberdeen 1926
AW*	Shrewsbury	Shropshire
AX*	Cardiff	Monmouthshire
AY*	Leicester	Leicestershire
AZ		Belfast 1928
B*		Lancashire
BA*	Manchester	Salford
BB*	Newcastle upon Tyne	
BC*	Leicester	
BD*	Northampton	Northamptonshire
BE*	Lincoln	Lincolnshire: Parts of Lindsey
BF	Stoke on Trent	
BG*	Liverpool	Birkenhead 1931
BH*	Luton	Buckinghamshire
BI		Monaghan
BJ*	Ipswich	East Suffolk
BK*	Portsmouth	
BL*	Reading	Berkshire
BM*	Luton	Bedfordshire
BN*	Manchester	Bolton
BO*	Cardiff	
BP*	Portsmouth	West Sussex
BR*	Newcastle upon Tyne	Sunderland
BS*	Aberdeen	Orkney
BT*	Leeds	Yorkshire: East Riding
BU*	Manchester	Oldham
BV	Preston	Blackburn 1930
BW	Oxford	Oxfordshire
BX*	Haverfordwest	Carmarthenshire
BY	London NW	Croydon
BZ		Down 1930
C*		Yorkshire: West Riding
CA*	Chester	Denbighshire
CB*	Manchester	Blackburn
CC*	Bangor	Caernarvonshire
CD	Brighton 1920	
CE*	Peterborough	Cambridgeshire
CF	Reading	West Suffolk 1908
CG	Bournemouth	Southampton County 1931
CH*	Nottingham	Derby
CI*		Queen's County

CJ*	Gloucester	Hertfordshire
CK*	Preston	
CL*	Norwich	
CM*	Liverpool	Birkenhead
CN	Newcastle upon Tyne	Gateshead 1920
CO*	Exeter	Plymouth
CP*	Huddersfield	Halifax
CR*	Portsmouth	Southampton
CS*	Glasgow	Ayr 1934
CT*	Lincoln	Lincolnshire: Parts of Kesteven
CU*	Newcastle upon Tyne	South Shields
CV	Truro	Cornwall 1929
CW*	Preston	Burnley
CX*	Huddersfield	
CY*	Swansea	
CZ		Belfast 1932
D*		Kent
DA*	Birmingham	Wolverhampton
DB*	Manchester	Stockport
DC*	Middlesbrough	
DD	Gloucester	Gloucestershire 1921
DE*	Haverfordwest	Pembrokeshire
DF 1926, DG 1930	Gloucester	
DH*	Dudley	Walsall
DI*		Roscommon
DJ*	Liverpool	St Helens
DK*	Manchester	Rochdale
DL*	Portsmouth	Isle of Wight
DM*	Chester	Flintshire
DN*	Leeds	York
DO*	Lincoln	Lincolnshire: Parts of Holland
DP*	Reading	
DR	Exeter	Plymouth 1926
DS*	Glasgow	Peebles
DT	Sheffield	Doncaster 1927
DU*	Coventry	
DV	Exeter	Devon 1929
DW*	Cardiff	Newport (Mon)

DX*	Ipswich	
DY*	Brighton	Hastings
DZ		Antrim County 1932
E*		Staffordshire
EA*	Dudley	West Bromwich
EB*	Peterborough	Isle of Ely
EC*	Preston	Westmorland
ED*	Liverpool	Warrington
EE*	Lincoln	Grimsby
EF*	Middlesbrough	West Hartlepool
EG*	Peterborough	Soke of Peterborough
EH*	Stoke on Trent	
EI*		County Sligo
EJ*	Haverfordwest	Cardiganshire
EK*	Liverpool	Wigan
EL*	Bournemouth	
EM*	Liverpool	Bootle
EN*	Manchester	Bury
EO*	Preston	Barrow-in-Furness
EP*	Swansea	Montgomeryshire
ER	Peterborough	Cambridgeshire 1922
ES*	Dundee	Perth
ET*	Sheffield	Rotherham
EU*	Bristol	Brecknockshire
EV	Chelmsford	Essex 1931
EW*	Peterborough	Huntingdonshire
EX*	Norwich	Great Yarmouth
EY*	Bangor	Anglesey
EZ		Belfast 1935
F*		Essex
FA*	Stoke on Trent	Burton on Trent
FB*	Bristol	Bath
FC	Oxford	
FD*	Dudley	
FE*	Lincoln	
FF*	Bangor	Merioneth
FG	Brighton	Fife 1925
FH*	Gloucester	
FI*		Tipperary: North Riding
FJ*	Exeter	
FK*	Dudley	Worcester

FL*	Peterborough	Soke of Peterborough
FM*	Chester	
FN*	Maidstone	Canterbury
FO*	Gloucester	Radnorshire
FP*	Leicester	Rutland
FR*	Preston	Blackpool
FS	Edinburgh 1931	
FT*	Newcastle upon Tyne	Tynemouth
FU	Lincoln	Lincolnshire: Parts of Lindsey 1922
FV	Preston	Blackpool 1929
FW	Lincoln	Lincolnshire: Parts of Lindsey 1929
FX*	Bournemouth	Dorset
FY*	Liverpool	Southport
FZ		Belfast 1938
G*		Glasgow 1921
GA, GB	Glasgow 1921	
GC	London SW	London 1929
GD	Glasgow 1925	
GE	Glasgow 1928	
GF	London SW	London 1930
GG	Glasgow 1930	
GH, GJ, GK	London SW	London 1930
GL	Truro	Bath 1932
GM	Reading	Motherwell and Wishaw 1921
GN, GO, GP	London SW	London 1931
GR	Newcastle upon Tyne	Sunderland 1933
GS	Luton	Perth 1928
GT	London SW	London 1931
GU	London SE	London 1929
GV	Ipswich	West Suffolk 1930
GW	London SE	London 1931
GX, GY	London SE	London 1932
GZ		Belfast 1942
H*		Middlesex
HA	Dudley	Smethwick 1907
HB	Cardiff	Merthyr Tydfil 1908
HC	Brighton	Eastbourne 1911
HD	Huddersfield	Dewsbury 1913
HE	Sheffield	Barnsley 1913

HF	Liverpool	Wallasey 1913
HG	Preston	Burnley 1930
HH	Carlisle 1914	
HI*		Tipperary: South Riding
HJ	Chelmsford	Southend-on-Sea 1914
HK	Chelmsford	Essex 1915
HL	Sheffield	Wakefield 1915
HM	London C	East Ham 1915
HN	Middlesbrough	Darlington 1921
HO	Bournemouth	Southampton (County) 1917
HP	Coventry 1919	
HR	Swindon	Wiltshire 1919
HS*	Glasgow	Renfrewshire
HT	Bristol 1920	
HU	Bristol 1924	
HV	London C	East Ham 1929
HW	Bristol 1927	
HX	London C	Middlesex 1930
HY	Bristol 1930	
HZ		Tyrone 1944
IA*		County Antrim
IB*		Armagh
IC*		County Carlow
ID*		County Cavan
IE*		County Clare
IF*		County Cork
IH*		County Donegal
IJ*		County Down
IK		County Dublin
IL*		Fermanagh
IM*		County Galway
IN*		County Kerry
IO*		County Kildare
IP*		County Kilkenny
IR*		King's County
IT*		Leitrim
IU		County Limerick
IW*		County Londonderry
IX*		County Longford
IZ		County Mayo 1920

J*		County Durham
JA	Manchester	Stockport 1929
JB	Reading	Berkshire 1932
JC	Bangor	Caernarvonshire 1931
JD	London C	West Ham 1929
JE	Peterborough	Isle of Ely 1933
JF	Leicester 1930	
JG	Maidstone	Canterbury 1929
JH	Reading	Hertfordshire 1931
JI*		Tyrone
JJ	Maidstone	London 1932
JK	Brighton	Eastbourne 1928
JL	Lincoln	Lincolnshire: Parts of Holland 1932
JM	Reading	Westmorland 1931
JN	Chelmsford	Southend-on-Sea 1930
JO	Oxford 1930	
JP	Liverpool	Wigan 1934
JR	Newcastle upon Tyne	Northumberland 1932
JS*	Inverness	Ross and Cromarty
JT	Bournemouth	Dorset 1933
JU	Leicester	Leicestershire 1932
JV	Lincoln	Grimsby 1930
JW	Birmingham	Wolverhampton 1931
JX	Huddersfield	Halifax 1932
JY	Exeter	Plymouth 1932
K*		Liverpool
KA	Liverpool 1925	
KB	Liverpool 1914	
KC	Liverpool 1920	
KD	Liverpool 1927	
KE	Maidstone	Kent 1920
KF	Liverpool 1930	
KG	Cardiff 1931	
KH	Hull 1925	
KJ	Maidstone	Kent 1931
KK	Maidstone	Kent 1922
KL	Maidstone	Kent 1924
KM	Maidstone	Kent 1925
KN	Maidstone	Kent 1917
KO	Maidstone	Kent 1927

KP	Maidstone	Kent 1928
KR	Maidstone	Kent 1929
KS*	Edinburgh	Roxburgh
KT	Maidstone	Kent 1913
KU	Sheffield	Bradford 1922
KV	Coventry 1931	
KW	Sheffield	Bradford 1926
KX	Luton	Buckinghamshire 1928
KY	Sheffield	Bradford 1931
L*		Glamorganshire
LA	London NW	London 1910
LB	London NW	London 1908
LC*	London NW	London
LD	London NW	London 1909
LE	London NW	London 1911
LF	London NW	London 1912
LG	Chester	Cheshire 1928
LH	London NW	London 1913
LI*		County Westmeath
LJ	Bournemouth 1929	
LK	London NW	London 1913
LL	London NW	London 1914
LM	London NW	London 1914
LN	London NW	London 1906
LO	London NW	London 1915
LP	London NW	London 1915
LR	London NW	London 1916
LS	Edinburgh	Selkirk 1923
LT	London NW	London 1918
LU	London NW	London 1919
LV	Liverpool 1932	
LW, LX, LY	London NW	London 1919
M		Cheshire
MA, MB	Chester	Cheshire
MC	London NE	Middlesex 1917
MD	London NE	Middlesex 1920
ME	London NE	Middlesex 1921
MF	London NE	Middlesex 1923
MG	London NE	Middlesex 1924
MH*	London NE	Middlesex
MI		County Wexford 1930

MJ	Luton	Bedfordshire 1932
MK	London NE	Middlesex 1925
ML, MM	London NE	Middlesex 1926
MN	not used	
MO	Reading	Berkshire 1922
MP	London NE	Middlesex 1927
MR	Swindon	Wiltshire 1924
MS*	Edinburgh	Stirling
MT, MU	London NE	Middlesex 1928–29
MV	London SE	Middlesex 1931
MW	Swindon	Wiltshire 1927
MX	London SE	Middlesex 1912
MY	London SE	Middlesex 1929
N*		Manchester
NA	Manchester 1913	
NB	Manchester 1919	
NC	Manchester 1920	
ND	Manchester 1923	
NE	Manchester 1925	
NF	Manchester 1926	
NG	Norwich	Norfolk 1930
NH*	Northampton	
NI*		County Wicklow
NJ	Brighton	East Sussex 1932
NK	Luton	Hertfordshire 1919
NL	Newcastle upon Tyne	Northumberland 1921
NM	Luton	Bedfordshire 1921
NN	Nottingham	Nottinghamshire 1921
NO	Chelmsford	Essex 1921
NP	Worcester	Worcestershire 1921
NR*	Leicester	Leicestershire 1921
NS	Glasgow	Sutherland
NT	Shrewsbury	Shropshire 1921
NU	Nottingham	Derbyshire 1923
NV	Northampton	Northamptonshire 1931
NW	Leeds 1921	
NX	Dudley	Warwickshire 1921
NY	Cardiff	Glamorganshire 1921
O*		Birmingham
OA	Birmingham 1913	
OB	Birmingham 1915	

OC	Birmingham 1933	
OD	Exeter	Devon 1931
OE	Birmingham 1919	
OF	Birmingham 1929	
OG	Birmingham 1930	
OH	Birmingham 1920	
OI*		Belfast
OJ	Birmingham 1932	
OK	Birmingham 1922	
OL	Birmingham 1923	
OM	Birmingham 1924	
ON	Birmingham 1925	
OO	Chelmsford	
OP	Birmingham 1926	
OR	Portsmouth	Southampton (County) 1922
OS	Glasgow	Wigtown 1921
OT	Portsmouth	Southampton (County) 1926
OU	Bristol	Southampton (County) 1928
OV	Birmingham 1931	
OW	Portsmouth	Southampton 1931
OX	Birmingham 1927	
OY	London NW	Croydon 1931
P*		Surrey
PA	Guildford	Surrey 1913
PB	Guildford	Surrey 1919
PC	Guildford	Surrey 1921
PD	Guildford	Surrey 1923
PE	Guildford	Surrey 1925
PF	Guildford	Surrey 1926
PG	Guildford	Surrey 1929
PH	Guildford	Surrey 1927
PI*		Cork
PJ	Guildford	Surrey 1931
PK	Guildford	Surrey 1928
PL	Guildford	Surrey 1930
PM	Guildford	East Sussex 1922
PN	Brighton	East Sussex 1927
PO	Portsmouth	West Sussex 1929

PP	Luton	Buckinghamshire 1923
PR	Bournemouth	Dorset 1923
PS*	Aberdeen	Zetland (Shetland)
PT	Newcastle upon Tyne	County Durham 1922
PU	Chelmsford	Essex 1923
PV	Ipswich 1932	
PW	Norwich	Norfolk 1923
PX	Portsmouth	West Sussex 1923
PY	Middlesbrough	Yorkshire: North Riding 1923
R*		Derbyshire
RA	Nottingham	Derbyshire 1926
RB	Nottingham	Derbyshire 1929
RC	Nottingham	Derby 1931
RD	Reading 1928	
RE	Stoke on Trent	Staffordshire 1921
RF	Stoke on Trent	Staffordshire 1924
RG	Newcastle upon Tyne	Aberdeen (City) 1928
RH	Hull 1930	
RI*		Dublin
RJ	Manchester	Salford 1931
RK	London NW	Croydon
RL	Truro	Cornwall 1924
RM	Carlisle	Cumberland 1924
RN	Preston 1928	
RO	Luton	Hertfordshire 1925
RP	Northampton	Northamptonshire 1924
RR	Nottingham	Nottinghamshire 1925
RS*	Aberdeen	Aberdeen (City)
RT	Ipswich	East Suffolk 1925
RU	Bournemouth 1924	
RV	Portsmouth	Portsmouth 1930
RW	Coventry 1924	
RX	Reading	Berkshire 1927
RY	Leicester 1925	
S*		Edinburgh
SA*	Aberdeen	
SB*	Glasgow	Argyll
SC	Edinburgh 1927	
SCY		Scilly Isles (Truro)
SD	Glasgow	Ayr

SE*	Aberdeen	Banff
SF	Edinburgh 1924	
SG	Edinburgh 1918	
SH*	Edinburgh	Berwick
SJ*	Glasgow	Bute
SK*	Inverness	Caithness
SL*	Dundee	Clackmannan
SM*	Carlisle	Dumfries
SN*	Dundee	Dunbarton
SO*	Aberdeen	Moray
SP	Dundee	Fife
SR*	Dundee	Angus
SS*	Aberdeen	East Lothian
ST*	Inverness	
SU*	Glasgow	Kincardine
SV*	spare	Kinross
SW*	Carlisle	Kirkudbright
SX*	Edinburgh	West Lothian
SY*	spare	Midlothian
T		Devon
TA	Exeter	Devon
TB	Liverpool	Lancashire
TC	Bristol	Lancashire
TD, TE	Manchester	Lancashire
TE	Manchester	Lancashire 1927
TF	Reading	Lancashire 1929
TG	Cardiff	Glamorganshire 1930
TH	Swansea	Carmarthenshire 1929
TI*		Limerick
TJ	Liverpool	Lancashire 1932
TK	Exeter	Dorset 1927
TL	Lincoln	Lincolnshire: Parts of Kesteven 1928
TM	Luton	Bedfordshire 1927
TN	Newcastle upon Tyne 1925	
TO	Nottingham 1924	
TP	Portsmouth 1924	
TR	Portsmouth	Southampton 1925
TS*	Dundee	
TT	Exeter	Devon
TU	Chester	Cheshire 1925

TV	Nottingham 1929	
TW	Chelmsford	Essex 1925
TX	Cardiff	Glamorganshire 1926
TY	Newcastle upon Tyne	Northumberland 1925
U*		Leeds
UA	Leeds 1927	
UB	Leeds 1929	
UC	London C	London 1928
UD	Oxford	Oxfordshire 1926
UE	Dudley	Warwickshire 1925
UF	Brighton 1925	
UG	Leeds 1923	
UH	Cardiff 1925	
UI*		Londonderry
UJ	Shrewsbury	Shropshire 1932
UK	Birmingham	Wolverhampton 1925
UL	London C	London 1929
UM	Leeds 1925	
UN	Exeter	Denbighshire 1927
UO	Exeter	Devon 1926
UP	Newcastle upon Tyne	County Durham 1927
UR	Luton	Hertfordshire 1928
US	Glasgow 1933	
UT	Leicester 1927	
UU, UV, UW	London C	London 1929
UX	Shrewsbury	Shropshire 1927
UY	Worcester	Worcestershire 1927
V*		Lanark
VA	Peterborough	Lanark 1923
VB	Maidstone	Croydon 1927
VC	Coventry 1929	
VD	series withdrawn	Lanark 1933
VE	Peterborough	Cambridgeshire 1928
VF	Norwich	Norfolk 1927
VG	Norwich 1927	
VH	Huddersfield 1927	
VJ	Gloucester	Herefordshire 1927
VK	Newcastle upon Tyne 1929	
VL	Lincoln 1928	
VM	Manchester 1928	

VN	Middlesbrough	Yorkshire: North Riding 1929
VO	Nottingham	Nottinghamshire 1928
VP	Birmingham 1928	
VR	Manchester 1929	
VS*	Luton	Greenock
VT	Stoke on Trent 1927	
VU	Manchester 1930	
VV	Northampton 1930	
VW	Chelmsford	Essex 1927
VX	Chelmsford	Essex 1929
VY	Leeds	York 1928
W*		Sheffield
WA	Sheffield 1919	
WB	Sheffield 1924	
WC	Chelmsford	
WD	Dudley	Warwickshire 1930
WE	Sheffield 1927	
WF	Sheffield	Yorkshire: East Riding 1926
WG	Sheffield	Stirling 1930
WH	Manchester	Bolton 1927
WJ	Sheffield 1930	
WK	Coventry 1926	
WL	Oxford 1925	
WM	Liverpool	Southport 1927
WN	Swansea 1927	
WO	Cardiff	Monmouthshire 1927
WP	Worcester	Worcestershire 1931
WR	Leeds	Yorkshire: West Riding 1915
WS*	Bristol	WS1 – WS500 Leith
		WS 501 – Edinburgh 1934
WT	Leeds	Yorkshire: West Riding 1923
WU	Leeds	Yorkshire: West Riding 1925
WV	Brighton	Wiltshire 1931
WW	Leeds	Yorkshire: West Riding 1927
WX	Leeds	Yorkshire: West Riding 1929
WY	Leeds	Yorkshire: West Riding 1921
X*		Northumberland
XA, XB, XC, XD, XE	spare	London 1920
XF	spare	London 1921

XG	spare	Middlesbrough 1930
XH	spare	London 1921
XI		Belfast 1921
XJ	spare	Manchester 1932
XK, XL, XM	spare	London 1922
XN, XO, XP	spare	London 1923
XR	spare	London 1924
XS*	spare	Paisley
XT, XU	spare	London 1924
XV	spare	London 1928
XW	spare	London 1924
XX, XY	spare	London 1925
Y*		Somerset
YA, YB, YC, YD	Taunton	Somerset 1921
YB	Taunton	Somerset 1924
YC	Taunton	Somerset 1927
YD	Taunton	Somerset 1930
YE, YF	London C	London 1927
YG	Leeds	Yorkshire: West Riding 1932
YH	London C	London 1927
YI		Dublin 1921
YJ	Brighton	Dundee 1932
YK, YL, YM	London C	London 1925
YN, YO, YP, YR	London C	London 1926
YS	Glasgow 1935	
YT, YU	London C	London 1927
YV, YW, YX	London C	London 1928
YY	London C	London 1932
Z		Dublin County 1927
ZA		Dublin 1933
ZB		Cork 1935
ZC		Dublin 1937
ZD		Dublin 1940
ZI		Dublin 1927
ZZ		Dublin and the Council of any County which adjoins Northern Ireland

By location

Index marks	Centre
BS, PS, RS, SA, SE, SO, SS	Aberdeen
CC, EY, FF, JC	Bangor
DA, JW, OA, OB, OC, OE, OF, OG, OH, OJ, OK, OL, OM, ON, OP, OV, OX, UK, VP	Birmingham
AA, CG, EL, FX, HO. JT, LJ, PR, RU	Bournemouth
AP, CD, DY, FG, HC, JK, NJ, PN, UF, WV, YJ	Brighton
AE, EU, FB, HT, HU, HW, HY, OU, TC, WS	Bristol
AX, BO, DW, HB, KG, NY, TG, TX, UH, WO	Cardiff
AO, HH, RM, SM, SW	Carlisle
AR, EV, HJ, HK, JN, NO, OO, PU, TW, VW, VX, WC	Chelmsford
CA, DM, FM, LG, MA, MB, TU	Chester
AC, DU, HP, KV, RW, VC, WK	Coventry
DH, EA, FD, FK, HA, NX, UE, WD	Dudley
ES, SL, SN, SP, SR, TS	Dundee
FS, KS, LS, MS, SC, SF, SG, SH, SX	Edinburgh
CO, DR, DV, FJ, JY, OD, TA, TK, TT, UN, UO	Exeter
CS, DS, GA, GB, GD, GE, GG, HS, NS, OS, SB, SD, SJ, SU, US, YS	Glasgow
AD, CJ, DD, DF, DG. FH, FO, VJ	Gloucester
PA, PB, PC, PD, PE, PF, PG, PH, PJ, PK, PL, PM	Guildford
BX, DE, EJ	Haverfordwest
CP, CX, HD, JX, VH	Huddersfield
AG, AT, KH, RH	Hull
AS, JS, SK, ST	Inverness
BJ, DX, GV, PV, RT	Ipswich
BT, DN, NW, UA, UB, UG, UM, VY, WR, WT, WU, WW, WX, WY, YG	Leeds
AY, BC, FP, JF, JU, NR, RY, UT	Leicester
BE, CT, DO, EE, FE, FU, FW, JL, JV, TL, VL	Lincoln
BG, CM, DJ, ED, EK, EM, FY, HF, JP, KA, KB, KC, KD, KF, LV, TB, TJ, WM	Liverpool
HM, HV, HX, JD, UC, UL, UU, UV, UW, YE, YF, YH, YK, YL, YM, YN, YO, YP, YR, YT, YU, YV, YW, YX, YY	London C
MC, MD, ME, MF, MG, MH, MK, ML, MM, MP, MT, MU	London NE

BY, LA, LB, LC, LD, LE, LF, LH, LK, LL, LM, LN, LO, LP, LR, LT, LU, LW, LX, LY, OY, RK	London NW
GU, GW, GX, GY, MV, MX, MY, GC, GF, GH, GJ, GK, GN, GO, GP, GT	London SE
BH, BM, GS, KX, NK, NM, PP, RO, TM, UR, VS	Luton
FN, JG, JJ, KE, KJ, KK, KL, KM, KN, KO, KP, KR, KT, VB	Maidstone
BA, BN, BU, CB, DB, DK, EN, JA, NA, NB, NC, ND, NE, NF, RJ, TD, TE, VM, VR, VU, WH	Manchester
AJ, DC, EF, HN, PY, VN	Middlesbrough
BB, BR, CN, CU, FT, GR, JR, NL, PT, RG, TN, TY, UP, VK	Newcastle upon Tyne
BD, NH, NV, RP, VV	Northampton
AH, CL, EX, NG, PW, VF, VG	Norwich
AL, AU, CH, NN, NU, RA, RB, RC, RR, TO, TV, VO	Nottingham
BW, FC, JO, UD, WL	Oxford
AV, CE, EB, EG, ER, EW, FL, JE, VA, VE	Peterborough
BK, BP, CR. DL, OR, OT, OW, PO, PX, RV, TP, TR	Portsmouth
BV, CK, CW, EC, EO, FR, FV, HG, RN	Preston
AN, BL, CF, DP, GM, JB, JH, JM, MO, RD, RX, TF	Reading
AK, DT, ET, HE, HL, KU, KW, KY, WA, WB, WE, WF, WG, WJ	Sheffield
AW, NT, UJ, UX	Shrewsbury
BF, EH, FA, RE, RF, VT	Stoke on Trent
CY, EP, TH, WN	Swansea
AM, HR, MR, MW	Swindon
YA, YB, YC, YD	Taunton
AF, CV, GL, RL	Truro
AB, NP, UY, WP	Worcester

Main roads of Britain

Motorways

A1(M)	Doncaster Bypass
A1(M)	South Mimms – Baldock
A1(M)	Scotch Corner – Tyneside
A3(M)	Havant – Horndean
A38(M)	Aston Expressway
A46(M)	M1/M69 Spur to Leicester

A48(M)	M4 Spur to Cardiff
A57(M)	Mancunian Way, Manchester
A58(M)	Leeds Inner Ring Road
A64(M)	Leeds Inner Ring Road East
A66(M)	A1(M) Spur to Darlington
A102(M)	Blackwall Tunnel Approach
A167(M)	Through Newcastle upon Tyne
A194(M)	A1(M) Spur to Tyne Tunnel
A308(M)	M4 Spur to Maidenhead
A329(M)	East of Reading
A404(M)	M4 Spur to Maidenhead
A601(M)	E–W link across M6 N of Lancaster
A627(M)	Oldham – Rochdale
A823(M)	Spur from M90
A6127(M)	Newcastle Central Motorway
A6144(M)	M63 Spur to Carrington
M1	London–Wetherby
M2	Rochester–Faversham
M3	Sunbury–Southampton
M4	London–Pont Abraham
M5	Birmingham–Exeter
M6	Rugby–Carlisle
M8	Edinburgh–Glasgow–Bishopton
M9	Edinburgh–Dunblane
M10	St Albans–M1 link
M11	London–Cambridge
(M16)	(Now M25 J23–J24)
M18	M1–M62 link; Rotherham–Humberside
M20	Swanley–Folkestone
M23	Hooley–Crawley
M25	London Orbital Motorway
M26	M20–M25 link
M27	Cadnam–Portsmouth
M32	M4 spur to Bristol
M40	London–Birmingham
M42	Bromsgrove–Measham
M45	Spur to Dunchurch
M48	Old M4 Severn crossing
M49	Bristol to new Severn crossing
M50	M5 spur to Ross

M53	Mersey Tunnel–Chester
M54	Telford Motorway
M55	M6 spur to Blackpool
M56	North Cheshire Motorway
M57	Liverpool Outer Ring Road
M58	Liverpool–Wigan
M60	Manchester Orbital Motorway
M61	Greater Manchester–Preston
M62	Liverpool–Humberside
M63	Manchester Ring Road
M65	Calder Valley Motorway
M66	Greater Manchester
M67	Hyde Bypass
M69	Coventry–Leicester
M73	East of Glasgow
M74, A74(M)	Glasgow–Gretna
M77	Spur to Glasgow
M80	Glasgow–Stirling
M85	Was Perth Eastern Bypass
M90	Forth Road Bridge–Perth
M180	Thorne–Brigg
M181	Spur to Scunthorpe
M271	Southampton–Romsey
M275	Spur M27–Portsmouth
M602	Eccles Bypass
M606	Spur to Bradford
M621	Leeds–Gildersome
M876	Bonnybridge–Kincardine Bridge
M898	Spur M8–Erskine Bridge

A-Roads

The main A-roads, some of which have been supported or supplanted by motorways, radiate from London or Edinburgh numbered in a clockwise direction as follows:

A   London to
1   Edinburgh
2   Dover
3   Portsmouth
4   Bristol
5   Holyhead
6   Carlisle

A   Edinburgh to
7   Carlisle
8   Greenock
9   Thirsk

Generally, the next order of roads springs from the above in a clockwise direction; thus we have

A   London to
10   King's Lynn
11   Norwich
12   Great Yarmouth via Ipswich
13   Southend-on-Sea

until we reach the **A2** ...

20   Folkestone
21   Hastings
22   Eastbourne
23   Brighton
24   Worthing

... and the **A3** ...

30   Land's End

... and the **A4** ...

40   Fishguard

... and so on.

That was the original plan, but there has been so much road-building and renumbering (apart from roads that were inconsiderate enough not to bend easily to the system) that we now have to make the best of it. B-roads are of lesser importance, are often coloured yellow on the map, and have 3- or 4-digit numbers. We have encountered the occasional C-road, but they usually keep themselves to themselves.

Other interesting roads
A34   Manchester–Winchester
A46   Bristol–Grimsby
A59   Liverpool–York

The United States of America

US States

State	ZIP	Abbr.	Capital	Nickname	Adm. to Union	No.	Residents	Alt. name	Origin of name	State motto
Alabama	AL	Ala	Montgomery	Heart of Dixie Cotton State Yellow-hammer State Camellia State	1412.1819	22	Alabamian, Alabaman	Lizards	A Native American word: 'here we rest' uttered by a chief on finding the well-stocked hunting grounds of the area. May originate from Choctaw meaning 'thicket-clearers' or 'vegetation-gatherers'	*Audemus Jura Nostra Defendere* We Dare Defend Our Rights
Alaska	AK		Willow South (orig Juneau)	The Last Frontier Land of the Midnight Sun The Mainland State	0301.1959	40	Alaskan		Corruption of Aleut word meaning 'great land' or 'that which the sea breaks against'	North to the Future
Arizona	AZ	Ariz	Phoenix	Grand Canyon State Apache State Aztec State Valentine State	1402.1912	48	Arizonan, Arizonian		From the Indian 'Arizonac', meaning 'little spring' or 'young spring'	*Ditat Deus* God Enriches

			Capital	Nicknames	Date	No.	Demonym	Nickname	Origin of name	Motto
Arkansas	AR	Ark	Little Rock	Land of Opportunity, Wonder State, Bear State	1806.1836	25	Arkansan	Tooth-picks	From the Quapaw Indians	*Regnat Populus* The People Rule
California	CA	Cal(if)	Sacramento	Golden State, Sunshine State	0909.1850	31	Californian	Gold-hunters	From a book, *Las Sergas de Esplandián*, by Garcia Ordóñez de Montalvo, c 1500	*Eureka* I Have Found It
Colorado	CO	Colo	Denver	Centennial State	0108.1876	38	Coloradan, Coloradoan	Rovers	From the Spanish, 'ruddy' or 'red'	*Nil Sine Numine* Nothing Without Providence
Connecticut	CT	Conn	Hartford	Constitution State, Nutmeg State	0901.1788	5	Connecticuter, Nutmegger	Wooden nutmegs	From an Indian word (Quinnehtukqut) meaning 'beside the long tidal river'	*Qui Transtulit Sustinet* He Who Transplanted Still Sustains
Delaware	DE	Del	Dover	First State, Diamond State, Small Wonder	0712.1787	1	Delawarean	Muskrats	A Native American tribe with whom William Penn negotiated. From Delaware River and Bay; named in turn for Sir Thomas West, Baron De La Warr	Liberty and Independence

Florida	FL	Fla	Tallahassee	Sunshine State Peninsula State Everglade State	0303.1845	27	Floridian, Floridan	Fly-up-the-creeks	Discovered by the Spaniards on a Palm Sunday and named after Pasqua Florida. From the Spanish, meaning 'feast of flowers' (Easter)	In God We Trust
Georgia	GA	Ga	Atlanta	Empire State of the South Peach State	0201.1788	4	Georgian	Buzzards	Named for the English King George II in whose name its first settlement was made.	Wisdom, Justice and Moderation
Hawaii	HI		Honolulu	Aloha State	2108.1959	50	Hawaiian, also kamaaina (native-born nonethnic Hawaiian), malihini (newcomer)		Uncertain – the islands may have been named by Hawaii Loa, their traditional discoverer. Or they may have been named after Hawaii or Hawaiki, the traditional home of the Polynesians	*Ua Mau Ke Ea O Ka Aina I Ka Pono* The Life of the Land is Perpetuated in Righteousness
Idaho	ID	Id, Ida	Boise City	Gem State Gem of the Mountains Panhandle State Spud State	0307.1890	43	Idahoan		Though popularly believed to be an Indian word, it is an invented name whose meaning is unknown	*Esto Perpetua* It is For Ever
Illinois	IL	Ill	Springfield	Prairie State Land of Lincoln	0312.1818	21	Illinoisan	Suckers	Algonquin for 'tribe of superior men'	State Sovereignty – National Union

State	Abbr	Abbr2	Capital	Nickname(s)		#	Resident	People	Origin of name	Motto
Indiana	IN	Ind	Indianapolis	Hoosier State	1112.1816	19	Indianan, Indianian, Hoosier	Hoosiers	Named in 1801 from the number of Native Americans who dwelt there. Meaning 'land of Indians'	The Crossroads of America
Iowa	IA	Ia, Io	Des Moines	Hawkeye State, Corn State	2812.1846	29	Iowan	Hawk-eyes	Probably from an Indian word meaning 'this is the place' or 'the Beautiful Land'	Our Liberties We Prize and Our Rights We Will Maintain
Kansas	KS	Kan	Topeka	Sunflower State, Jayhawker State	2901.1861	34	Kansan	Jay-hawkers	From a Sioux word meaning 'people of the south wind'	As Astra Per Aspera To The Stars Through Difficulties
Kentucky	KY	Ky	Frankfort	Bluegrass State	0106.1792	15	Kentuckian	Corn-crackers	From an Iroquoian word 'Ken-tah-ten' meaning 'land of tomorrow'	United We Stand, Divided We Fall
Louisiana	LA	La	Baton Rouge	Pelican State, Creole State, Sugar State, Bayou State, Sportsman's Paradise	3004.1812	18	Louisianan, Louisianian	Creoles	Named in 1682 by M de la Sale to honour King Louis XIV of France	Union, Justice and Confidence

State			Capital	Nickname			Demonym		Description	Motto
Maine	ME	Me	Augusta	Pine Tree State	1503.1820	23	Mainer	Foxes	Named after the French province in 1638. First used to distinguish the mainland from the offshore islands. It has been considered a compliment to Henrietta Maria, queen of Charles I of England. She was said to have owned the province of Mayne in France	*Dirigo* I Direct
Maryland	MD	Md	Annapolis	Old Line State Free State	2804.1788	7	Marylander	Craw-thumpers	Named by Lord Baltimore in 1633 to compliment Henrietta-Maria, Queen of Charles II of England. Annapolis compliments Queen Anne, in whose reign it became the seat of local government.	*Fatti Maschii, Parole Femine* Manly Deeds, Womanly Words
Massachusetts	MA	Mass	Boston	Bay State Old Colony State	0602.1788	6	Bay Stater		Boston named after Boston (Lincolnshire) in England, whence many of its inhabitants came. From Massachusett tribe of Native Americans, meaning 'at or about the great hill'	*Ense Petit Placidam Sub Libertate Quietem* By the Sword We Seek Peace, But Peace Only Under Liberty

State		Abbr	Capital	Nicknames	Date	No.	Demonym	Mascot	Name meaning	Motto
Michigan	MI	Mich	Lansing	Wolverine State, Auto State, Greta Lake State	2601.1837	26	Michigander, Michiganite	Wolverines	From Indian word 'Michigana' meaning 'great or large lake'	*Si Quaeris Peninsulam Amoenam Circumspice* If You Seek a Pleasant Peninsula, Look About You
Minnesota	MN	Minn	St Paul	North Start State, Gopher State, Land of 10,000 Lakes	1105.1858	32	Minnesotan	Gophers	Laughing waters. From a Dakota Indian word meaning 'sky-tinted water'	*L'Étoile du Nord* The North Star
Mississippi	MS	Miss	Jackson	Magnolia State, Bayou State	1012.1817	20	Mississipian	Tadpoles	Sea of waters. From an Indian word meaning 'Father of Waters'	*Virtue et Armis* By Valour and Arms
Missouri	MO	Mo	Jefferson City	Show Me State, Bullion State	1008.1821	24	Missourian	Pukes	Named after the Missouri Indian tribe. 'Missouri' means 'town of the large canoes'	*Salus Populi Suprema Lex Esto* The Welfare of the People Shall Be the Supreme Law
Montana	MT	Mont	Helena	Treasure State, Big Sky Country	0811.1889	41	Montanan		Chosen from Latin dictionary by J M Ashley. It is a Latinized Spanish word meaning 'mountainous'	*Oro y Plata* Gold and Silver

State			Capital	Nickname	Date	No.	Demonym	People nickname	Origin	Motto
Nebraska	NE Nebr	Lincoln	Cornhusker State, Beef State, Tree Planter State	0103.1867	37	Nebraskan	Bug-eaters	From an Oto Indian word meaning 'flat water'	Equality Before the Law
Nevada	NV Nev	Carson City	Sagebrush State, Silver State, Battle-born State	3110.1864	36	Nevandan, Nevadian	Sage hens	Names after the Sierra Nevada chain of mountains. Spanish: 'snowcapped'	All For Our Country
New Hampshire	NH NH	Concord	Granite State	2106.1788	9	New Hampshirite	Granite boys	From the English county of Hampshire. Previously named Laconia; renamed in 1629 by J Mason, Governor of Hampshire to whom it was conceded	Live Free or Die
New Jersey	NJ NJ	Trenton	Garden State	1812.1787	3	New Jerseyite, New Jerseyan	Blues, Clam-catchers	From the Channel Isle of Jersey. Named in honour of Sir G Carteret who defended Jersey against parliamentary forces (1664)	Liberty and Prosperity
New Mexico	NM NMex	Santa Fé	Land of Enchantment, Sunshine State	0601.1912	47	New Mexican		From the country of Mexico	Crescit Eundo It Grows as it Goes

			Capital	Nickname(s)	Date	No.	Demonym	Residents	Origin of name	Motto
New York	NY	NY	Albany	Empire State	2607.1788	11	New Yorker	Knicker-bockers	Previously named New Amsterdam by the Dutchman Peter Stuyvesant; renamed in 1664 to compliment James Duke of York, afterwards James II.	Excelsior, Ever Upward
North Carolina	NC	NC	Raleigh	Tar Heel State Old North State	2111.1789	12	North Carolinian	Tar boilers Tuckoes	Names to Compliment Charles II who granted the whole country to eight needy courtiers.	*Esse Quam Videri* To Be Rather Than To Seem
North Dakota	ND	ND	Bismarck	Sioux State Flickertail State Peace Garden State	0211.1889	39	North Dakotan		From the Sioux tribe, meaning 'allies'	Liberty and Union, Now and Forever, One and Inseperable
Ohio	OH	O	Columbus	Buckeye State	0103.1803	17	Ohioan	Buck-eyes	From an Iroquoian word meaning 'great river'	With God, All Things Are Possible
Oklahoma	OK	Okla	Oklahoma City	Sooner State	1611.1907	46	Oklahoman		From two Choctaw Indian words meaning 'red people'	*Labor Omnia Vincit* Labour Conquers All Things

State	Abbr	Abbr2	Capital	Nickname	Date	Order	Resident	People nickname	Origin of name	Motto
Oregon	OR	Ore(g)	Salem	Beaver State, Sunset State	1402.1859	33	Oregonian	Web feet, Hard cases	Unknown – although generally accepted that the word, first used by Jonathon Carver in 1778, was taken from the writings of Maj. Robert Rogers, an English army officer. Astoria named after Mr Astor, the New York merchant, who established a fur-trading station here in 1811. Carson City named after the Rocky Mountain trapper and guide Kit Carson (d1871)	The Union
Pennsylvania	PA	Pa	Harrisburg	Keystone State	1212.1787	2	Pennsylvanian	Pennanites, Leather-heads	In honour of Adm. Sir William Penn, father of William Penn who gave the state its constitution in 1681. It means 'Penn's Woodland'. Harrisburg named from Mr Harris who settled it in 1733 under a grant from the Penn family	Virtue, Liberty and Independence
Rhode Island	RI	RI	Providence	Little Rhody, Ocean State, Plantation State	2905.1790	13	Rhode Islander	Gun flints	From the Greek Island of Rhodes	Hope

			Capital	Nickname(s)	Date	No.	Resident	Nickname	Name origin	Motto
South Carolina	SC	SC	Columbia	Palmetto State, Gamecock State	2305.1788	8	South Carolinian	Weasels	Charleston founded 1670 named for the English King Charles II	*Animus Opibusque Parati* Prepared in Mind and Resources
South Dakota	SD	SD	Pierre	Coyote State, Sunshine State, Artesian State, Mount Rushmore State	0211.1889	40	South Dakotan		From the Sioux tribe, meaning 'allies'	Under God the People Rule
Tennessee	TN	Tenn	Nashville	Volunteer State	0106.1796	16	Tennessean, Tennesseean	Whelps	Of Cherokee origin; the exact meaning is unknown	Agriculture and Commerce
Texas	TX	Tex	Austin	Lone Star State	2912.1845	28	Texan	Beef-heads	'The place of protection' so called because General Lallemant there protected a French refugee colony in 1817 From an Indian word meaning 'friends'	Friendship
Utah	UT	Utah	Salt Lake City	Beehive State, Mormon State	0401.1896	45	Utahan, Utahn		From the Ute tribe, meaning 'people of the mountains'	Industry
Vermont	VT	Vt	Montpelier	Green Mountain State	0403.1791	14	Vermonter	Green Mountain boys	From the French 'vert mont', meaning 'green mountain'	Freedom and Unity

State			Capital	Nickname		Order	Date	Demonym		Name meaning	Motto
Virginia	VA	Va	Richmond	Old Dominion State, Cavalier State, Mother of Presidents		2606.1788	10	Virginian	Beadies	Named by Sir Walter Raleigh in 1584 to compliment the Virgin Queen (Elizabeth I)	Sic Semper Tyrannis / Thus Always to Tyrants
Washington	WA	Wash	Olympia	Evergreen State, Chinook State		1111.1788	42	Washington		In honour of George Washington	Alki / Bye and Bye
West Virginia	WV	WVa	Charleston	Mountain State, Panhandle State		2006.1863	35	West Virginian		In honour of Elizabeth, 'Virgin Queen' of England	Montani Semper Liberi / Mountaineers Are Always Free
Wisconsin	WI	Wis	Madison	Badger State, America's Dairyland		2905.1848	30	Wisconsinite	Badgers	French corruption of an Indian word whose meaning is disputed	Forward
Wyoming	WY	Wyo	Cheyenne	Equality State		1007.1890	44	Wyomingite		From the Delaware Indian word, meaning 'mountains and valleys alternating'; the same as the Wyoming Valley in Pennsylvania	Equal Rights

Major US interstate highways

Two-digit even-numbered Interstates run east-west with low numbers in the south and high numbers in the north.

Two-digit odd-numbered Interstates run north-south with low numbers in the west and high numbers in the south.

Three-digit Interstates are generally spurs into cities and by-passes round cities.

I 4   St Petersburg FL–Orlando FL–Daytona Beach FL

I 10   Los Angeles CA–Phoenix AZ–Tucson AZ–El Paso TX–San Antonio TX–Houston TX–Baton Rouge LA–Mobile LA–Tallahassee FL–Jacksonville FL

I 20   Pecos TX–Abilene TX–Dallas/Fort Worth TX–Shreveport LA–Jackson MS–Birmingham AL–Atlanta GA–Augusta GA–Columbia SC–Florence SC

I 40   Barstow CA–Flagstaff AZ–Albuquerque NM–Amarillo TX–Oklahoma City OK–Little Rock AR–Memphis TN–Nashville TN–Knoxville TN–Winston-Salem NC–Durham NC–Raleigh NC–Wilmington NC

I 70   Across central Utah–Grand Junction CO–Denver CO–Topeka KS–Kansas City MO–St Louis MO–Indianapolis IN–Columbus OH–south of Pittsburgh PA–Baltimore MD

I 80   San Francisco CA–Sacramento CA–Reno NV–Salt Lake City UT–Laramie WY–Cheyenne WY–Omaha NE–Des Moines IA–south of Chicago IL–Toledo OH–Cleveland OH–New York City NY

I 84   Portland OR–Boise ID–north of Salt Lake City UT

I 90   Seattle WA–Spokane WA–Missoula MT–Billings MT–Sheridan WY–Rapid City ND–Sioux Falls SD–Madison WI–Chicago IL–Toledo OH–Cleveland OH–Buffalo NY–Syracuse NY–Boston MA

I 94   Billings MT–Minneapolis/St Paul MN–Madison WI–Milwaukee WI–Chicago IL–Kalamazoo MI–Detroit MI–Port Huron MI

I 5   Canadian border south of Vancouver BC–Seattle WA–Portland OR–Sacramento CA–Los Angeles CA–San Diego CA

I 15   Canadian border east of Glacier National Park MT–Great Falls MT–Pocatello ID–Salt Lake City UT–St George UT–Las Vegas NV–Los Angeles CA

I 25 Buffalo WY–Casper WY–Cheyenne WY–Denver CO–Colorado Springs CO–Santa Fé NM–Albuquerque NM–El Paso TX

I 29 Canadian border south of Winnipeg MB–Grand Forks ND–Fargo ND–Watertown SD–Sioux Falls SD–Sioux City IA–Omaha NE–St Joseph MO–Kansas City MO

I 35 Duluth MN–Minneapolis/St Paul MN–Des Moines IA–Kansas City MO–Wichita KS–Oklahoma City OK–Dallas/Ft Worth TX–San Antonio TX–Laredo TX

I 55 Chicago IL–St Louis MO–Memphis TN–New Orleans LA

I 65 Chicago IL–Indianapolis IN–Louisville KY–Nashville TN–Birmingham AL–Montgomery AL–Mobile AL

I 75 Sault Ste Marie MI–Flint MI–Toledo OH–Cincinnati OH–Lexington KY–Knoxville TN–Chattanooga TN–Atlanta GA–Macon GA–Tampa/St Petersburg FL–Naples FL–Fort Lauderdale FL

I 81 Canadian border (ON)–Watertown NY–Syracuse NY–Harrisburg PA–Roanoke VA–Knoxville TN

I 95 Canadian border (NB)–Bangor ME–Boston MA–Providence RI–Bridgeport CT–New York City NY–Philadelphia PA–Wilmington DE–Baltimore MD–Washington DC–Richmond VA–Fayetteville NC–Florence SC–Savannah GA–Jacksonville FL–Miami FL

US interstate highways

Rank	Route	Daily traffic (1996)	County	Metropolitan area	State
1	405	332,100	Orange	Los Angeles	CA
2	90	331,703	Cook	Chicago	IL
3	75	327,900	Fulton	Atlanta	GA
4	10	322,200	Los Angeles	Los Angeles	CA
5	405	316,200	Los Angeles	Los Angeles	CA
6	5	305,100	Orange	Los Angeles	CA
7	5	297,800	Los Angeles	Los Angeles	CA
8	75	292,600	Cobb	Atlanta	GA
9	5	289,114	King	Seattle	WA
10	580	287,400	Alameda	San Francisco	CA
11	95	278,000	Broward	Miami	FL
12	80	277,700	Alameda	San Francisco	CA
13	80	273,700	San Francisco	San Francisco	CA
14	95	267,306	Bergen	New York	NJ
15	95	267,000	Fairfax	Washington	VA
16	94	266,744	Cook	Chicago	IL
17	85	256,300	Gwinnett	Atlanta	GA
18	210	254,700	Los Angeles	Los Angeles	CA
19	605	254,500	Los Angeles	Los Angeles	CA
20	395	254,369	—	Washington	DC
21	85	253,650	DeKalb	Atlanta	GA
22	610	251,420	Harris	Houston	TX
23	495	250,350	Montgomery	Washington	MD

Top 25 Wide US Interstate Highways (Motorways) with 12 or more through lanes

Rank	Route	Lanes	County	Metropolitan area	State
1	75	15	Cobb	Atlanta	GA
2	405	14	Orange	Los Angeles	CA
3	15	14	San Diego	San Diego	CA
4	75	14	Fulton	Atlanta	GA
5	95	14	Bergen	New York	NJ
6	95	14	New York	New York	NY
7	270	13	Montgomery	Washington	MD
8	395	13	Arlington	Washington	VA
9	395	13	Alexandria	Washington	VA
10	5	13	King	Seattle	WA
11	10	12	Maricopa	Phoenix	AZ
12	5	12	Orange	Los Angeles	CA
13	8	12	San Diego	San Diego	CA
14	84	12	Hartford	Hartford	CT
15	95	12	Broward	Miami	FL
16	75	12	Broward	Miami	FL
17	95	12	Duval	Jacksonville	FL
18	85	12	DeKalb	Atlanta	GA
19	285	12	DeKalb	Atlanta	GA
20	85	12	Gwinnett	Atlanta	GA
21	90	12	Cook	Chicago	IL
22	96	12	Wayne	Detroit	MI
23	278	12	Kings	New York	NY
24	278	12	Richmond	New York	NY
25	610	12	Harris	Houston	TX

Native Americans and their modern areas

Algonquin Stock

Abnaki	Maine
Passamaquoddy	Maine
Penobscot	Maine
Arapaho	Central Plains
Blackfoot	Northern Plain
Cheyenne	Minnesota
Chippewa	Great Lakes

Cree	Canada
Maskegon	Canada
Delaware	Pennsylvania
Munsee	Pennsylvania
Illinois	Illinois
Kickapoo	Wisconsin
Menominee	Wisconsin
Micmac	Wisconsin
Mohegan	New England
Narraganset	New England
Naintic	New England
Pequot	New England
Ottawa	Canada
Algonkin	Canada
Potawatomi	Wisconsin
Powhatan	Virginia
Sauk	Michigan
Fox	Michigan
Shawnee	Tennessee

Athabascan Stock

Apache	New Mexico
Carrier	British Columbia
Chipewyan	N W Canada
Hupa	California
Kutchin	N W Canada
Navaho	Arizona
Slave	Great Bear Lake

Caddoan Stock

Caddo	Texas
Pawnee	Nebraska
Wichita	Oklahoma

Inuit Stock

Aleut	Aleut Islands (Alaska)
Inuit	Arctic Coast

Iroquoian Stock

Cherokee	South Appalachians

Huron	Ontario
Iroquois	New York State
Cayuga	New York State
Mohawk	New York State
Oneida	New York State
Onondaga	New York State
Seneca	New York State
Tuscarora	N Carolina

Muskhogean Stock

Chickasaw	Mississippi
Choctaw	Mississippi
Creek	Alabama
Seminole	Alabama
Natchez	Mississippi

Piman Stock

Papago	Arizona
Pima	Arizona

Salishan Stock

Bellacoola	British Columbia
Cowichan	British Columbia
Flathead	Montana
Kalispel	Idaho
Nasqualli	Washington
Puyallup	Washington
Shuswap	British Columbia
Thompsons	British Columbia

Shoshonean Stock

Comanche	Kansas
Hopi	Arizona
Paiute	Nevada
Shoshonee	Idaho
Ute	Utah

Siouan (Siouxian) Stock

Assiniboine	Lake Superior
Catawba	Carolina
Crow	Dakota
Dakota (The Sioux)	Minnesota
Hidatsa	N Dakota

Mandan	N Dakota
Omaha	Missouri
Osage	Arkansas
Winnebago	Wisconsin

Various Indefinite Stocks

Haida	British Columbia
Keresan	New Mexico
Kiowa	Colorado
Kwakiutl	New Mexico
Mission	California
Modoc	British Columbia
Mohave	California
Nez Percés	Idaho
Nootka	Vancouver Island
Pomo	California
Tanoan	New Mexico
Teingit	Alaska
Tsimshian	British Columbia
Yakima	Washington
Yuma	California
Zuni	New Mexico

Worldwide

Huge bridge spans

The span of a bridge is usually taken to be the distance, centre to centre, between adjacent towers, pylons, piers or other supports. There are longer multi-span bridge complexes with natural or artificial islands, but it is the single span that counts for the record book. Suspension bridges support the deck by cables hanging vertically from massive primary cables that are carried over the top of piers and anchored on the ground. These primaries form a mathematical shape called a catenary (from the Latin for chain). Cable-stayed bridges on the other hand support the deck directly which means that, as the length of the span increases, the cables radiate out at increasing angles from their supports. For this reason the cables become more horizontal and less efficient with increasing length. Cable-stayed bridges are therefore unable to support spans as long as classical suspension bridges.

The dramatic beauty of giant bridges and the height they need to cover great spans have given them a perverse appeal to suicides. The Golden Gate bridge in San Francisco holds the record with over 1,200 suicides since it was built in 1937. The terminal velocity of the bodies is so great (not all of them are recovered) that they show signs of internal damage – ruptured spleens, pierced lungs and so on. Very few jumpers have survived, and they have always gone in feet first. In Britain, Brunel's elegant Clifton suspension bridge in Bristol has something of the same romance for those in despair.

There have been some famous engineering mistakes making bridges. The first Tacoma Narrows bridge (nicknamed Galloping Gertie) in Washington State, USA, was very fine but its thin deck caught the wind and twisted. It shook itself to bits in 1940. The Norman Foster/Anthony Caro Millennium Bridge for pedestrians over the Thames in London (2000, reopened 2002) was a stunning innovative design with the suspension cables to each side rather than above the deck. It also resonated with its heavy foot traffic, a phenomenon made worse by people's tendency to fall into step to counteract the swaying. The problem was eventually fixed by engineers, Ove Arup, using discreet mass dampers.

Suspension spans

Name	Location	Year	Span (ft)	(m)
Akashi Kaikyo	Shikoku, Japan	1998	6,529	1,990
Great Belt East (Storebaelt East Bridge)	Korsor, Denmark	1998	5,328	1,624
Runyang South	Zhenjiang, China	2005	4,888	1,490
Humber Estuary	Kingston upon Hull, England	1981	4,626	1,410
Jiangyin (Yangtze)	Jiangsu, China	1999	4,544	1,385
Tsing Ma	Hong Kong, China	1997	4,518	1,377
Verrazano Narrows	Brooklyn–Staten Island, USA	1964	4,260	1,298
Golden Gate	San Francisco Bay, USA	1937	4,200	1,280
Höga Kusten	Kramfors, Sweden	1997	3,970	1,210
Mackinac Straits	Mackinaw City, Michigan, USA	1957	3,800	1,158
Minami Bisan-Seto	Japan	1988	3,609	1,100
Bosporus II Faith Sultan Mehmet	Istanbul, Turkey	1992	3,576	1,090
Bosporus I	Istanbul, Turkey	1973	3,524	1,074
George Washington	Hudson River, New York City, USA	1931	3,500	1,067
Kurushima III	Japan	1999	3,379	1,030
Kurushima II	Japan	1999	3,346	1,020
Ponte 25 de Abril (Tagus) (road and rail)	Lisbon, Portugal	1966	3,323	1,013
Firth of Forth (road)	Nr Edinburgh, Scotland	1964	3,300	1,006
Kits Bisan-Seto	Japan	1988	3,248	990
*Severn River	Severn Estuary, England	1966	3,240	988

* The main span of the 3.2 mile long Second Severn bridging, opened in 1996, is 1,496ft (456m).

Cantilever spans

			Span	
Name	Location	Year	(ft)	(m)
Pont de Québec (rail-road)	St Lawrence, Canada	1917	1,800	548.6
Ravenswood	W Virginia, USA		1,723	525.1
Firth of Forth (rail)	Nr Edinburgh, Scotland (two spans of 1710 ft each)	1890	1,710	521.2
Minato (Nanko)	Osaka, Japan	1974	1,673	510.0
Commodore Barry Delaware River	Chester, Pennsylvania, USA	1975	1,644	501.0
Greater New Orleans	Louisiana, USA (I 1958, II 1988)	1958	1,575	480.0
Howrah (rail-road)	Calcutta, India	1936–43	1,500	457.2
Transbay (Oakland)	San Francisco, California, USA	1936	1,400	426.7
Baton Rouge	Mississippi River, Louisiana, USA	1968	1,235	376.4
Astoria	Oregon, USA	1966	1,235	376.4
Nyack-Tarrytown (Tappan Zee)	Hudson River, NY, USA	1955	1,212	369.4
Longview	Columbia River, Washington, USA	1930	1,200	365.7
Baltimore	Maryland, USA	1976	1,200	365.7
Queensboro	East River, NY City, USA	1909	1,182	360.2
Carquinez Strait	Nr San Francisco, California, USA	1927	1,100	335.2
Second Narrows	Burrard Inlet, Vancouver, BC, Canada	1959	1,100	335.2

Steel arch spans

			Span	
Name	Location	Year	(ft)	(m)
Lupu	Shanghai, China	2003	1,804	550.0
New River Gorge	Fayetteville, W Virginia, USA	1977	1,700	518.0
Bayonne (Kill van Kull)	Bayonne, NJ–Staten Island, USA	1931	1,675	510.5
Sydney Harbour	Sydney, Australia	1932	1,650	502.9

The 'floating' bridging at Evergreen Point, Seattle, Washington State, USA (1963), is 12,596ft (3,839m) long, of which 7,578ft (2,310m) floats.

The longest stretch of bridgings of any kind is that carryig the Interstate 55 and Interstate 10 highways at Manchac, Louisiana (1979), on twin concrete trestles over 34.31 miles (55.21km).

Tallest inhabited buildings

				Height	
Building	City	Storeys	Year	(ft)	(m)
Petronas Towers I and II	Kuala Lumpur, Malaysia	88	1998	1,482	451.9
Sears Tower	Chicago[1], USA	110	1974	1,454	443
Jin Mao	Shanghai, China	86	1998	1,378	420
International Finance Centre	Hong Kong		2003	1,352	412
CITIC Plaza	Guangzhou, China		1996	1,283	391
Shun Hing Square	Shenzhen, China		1996	1,260	384
Empire State Building	5th Av and 34th Street, New York City[2]	102	1931	1,250	381
Central Plaza	Hong Kong		1992	1,227	373
Bank of China Tower	Hong Kong		1989	1,209	368
Emirates Tower One	Dubai		2000	1,165	355
The Centre	Hong Kong		1998	1,148	350
Tuntex and Chein-Tai Tower	Taiwan		1998	1,140	347
Standard Oil Building	Chicago, Illinois	80	1973	1,136	346
Kingdom Centre	Riyadh, Saudi Arabia		2001	1,132	345
John Hancock Center	Chicago	100	1969	1,127	343
Baurj al Arab Hotel	Dubai		1999	1,053	321
Texas Commerce Plaza	Houston, Texas	75		1,049	320
Chrysler Building	Lexington Av and 42nd Street, New York City	77	1930	1,046	318
American International Building	70 Pine St, New York City	66		950	289
First Bank Tower	First Canadian Place, Toronto, Ontario	72		935	285
40 Wall Tower	New York City	71		927	282
Citicorp Center	New York City	59	1977	914	279
Walter Tower Plaza	Chicago, Illinois	74	1975	859	262
United California Bank	Los Angeles, California	62	1974	858	261
United California Bank	New York City	66		851	259

[1] with TV antennae, 1,707ft (520m)
[2] with TV tower (added in 1950-1), 1,414ft (430.9m)
Note: The Two World Trade Centre towers, One/North (1972) 110 stories high, 1,368ft (415m), or 1,716ft (521m) with TV antennae; and Two/South (1973) 110 stories high, 1,362ft (413m), were destroyed by two terrorist hijacked aircraft on 11 September 2001.

Highest dams

Name	River	Country (and date of completion)	Height (ft)	Height (m)
Rogunsky	Vakhsh	Tajikistan	1,066	325
Nurek	Vakhsh	Tajikistan (1980)	1,040	317
Grande Dixence	Dixence–Rhône	Switzerland (1961)	935	285
Ingurskaya	Inguri	Georgia (1980)	892	272
Vajont	Piave	Italy (1980)	859	262
Chicoasén	Grijalva	Mexico (1980)	856	261
Tehri	Bhagivathi	India (1989)	856	261
Mica	Columbia	Canada (1976)	803	245

The world's largest dam is the Syncrude Tailings dam in Alberta, Canada, which will have a volume of 706 million cubic yards (540 million cubic metres).

The Three Gorges Chang Jiang (Yangtze) Dam, China, with a crest length of 6,505ft (1,983m) is due for completion in 2009.

The Yacretá-Apipe dam across the River Paraná, Argentina–Paraguy, is being completed to a length of 43.24 miles (69,600m).

Longest ship canals

See table overleaf.

The first section of China's Grand Canal, running 1107 miles (1782km) from Beijing to Hangzhou, was opened AD 610 and completed in 1283. Today it is limited to 2000 tonne vessels.

The St Lawrence Seaway comprises the Beauharnois, Welland and Welland Bypass and Seaway 54–59 canals, and allows access to Duluth, Minnesota, USA via the Great Lakes from the Atlantic end of Canada's Gulf of St Lawrence, a distance of 2,342 miles (3,769km). The St Lawrence Canal, completed in 1959, is 182 miles (293km) long.

Structure	Year	No. of locks	Min. depth (ft)	Min. depth (m)	Length (miles)	Length (km)	Notes
White Sea–Baltic (formerly Stalin), of which Canalised river 32 miles (51.5km)	1933	19	5	16.5	146.02	235	Links with Barents Sea and White Sea to the Baltic with a chain of a lake, canalised river, and 32 miles (51.5km) of canal.
Suez	1869	0	42.3	12.9	100.60	162	Eliminates the necessity for 'rounding the Cape'.
V I Lenin Volga-Don	1952	13	n/a	n/a	62.20	100	Interconnects Black, Azov and Caspian Seas.
Kiel (or North Sea)	1895	2	45.0	13.7	60.90	98	Shortens the North–Sea–Baltic passage; south of German–Danish border. Major reconstruction 1914.
Houston	1940	0	34.0	10.4	56.70	91	Makes Houston, although 50 miles from the coast, the United States' eighth busiest port.
Alphonse XIII	1926	13	25.0	7.6	53.00	85	Gives Seville access to sea. True canal only 4 miles (6.4km) in length.
Panama	1914	6	41.0	12.5	50.71	82	Eliminates necessity for 'rounding the Horn'. 49 miles (78.9km) of the length was excavated.
Manchester Ship	1894	4	28.0	8.5	39.70	64	Makes Manchester, although 54 miles (86.9km) from the open sea, Britain's third busiest port.
Welland	1932	7	29.0	8.8	27.00	43.5	Circumvents Niagara falls and Niagara River rapids.
Brussels (Rupel Sea)	1922	4	21.0	6.4	19.80	32	Makes Brussels an inland port.

Tallest structures

			Height	
Structure	Location	Year	ft	m
*Warszawa Radio Mast	Konstantynow, Poland	1974	2,120	646
KVLY (formerly KTHI)-TV Mast	Blanchard, North Dakota (guyed)	1963	2,063	629
Indosat Telkom Tower	Jakarta, Indonesia		1,831	558
CN Tower	Metro Centre, Toronto, Canada	1975	1,822	555
Ostankino Tower	Moscow	1967	1,772	540
WRBL-TV and WTVM	Columbus, Georgia, USA	1962	1,749	533
WBIR-TV	Knoxville, Tennessee, USA	1963	1,749	533
Moscow TV Tower	Moscow		1,732	528
KFVS-TV	Cape Girardeau, Missouri, USA	1960	1,673	510
WPSD-TV	Paducah, Kentucky, USA		1,638	499
WGAN-TV	Portland, Maine, USA	1959	1,619	493
KSWS-TV	Roswell, New Mexico, USA	1956	1,610	490
WKY-TV	Oklahoma City, Okla, USA		1,600	487
KW-TV	Oklahoma City, Okla, USA	1954	1,572	479
BREN Tower	Nevada, USA	1962	1,527	465

* Collapsed during renovation, August 1991. New structure planned on site at Solkajawaski. The USA has 8 other guyed TV towers above 1,822ft (555m).

Longest vehicular tunnels

			Length	
Structure	Location	Year	miles	km
*Seikan (rail)	Tsugaru Channel, Japan	1988	33.46	53.85
*Channel Tunnel (rail)	Cheriton, Kent–Sangatte, Calais	1994	31.35	50.45
Moscow metro	Belyaevo–Bittsevsky, Moscow, Russia	1979	23.50	37.90
Northern Line tube	East Finchley–Morden, London	1939	17.30	27.84
Iwate (rail)	Japan	2002	16.03	25.81
Laerdal-Aurland Road Link		2000	15.22	24.51
*Oshimizu (rail)	Honshu, Japan	1982	13.78	22.17
Simplon II (rail)	Brigue, Switzerland–Iselle, Italy	1922	12.31	19.82
Simplon I (rail)	Brigue, Switzerland–Iselle, Italy	1906	12.30	19.80
Vereina	Switzerland	1999	11.84	19.06
*Shin-Kanmon (rail)	Kanmon Strait, Japan	1975	11.61	18.68
Great Appennine (rail)	Vernio, Italy	1934	11.50	18.50

St Gotthard (road)	Göschenen–Airolo, Switzerland	1980 (re-opened 2001)	10.51	16.91
Rokko (rail)	Japan	1972	10.00	16.00
Hong Kong Subway	Hong Kong	1975–80	9.94	16.00
Henderson (rail)	Rocky Mts, Colorado, USA	1975	9.85	15.80
St Gotthard (rail)	Göschenen-Airolo, Switzerland	1872–82	9.26	14.90
Lötschbery (rail)	Kandersteg-Goppenstein, Switzerland	1906–13	9.03	14.50
Arlberg (road)	Langen-St Anton, Austria	1978	8.70	14.00
Hokkuriku (rail)	Tsuruga-Imajo-Japan	1957–62	8.61	13.85

* Sub-aqueous

The longest non-vehicular tunnelling in the world is the Delaware Aqueduct in New York State, USA, constructed in 1937–44 to a length of 105 miles (168.9km).

St Gotthard (rail) tunnel (2010) will be 35.46 miles (57.07km).

British rail tunnels

Structure	Location	Length	
		miles	yards
Severn	Bristol–Newport (1873–86)	4	484
Totley	Manchester–Sheffield	3	950
Standedge	Manchester–Huddersfield	3	66
Sodbury	Swindon–Bristol	2	924
Strood	Medway, Kent	2	426
Disley	Stockport–Sheffield	2	346
Ffestiniog	Llandudno–Blaenau Ffestiniog	2	338
Bramhope	Leeds–Harrogate	2	241
Cowburn	Manchester–Sheffield	2	182

The longest road tunnel in Britain is the Mersey Queensway Tunnel (1934), 2 miles 228 yards (3.42km) long. The longest canal tunnel, at Stanedge, W Yorkshire, is 3 miles and 417 yards (5.12km) long; it was completed in 1811, closed in 1944 and reopened in 2001.